THE BUDDHIST GUIDE TO NEW YORK

JEFF WILSON

ILLUSTRATIONS BY **MIKE TAYLOR**

 ST. MARTIN'S GRIFFIN ❧ NEW YORK

THE BUDDHIST GUIDE TO NEW YORK

WHERE TO GO, WHAT TO DO,

AND HOW TO MAKE THE MOST

OF THE FANTASTIC RESOURCES

IN THE TRI-STATE AREA

THE BUDDHIST GUIDE TO NEW YORK: WHERE TO GO, WHAT TO DO, AND HOW TO MAKE THE MOST OF THE FANTASTIC RESOURCES IN THE TRI-STATE AREA

www.stmartins.com

Book design by Victoria Kuskowski

Library of Congress Cataloging-in-Publication Data

Wilson, Jeff (Jeff Townsend)
  Buddhist guide to New York : where to go, what to do, and how to make the most of the fantastic resources in the Tri-State Area / Jeff Wilson.
    p. cm.
  Includes index.
  ISBN 0-312-26715-0
    1. Buddhism—New York Region. 2. Spiritual life—Buddhism. 3. Buddhist centers—New York Region—Guidebooks 4. Temples, Buddhist—New York Region—Guidebooks. I. Title.

BQ739.N48 W55 2000
294.3'09747'1—dc21

                                                                00-040253

First Edition: December 2000

10 9 8 7 6 5 4 3 2 1

Buddham saranam gacchami

Dhammam saranam gacchami

Sangham saranam gacchami

Sentient beings are numberless; I vow to save them all.

Delusions are endless; I vow to illuminate them all.

The teachings are infinite; I vow to learn them all.

The Buddha way is inconceivable; I vow to attain it.

CONTENTS

PART THREE: **WHAT OTHER BUDDHIST RESOURCES ARE AVAILABLE?**

ACKNOWLEDGMENTS

The highest principle of Buddhism is that all things are interconnected, with no beginning or end. With that recognition in mind, it's impossible to acknowledge all of the influences and assistance that went into making this project a success. I'll just take a moment to thank a few people whose help and support were most prominent; I apologize to all whose names should appear here but don't. Your contributions are no less important.

First, I'd especially like to thank my editor, Kristen Macnamara, for not only believing in this project but also believing in me, even when I wasn't so sure myself. This book would not exist without her hard work, care, and support.

Second, I'd like to thank my parents. Their many years of love, self-sacrifice, and encouragement have produced whatever positive qualities and achievements I can lay claim to. I also owe a debt of gratitude to my brother, grandparents, aunts, uncles, cousins, and other family members that I'll never fully be able to return.

Third, I'd like to acknowledge the support of my many friends, particularly Sara Fajardo and Christy Damio, who've put up with me for an inordinate amount of time. Their talents, enthusiasm, and intelligent criticisms are all part of the foundation of my work.

Thanks to Mike Taylor for his delightful illustrations.

A special thanks needs to go to all the people whom I interviewed, chatted up, meditated with, learned from, and was benefited by in the process of compiling this information. I met so many bodhisattvas that I could never name them all. Thank you for your cooperation and for revealing the richness and wonder of Buddhism in greater New York to me.

Thanks to St. Martin's Press, Helen Tworkov, Mary Martin Niepold, Phil Ryan, Laurie Moffat, Paul Morris, James Shaheen, Joel Whitney,

Pat O'Hara, Chung Ok Lee, Nicky Vreeland, Jasmine Gates, Ben Smyth, Joni Ang, Emily Manista, Amy Minter, Michael Bachrach, Marjorie Bowens-Wheatley, Richard Nugent, Gary Jacinto, Rande Brown, The Skeptical Sangha, Jean Brown, T. Griffith Foulk, Mary LaChappelle, Stephen Kendrick, and Bob Mauterstock.

Comments on the book and Buddhist experience in New York are welcome and can be addressed to my E-mail, MayuTzu@aol.com.

Namo Amida Butsu.

INTRODUCTION

On August 15, 1999, more than seven thousand New Yorkers gathered in Central Park, braving crowds, summer heat, and rainy forecasts to sit attentively together for several hours. The attraction wasn't the Backstreet Boys or the Rolling Stones; it wasn't a sporting event, political rally, or contest giveaway. The strikingly diverse group included hip Village kids, Gucci-clad Upper East Siders, working-class Bed-Stuy residents, and immigrants from a dozen Asian countries. They all came together to spend a little time in the presence of the Dalai Lama, an elderly Buddhist saint from a remote, landlocked region on the other side of the planet. It was a remarkable testament to the explosively growing interest in Buddhism among New Yorkers of all backgrounds.

Buddhism is the turn of the millennium's pop spiritual movement, attracting the Beastie Boys, Hollywood celebrities, and millions of baby boomers and gen Xers across the nation. It's also a more than 2,500-year-old contemplative tradition of compassion and wisdom with roots stretching back more than 150 years in this country.

In the five boroughs of New York City alone, there are more than one hundred Buddhist temples, centers, and meditation groups spanning the entire range of Buddhist teachings, as well as dozens of Buddhist-oriented book- and supply stores, restaurants, and art dealers. Nowhere else in the history of Buddhism have so many different traditions and resources been available to a single population. New York simultaneously hosts cutting-edge Buddhist psychotherapist Mark Epstein and traditional Tibetan medicine man Eliot Tokar. There's a larger than life-size statue of a Buddhist saint (which survived the atomic bombing of Hiroshima) on the Upper West Side, as well as a museum devoted entirely to Tibetan art on Staten Island. In the East Village celibate monks and nuns maintain a Tibetan-style monastery, while a few blocks away the Village Zendo is run by an Irish American lesbian Zen master.

Celebrity Buddhists Richard Gere and Philip Glass are meditating at the same time as prisoners in Sing Sing. From the performing arts to cuisine to the hundreds of turtles ritualistically released into Central Park ponds by Chinese Buddhists each year, Buddhism has made an indelible mark on the life and character of New York City.

With this surge in interest and growing self-consciousness of Buddhism as a vital part of the metropolitan New York landscape, the demand for a comprehensive and accessible guide to Buddhist resources in the area has become great. This book seeks to answer a wide range of questions in an informative and lively way, but most of all to be useful to the average spiritual seeker in New York City trying to understand how to take advantage of the myriad and often confusing resources that they're offered. How do I choose a suitable Buddhist center to attend? What is proper protocol when visiting a Buddhist temple for the first time? What can I expect to get out of the experience? How should I dress? How should I address a Buddhist monk or nun? What is the Buddhist view of God? Are any of these organizations cults? What is Zen? What if I'm no good at meditating? All of these and many other concerns are addressed.

The first section of this book offers experienced answers to these and other questions, as well as giving the newcomer a short guided tour through the dazzling labyrinth of Buddhist thought and imagery one is likely to encounter. These questions may or may not be relevant to your particular situation, so don't feel that you absolutely must figure out the difference between Mahayana and Theravada philosophy before you set foot in a local Buddhist center! There's no need to read all of this straight through—just read what interests you, and come back to other answers later when these issues arise for you.

The second, longer section of the book directly explores the incredible variety of Buddhist resources available to you. There are detailed descriptions of the local Buddhist centers, outlining their locations, schedules, facilities, membership, atmosphere, applicable fees, and any other details that might prove useful. Now you'll know before you arrive whether you should bring money, if you should wear a skirt, how much personal attention you'll receive as a newcomer, and whether the center offers the sort of experience you're seeking. There are also shorter listings of other Buddhist centers in New York State, Connecticut, and New Jersey in case you want to search farther afield.

This section continues with additional listings of other useful Buddhist resources, including organizations, bookstores, magazines, doctors, museums, restaurants, and more. With this information at your fingertips you can find a good place to buy a Tibetan rug, meet a diminutive Buddhist nun who runs a vegetarian restaurant with a shrine dedicated to a fierce warrior deity, learn Korean, get your Ph.D. in Buddhist studies, and discover the intimate connection between Ben & Jerry's chocolate fudge brownie ice cream and New York City's Zen Buddhists.

There's a whole world of exciting and meaningful Buddhist experiences waiting for you in the New York metropolitan area. Whether you just want to dip your toe in the shallow end or are looking for a deeply transforming spiritual path, *The Buddhist Guide to New York* is a tool you can use to explore Buddhism for yourself and see what this ancient tradition can do for you.

HOW TO USE THIS BOOK

The Buddhist Guide to New York is meant to be a sort of primer on what to expect before you visit your local Buddhist group. It's written in the most basic, accessible language possible, so that people with no knowledge of Buddhism can use this book just as easily as enlightened gurus. For already-established Buddhists, it's also meant to make more resources available to the average practitioner, and hopefully strengthen ties between different groups by helping them learn about each other.

The book starts with an introduction to Buddhism and Buddhist groups you're likely to run into. Then you'll find a section on general etiquette at Buddhist centers, so you won't have to worry about making a major faux pas on your first visit. The bulk of the book contains descriptive entries about specific Buddhist groups and resources, divided into geographical or subject sections. Finally, other resources such as restaurants, supply stores, magazines, and special gatherings are listed.

What this book isn't is a teaching tool. Though there's plenty of information about Buddhism, there aren't any comprehensive teachings or how-to instructions for Buddhist practices. The Buddhist boom of the '90s has already produced a glut of instructional books, from stuff for beginners to advanced tantric practices. And in any case, visiting any one of the centers in this book is a better method of learning "how to" than reading a whole library of books *about* Buddhism.

The entries for each group follow a basic pattern. You'll get the name of the group, its address and contact information (including E-mail and Web site address if available), a short description of the type of Buddhism the group practices, and mention of the primary languages spoken by participants in the group. This is followed by a more fleshed-out description of the center, which provides information such as the group's practice, leadership, hours of operation, fees, rules, and any

other information deemed important or interesting. Unless otherwise stated, behavior at the individual centers conforms to that explained in the general etiquette section. For space reasons these descriptions are kept relatively short, but you should still find the sort of information you need to get a feel for what the group is like.

Because schedules change a lot, you should call or write to the center of your choice before attending, if possible. The information in this book is accurate as of this writing, but there's always the chance that some groups included here will shut down, move, undergo substantial changes in their practice style, or simply adjust their meeting times to fit a new schedule. In some cases, information has been left out for privacy reasons, though you should still find enough so that you can contact the group in question yourself. Also, though all attempts at accuracy and fairness have been made, the presentations here are ultimately filtered through the author's experience, and may not reflect the sort of experience you have when interacting with any particular group. Reading it all with a grain of salt may save you trouble or disappointment further down the road.

The book is broken down into geographical areas. The five boroughs of New York City are treated separately, as are New York State, Connecticut, and New Jersey. The descriptions of centers outside New York City are shorter and less descriptive, but should still give you enough information to gauge whether they're something you might be interested in. As always, if you don't find out everything you want to know here, just pick up the phone and go to the source.

Besides the individual entries for each center, there are some resources grouped together under common themes, such as museums and cultural resources, Tibetan support groups, and resources for parents. There are also longer essays on a variety of Buddhist subjects. You don't need to read these to start practicing right away, but they're included to answer some common questions about Buddhism and provide a little background material.

At the back of the book is a glossary explaining all the foreign terms used here, and an index for quick reference. If you've already got an idea of what you're looking for, this may actually be the best place to start.

A note on who's been included and who's been left out: basically, groups that consider themselves Buddhist or whose practice is a direct derivation from traditional Buddhism are included here. Left out are more heterogeneous groups, such as qi gong practitioners, New Age groups, most martial arts dojos, and Theosophy. No slight is meant toward such groups, but this book is intended to provide access to specifically Buddhist teachings. Also, though an exhaustive attempt to include all known resources in the tri-state area has been made, some groups have surely fallen through the cracks. If you know of other groups that should be included here, feel free to send information to the author for future editions of this guide.

Ultimately, the information contained in this book is for your benefit. Read as much or as little as you like, and remember that it won't all be helpful to you and your particular situation. Be prepared to encounter situations not covered here, and groups that have changed since this book was published. Buddhist teaching can be summed up as "everything changes," and that certainly holds true in the active and evolving world of New York City Buddhism.

GENERAL ETIQUETTE WHEN VISITING BUDDHIST CENTERS

Your first time walking into a Buddhist temple can be pretty unnerving. What's with all the chanting? Should I talk to the monks? How am I supposed to remember when to bow, when to sit, what to say? Depending on which group you drop in on and what your background is, that first visit can seem like a trip to another planet. But before you start wishing you had Captain Kirk along with you, here are some simple pointers that should make it easier for you.

Obviously, you should read the entry for whichever group you're interested in, checking to see if there are any special requirements listed. You may want to call ahead or visit the center's Web site, since things change and the rules listed here may not apply anymore next month.

Regardless of where you go first, it's always advisable to wear comfortable, loose-fitting clothes so that you'll be able to sit in meditation without feeling constricted. Formality differs from group to group, but it's always best to wear more conservative attire, without a lot of flashy colors. Wear layers if possible—many centers are unfortunately hot or cold, and overly zealous heating and air-conditioning can often make things worse. And skirts aren't usually a good choice—they're either so long that they interfere with proper sitting on a cushion, or too short to sit cross-legged and keep any semblance of modesty. Also, most groups require that you take your shoes off outside or in the hall before entering, and since you're almost certain to be meditating at some point, remember to wear easily removable footwear.

A new plague that's begun creeping into the zendos of New York City is cell phones and beepers. They're even less welcome in temple than they are at the opera, so please turn them off before services start. The last thing someone wants when they're trying to meditate is a phone

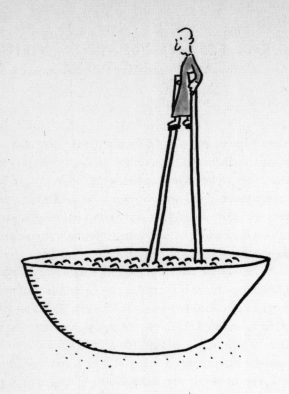

ringing in his or her ear. You should also turn off the alarm on your watch, if possible.

One thing you may want to do is bring a little money with you. Many groups ask for a small donation to help cover costs—some even require it. Putting a few dollars in the bowl by the door as you leave is a nice way to show your appreciation for the effort Buddhist teachers put out (and traditionally this is believed to create good karma). In many cases centers will also have some books for sale that may interest you. But don't ever bring more than twenty dollars or so unless you expect to pay for a specific activity that costs more; because temples are open to the public they occasionally attract pickpockets who may wish to free your wallet instead of your mind.

Some rules of thumb are pretty obvious: Don't smoke or bring alcohol into temples or centers. In fact, it's best not to bring any food at all—refreshments are usually provided in the situations where they're appropriate. Some temples provide the opportunity to symbolically offer food to the Buddhas; in these cases just observe what's appropriate and bring it next time. Don't swear, and try to cut down on slang, as many teachers may have somewhat limited English to begin with. If someone bows to you, bow back; if the person extends a hand, shake it. Don't ask to touch anybody's shaved head, and don't touch the Buddha statues. And while you may have read about the old Chinese Zen masters turning authority on its head, don't run around smacking the teachers or burning the Buddha statues. It won't make a good impression.

In some groups you may find yourself reading from a sutra or holy text. Generally, it's important to treat these books as sacred—don't put them on the floor, step over them, or treat them casually.

Some people are intimidated by Buddhist monks and nuns. They're afraid that they'll offend them somehow by causing them to break some sort of religious taboo, or newcomers project all sorts of fantasies of enlightenment onto them and start seeing them as superhuman. Don't stress out. Monks and nuns are just people too, and they'll indicate to you if your behavior isn't appropriate. If a monk follows a set of rules that doesn't allow him to be alone with a woman, he'll tell you. Or if he can't eat after noon, the practice of some schools, he'll decline your offered refreshments politely.

As far as knowing what to do, the best policy is to tell someone that you're a first-timer and ask for instruction before the service begins. Failing that, just watch what everybody else is doing and go with the flow. Don't expect to understand everything the first time, or to get it all right. Nobody is going to yell at you if you can't pronounce the liturgy or have to sneeze during meditation. Just do your best and you'll be fine.

On the other hand, don't expect anything miraculous to happen the first time either. You're not going to see somebody's aura or achieve instant enlightenment. The monks won't levitate and nobody's going to open your third eye. Spiritual progress comes as the result of sustained practice and is rarely accompanied by bells and whistles. If you walk out the first time believing that you're enlightened, you're probably more deluded than ever.

Sometimes you'll find yourself in a situation where you're practicing with a group that's largely made up of people from an ethnic group other than your own. If so, be aware that cultural differences may come up, and in most cases you should do your best to respect them. Asian immigrants may be more interested in trying to preserve something of value to them from the Old World, and meeting the needs of curious Americans may not be high on their list of priorities. In almost all cases outsiders who show sincere interest will be welcomed, and there's a lot to be learned from practicing in a cultural atmosphere that's different from your own. Just remember that you're a guest on their turf, and act accordingly.

Another mistake some new Buddhists make is inappropriately pestering teachers or demanding answers to all their questions. Most teachers are happy to answer a question or two after services, but keep in mind that they may be tired at the end of the day, have other people they need to talk to, or simply aren't in the mood to be interrogated. Also, many questions are best figured out on one's own, through further practice. Sensei Bonnie Treace from Zen Center of New York once told a particularly insistent questioner to "shut up and sit!" Sometimes that's the most compassionate advice one can receive.

One issue that should be discussed is that of authority and cults. Occasionally some groups employ rather strong rhetoric, proclaiming that obedience to their teacher is of utmost importance, or implying that if you disagree with their practices that you are especially stupid and unenlightened. Be aware that there are people ready to take advantage of newcomers' naïveté and inexperience. If anyone ever asks you to do something you're uncomfortable with, be cautious. Legitimate teachers should never ask you to lie for them, hide the truth, or ask for sexual favors or exorbitant donations in exchange for teachings or rituals. Be wary of excessive flattery, claims that practicing the way a particular group demands is the only way to reach salvation, or recommendations that you disassociate yourself from your family, friends, or profession. Such situations come up rarely. The vast majority of Buddhist teachers and groups are legitimate and have your welfare in mind, but there have also always been a handful of charlatans waiting to prey on the unsuspecting. If you ever have doubts about a particular community, it may be best simply to leave—in New York there are always many other groups to choose from.

Another thing to keep in mind is that incense and flowers are pretty much universal in Buddhist locations. If you have allergies or chemical sensitivities, be sure to call ahead and see exactly what sort of stuff is floating around in the air of your neighborhood temple. Also, chances are you'll end up meditating in a room next to people who may be wearing perfume or cologne, so be aware if this poses a danger to your health. For that matter, folks, please try not to wear strong scents to the zendo—it's hard to focus the mind when you're stuck two feet from someone with an overpowering odor of CK One. It doesn't hurt to shower first either, of course, especially in the summertime. . . .

One good idea is to get yourself placed on the mailing list of centers that interest you. That way you can find out about upcoming events, changes in the center's schedule and leadership, and often receive teachings and news through the group's newsletter. Most groups are happy to put you on their list; just mention it to someone after the service is over.

Finally, if you get to the temple and really just don't like what you find, please try to be polite about it. Don't walk out in the middle of a meditation session—try to wait until a break and then go. You may want to try again another time, as sometimes you may have arrived on a special festival or retreat day and encountered an unusual program. And if the first group doesn't work for you, don't give up. Keep trying until you find one that fits your needs, aesthetic preferences, and schedule. There are so many Buddhist options available in New York City that there's almost certainly one out there that's just right for you. Your Buddhist adventure is just beginning!

PART ONE

WHAT IS BUDDHISM?

BUDDHISM FOR BEGINNERS

So, what's Buddhism all about, anyway? Do you have to sit around with your legs crossed, endlessly chanting "om"? Isn't Dharma a TV sitcom character? Here are some basic Buddhist ideas and terms to get you started, plus answers to ten of the most common questions non-Buddhists ask. You don't need to know any of this stuff before you visit your first temple or Zen center, but it could be helpful.

BUDDHISM 101

THE FOUR NOBLE TRUTHS

A good place to start is with the Four Noble Truths, the bedrock of the Buddha's religious philosophy. After his enlightenment, when he decided to share what he'd discovered with the world, it was these basic principles that the Buddha put forth in his first sermon. Thousands of years later, they're still the fundamental guiding principles of the Buddhist community.

These truths are noble because they're practiced by noble people, not because they're particularly holy or comforting. In fact, they deal with suffering as well as happiness, with depravity and delusion as much as with morality and wisdom. Life is rocky, and what we need is tools to help get through the bumpy parts. That's just what the Four Noble Truths are meant to do. Thoroughly understood and put into practice,

they offer freedom from the addictions, neuroses, mistakes, and misconceptions that prevent us from living fully wise and compassionate lives.

The First Noble Truth is basically a big wake-up call: Everybody, no matter who or what they are, has suffering, stress, and disappointment in their life. That's quite a different lesson from what the media usually tries to teach. A lot of American culture these days is about chasing after material things we hope will bring us happiness, but let's face it—the

right car or lipstick or shampoo isn't going to solve your problems for you. That doesn't deny that sometimes we're happy and things seem to be going our way but rather reveals a hard truth that no one is immune to the "slings and arrows of outrageous fortune." It doesn't matter how rich, how beautiful, or how powerful you are—Bill Gates, Cindy Crawford, and Bill Clinton all experience some level of dissatisfaction, anger, and depression each day of their lives. The current boom of interest in Buddhism among the glamorous Hollywood elite ought to be proof enough of that.

The Second Noble Truth pushes this idea further. We suffer pain, stress, and disillusionment because of our wrong ideas about life, other people, and especially ourselves. We cling to things that can't bring us true happiness: material goods, money, our health or achievements, and so on. We want things to be perfect, and if we do manage to perfect some aspect of our lives—our job, our relationships, our skills, or whatever—we want it to remain that way forever. It's this twin denial of reality—believing that exterior things can bring us lasting happiness, and that somehow things won't change and get messy—that's at the root of most of our self-created suffering, confusion, and despair.

Fortunately, the Third Noble Truth isn't such a downer. After these tough first two truths, the Third Noble Truth offers the comfort of hope and encouragement: All this suffering is just a mental mistake, one that we can correct. Life doesn't have to be filled with pain, alienation, or stress. Peace of mind and good conduct can be learned by anyone, no matter how confused or misguided they may be right now. You can be a Buddha too.

Many people see the Buddha as a sort of metaphysical doctor, tending to the ills of the world. The First Noble Truth is his pronouncement of disease, the second is his diagnosis of the cause, and the third truth is his declaration that a cure exists. The Fourth Noble Truth is the Buddha's prescription for healing the mind and spirit: By practicing good deeds, training the mind, and developing wisdom, we can free ourselves from the troubles we create through greed, anger, and delusion. This process is usually referred to as following the Holy Eightfold Path.

THE HOLY EIGHTFOLD PATH

Each school of Buddhism has its own unique teachings regarding the path to enlightenment. But a common unifying factor is the Holy Eight-

fold Path, the original formula created by the Buddha and still observed by millions today. This teaching forms the fourth and final of the Noble Truths and represents the Buddha's recommendations for transforming greed into generosity, anger into compassion, and misunderstanding into wisdom.

The eight steps on this path are:

1. Correct view: recognizing the Four Noble Truths and the interconnected nature of all things.
2. Correct determination: resolving to root out bad habits and achieve peace.
3. Correct speech: avoiding gossip, slander, and lying.
4. Correct livelihood: pursuing an occupation that doesn't clash with your values and ideally affords opportunities to benefit others and discover wisdom.
5. Correct action: not harming others, be it through violence, theft, sexual misconduct, or losing control while under the influence of alcohol or drugs.
6. Correct effort: striving to practice the teachings, particularly by giving up deluded ways of thinking in favor of wholesome thoughts.
7. Correct mindfulness: being aware of negative thoughts when they arise, before they become harmful actions, and observing how the mind works.
8. Correct concentration: developing stability of mind.

Together, this mix of morality, mindfulness, and wisdom is the key to living a Buddhist life.

KARMA AND REBIRTH

Most people have at least heard of karma, though they may not have a clear idea what it means. Basically, karma is the active force that arises out of our thoughts, words, and actions, and which always leads to consequences. It's a sort of spiritual law of cause and effect, with the implication that prior conditioning increases the likelihood that you'll repeat an action, whether it's beneficial or harmful. Thus if you commit a misdeed—say you lie to cover up something you did—you set in action a chain of events that will eventually rebound negatively against you. Likewise, if you do something good—perhaps you contribute money to charity—that good karma will eventually return to you somehow. Exactly how each cause will manifest as an effect can't be known ahead of time—your lie may be exposed and cause you humiliation, or you may get away with it, but then worry constantly about being found out; perhaps your generosity will make you feel good and happy for the rest of the day, or maybe later someone will help you out when you're in need. The point is that actions all have consequences, and the quality of our life can be controlled to a large degree by regulating whether we are committing wholesome or unwholesome deeds.

Karma has an additional spiritual and mental level beyond that of reacting to actual things we do. If you think negative thoughts—perhaps you gripe all the time about how long your commute is, or you think about how cool it would be if your boss got hit by a bus—you will experience mental suffering and anguish. On the other hand, positive thoughts—such as reflecting on how much other people have contributed to your life, or resolving to help other people in need—produce mental and spiritual comfort and can lead to positive actions that create further positive karma. Holding on to greed, anger, or delusion pollutes the mind and therefore degrades the way in which we relate to the world. Approaching things with a fresh, forgiving, or positive attitude can measurably increase the amount of goodness we notice in the world and lead us to act in loving, compassionate ways.

Here's how the Buddha succinctly put it:

We are what we think. All that we are arises with our thoughts, and with our thoughts we create the world. Speak or act with an impure mind, and trouble will follow you as a cart follows the ox who draws it. Speak and act with a pure mind, and happiness will follow you like your shadow, never leaving. "He abused me, he beat me, he robbed me"—cling to such thoughts and you live in hate. "He abused me, he beat me, he robbed me"—release such thoughts, and live in peace.

Buddhist metaphysics is based on the idea that when we die, our minds are compelled by our accumulated karma to seek a new rebirth. Depending on whether we've built up good or bad karma, we may be reborn in positive or negative situations. Thus the fortune we experience now is based not only on deeds and thoughts from this life but countless previous ones as well. And the actions we undertake in this life will reverberate for centuries. Because all causes inevitably have effects, we're continually reborn in new forms until we shake off our old karmic patterns of misdeeds and unhealthy mind states. Through practicing Buddhism we learn how to achieve liberation from our past and gain full control over our lives.

Rebirth occurs not only between lives but from moment to moment as well. In each moment thoughts are passing away and new ones are replacing them. These new thoughts are conditioned by the previous ones and give rise to repeated patterns of behavior. If we can learn to turn our greed, pain, egocentricity, and delusion into generosity, forgiveness, selflessness, and wisdom, then we'll experience happiness and freedom from the cycle of negative thoughts. This mental freedom, seasoned with wisdom and compassion, is the goal of Buddhism. Buddhists call it by various names, such as nirvana, enlightenment, or awakening.

THE THREE JEWELS AND BECOMING A BUDDHIST

Many people ask how one "converts" to Buddhism. Basically, you don't become a Buddhist by renouncing your current religion or by adhering to a new dogma. Rather, it's accomplished by voluntarily turning to Buddhism for answers to your deep spiritual questions, an act that's traditionally referred to as seeking refuge with the Three Jewels. These Three Jewels are the Buddha, the teachings, and the community of practitioners.

When life has brought us to a crisis point, we seek help from that which we trust. If our trust is placed in Buddhism, then we can rightfully call ourselves Buddhists, whether or not our practice is particularly strong, our knowledge deep or shallow. Going to the Three Jewels for refuge is the most basic Buddhist activity, one repeated in temples and communities around the world every day, and performed again and again throughout the lifetime of each Buddhist.

The Three Jewels are called such because they're the precious core of Buddhism. The Buddha is the historical founder of Buddhism. Buddhists look to him as a role model and guide, a compassionate teacher and moral leader. But the title "Buddha" can also signify the other legendary Buddhas, as well as the innately enlightened aspect of our own minds. Thus when we seek refuge with the Buddha, we're trying to follow his example, and attempting to rely upon the Buddha nature that lies within us.

The teachings are known as the dharma, a complex Sanskrit term that includes concepts of law, natural order, lessons, methods, and wise writings and sayings. When Buddhists talk about the dharma, they mean both the specific teachings that were preached by the Buddha and refined by his followers, and the natural spiritual law of the universe, akin to the physical and chemical laws of science. The Buddha didn't invent the dharma—it's just how things naturally work, and he happened to discover this fundamental aspect of life and teach it to others. So by taking refuge in the dharma, we are following the teachings of Buddhism in order to better understand the way the world and our minds work.

The community of Buddhists is known as the sangha, another Sanskrit word. In its widest sense, all Buddhists are members of the sangha, and by taking refuge in the sangha we seek help and comfort from people walking the same spiritual path as ourselves. Sometimes the term sangha is used in a narrower sense to refer to a specific group of practitioners, or to refer to just the community of monks and nuns.

A good resource for further investigation is Walpola Rahula's *What the Buddha Taught*.

TEN FREQUENTLY ASKED QUESTIONS

WHO WAS THE BUDDHA?

The Buddha was a religious teacher who lived in India about 2,500 years ago. According to the stories of his life that have been handed down to us, the Buddha was a prince named Siddhartha Gautama. Based on a fortune-teller's prediction, his father feared that Siddhartha would become a guru instead of a king, and therefore had him kept in the palace, surrounded at all times by luxury and happiness. But one day the prince saw some suffering people and a wandering holy man and realized that there were more important things in life than material richness and power. He renounced his princehood and left his family to seek a religious solution to the problems of the world.

Siddhartha wandered around India, studying with different gurus and trying various ascetic and meditative practices. But nothing seemed to deliver the real release from suffering that he sought. Finally he discovered for himself a middle path between luxury and asceticism, and while meditating he achieved enlightenment—he understood the causes that bring about suffering, discovered the means to end them, and finally freed himself of angst and anguish. It is at this moment, at the age of thirty-five, that he became a Buddha: literally, an "awakened one."

The Buddha went on to found a large community of followers, including monks, nuns, and laypeople. He traveled the countryside for decades, preaching his doctrine of freedom through compassion, mindfulness, and wisdom. He finally died of food poisoning at the age of eighty.

After the Buddha passed away his remains were cremated and distributed among his followers. His community continued to grow and spread, eventually splitting into many different subgroups that viewed him and his teachings in different ways. Some people saw him as a human being who achieved extraordinary abilities through his peerless virtue and wisdom. Others saw him as a more transcendent being, an eternal guide and teacher who had always been enlightened. Today there are probably as many different ideas about who and what the Buddha was as there are about Jesus Christ.

The Buddha wasn't a god. Despite the miracles he is said to have performed and the belief of some that he represents an eternal principle of wisdom, Buddhists do not believe he was a deity or messiah. Buddha didn't create the world and doesn't control it—he was a great teacher who showed humanity the way to peace and insight. Others have done so before him and more Buddhas will appear in due time, because the truth that the Buddha discovered is an intrinsic part of reality, of being human, and it can be realized at any time if we only make the effort to practice as the Buddha recommended.

For a full account of the Buddha's life told in an accessible, novelistic style, try Thich Nhat Hanh's *Narrow Path, White Clouds*.

DO I HAVE TO MEDITATE IN ORDER TO BE A BUDDHIST?

No. To be honest, the majority of Buddhists living in Asia meditate very infrequently, if at all. Meditation is traditionally seen as a very difficult activity practiced by the religious elite—monks, nuns, and some advanced laypeople. Most Asian Buddhists would probably stress that morality is more important than meditation.

In America, meditation is strongly identified with Buddhism, to the extent that many American Buddhists consider meditation to be the core of Buddhist practice. This is a rather unique situation in the history of Buddhist transmission to a new country, which led the famous Zen teacher Shunryu Suzuki Roshi to remark that American Buddhists are "neither monks nor laypeople."

Meditation is a powerful tool for exploring the self and developing insight into reality. It's highly recommended that all people interested in Buddhism at least give meditation a try. But it's hardly the only useful technique for self-transformation that Buddhism offers; some people will fare better with chanting, visualization, study, bowing, or other Buddhist activities. Don't let the rigor of meditation practice deter you from exploring the riches of Buddhist practice, philosophy, and culture.

IS THERE A BUDDHIST BIBLE?

The short answer is that there's no one Buddhist "Bible" that can be quickly pointed to, and there are different interpretations of the many different scriptures. The canonical literature of Buddhism dwarfs the Christian Bible many times over—it is literally impossible to read all the sutras, shastras, tantras, and other primary texts within a single human lifetime. Also, these texts are not considered the "word of God" as the Bible is, but are books of wisdom, and many are the words of the Buddha.

Each particular school of Buddhism venerates specific texts as its central literature. In general, we can say that there are two main collections of Buddhist writing, the Pali-language Tipitaka and the various Mahayana versions known as the Tripitaka. Both Tipitaka and Tripitaka mean "three baskets," a reference to the organization of these roughly parallel collections. Each is composed of three sections: a Vinaya section containing rules and regulations for the priesthood (as well as many stories from the time of the Buddha), a Sutra section containing teachings and stories of the Buddha and his disciples, and an Abhidharma section containing further elaborations of Buddhist philosophy developed by later Buddhist practitioners.

The Tipitaka is the holy literature of the Theravada school and is widely considered to be the oldest Buddhist writing. It is studied in Sri Lanka, Cambodia, Thailand, Laos, Burma, and parts of Vietnam and Bangladesh. The Theravada school also recognizes the religious importance of some other texts, but only those contained within the Tipitaka are considered truly canonical.

The scriptures of the Mahayana schools (basically all forms of Buddhism other than Theravada) are much more difficult to categorize. The Tripitakas preserved in Tibetan, Chinese, and other languages differ in many aspects, with a wide variety of texts, including those dating from the time of the Pali Tipitaka to much later writings by sages from various countries. Because of the liberal nature of Mahayana Buddhism, it has accepted many more writings as valid than the Theravadins and has often been willing to incorporate new works into the canon if they represent authentic wisdom and practice.

Views toward the scriptures differ between schools and individuals. Some are considered to have been taught by the historical Buddha or other esoteric Buddhas, some were taught by his followers, and there are also many writings from later teachers and meditators. Zen Buddhism is famous for supposedly denigrating the scriptures, but this is primarily rhetoric—Zen practice typically involves scriptural study, adherence to the Vinaya discipline, as well as study of the unique texts of the Zen tradition.

Heart of Understanding, by Thich Nhat Hanh, contains the Heart Sutra, a short, important Buddhist text. *The Middle Length Discourses of the Buddha* by Bhikkhu Nanamoli is a collection of ancient Buddhist wisdom. Try *Zen Flesh, Zen Bones* by Paul Reps for a quick Zen fix.

WHAT IS THE BUDDHIST VIEW OF GOD?

The quick answer is "None." God, as commonly understood by Westerners—an all-powerful eternal being who created and rules the universe, and whose worship is the primary goal of religion—is a concept wholly absent from the Buddhist approach to religion. Buddhism views everything that exists as ever changing, and holds that the universe has both no beginning (because something would have had to come before whatever caused it) and no end. Furthermore, in Buddhism the active agent directing all events is karma, an impersonal force that arises as the natural result of one's good and bad actions, not an intelligent personality that guides and judges the world according to its own whims.

The better answer, though, is a little more complex. The majority of Asian Buddhists do believe in the existence of gods—that is, beings of greater than normal power and life span who can control the weather, seasons, and so on. Whether these are the Hindu gods, Shinto gods, or others depends on the cultural environment of the individual Buddhist. These are ancient indigenous beliefs that Buddhism has incorporated and by and large hasn't tried to eliminate—but it's important to recognize that these beliefs come from outside Buddhism and aren't actively propagated by it. In the orthodox view these beings are seen as part of the natural order of things, not superior to it, and they're acknowledged as limited beings whose worship can't grant ultimate peace or happiness.

Many Buddhists take this idea further and claim that the various gods are manifestations of one's own psyche, personified symbols of mental states and not actual independent beings in their own right. Another Buddhist view is that the gods are Buddhas in disguise, playing the part of gods in order to teach people who would otherwise fail to be attracted to religious truth.

IS IT POSSIBLE TO BE A BUDDHIST AND REMAIN CHRISTIAN/JEWISH/WHATEVER?

Interestingly, despite the traditional Buddhist disavowal of the importance of a God-centered approach to religion, there are many people practicing Buddhism in America today who claim to believe in God. Nearly all were raised with some idea of God as an important part of religion, and as they've moved into Buddhism, they've held on to this orientation. So now we find folks who cheerfully identify themselves as Christian Buddhists, Jewish Buddhists, and so on. From one perspective this is a rather unusual situation, as Christianity and Judaism are very different religious worldviews with quite different beliefs, goals, and rules from Buddhism. It isn't really possible to retain a rigid, fundamentalist idea of Western religion—for instance, to believe that all who do not accept Jesus Christ as their personal lord and savior will burn in eternal hell—and be a Buddhist.

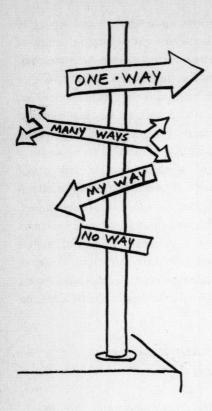

However, there are a great many more liberal approaches to Christianity and Judaism found in America, and some of them do seem at least somewhat compatible. From another perspective, this mixture is just the natural assimilation of Buddhism, an unusually adaptable and tolerant religion, into the native spirituality of a new country. Precisely because Buddhism doesn't demand adherence to its own God or gods, many Western Buddhists have found room in their spiritual lives to incorporate Christian or Jewish prayer and worship into their overall religious practice. It's too soon to tell if this will be a productive or destructive development—hopefully the combination will prove beneficial to those who choose this path.

Two good books on Buddhism and Christianity are *The Good Heart* by the Dalai Lama and *Living Buddha, Living Christ* by Thich Nhat Hanh. *That's Funny, You Don't Look Buddhist* by Sylvia Boorstein is written from a Jewish-Buddhist perspective. And for the strict atheists out there, there's *Buddhism without Beliefs* by Stephen Batchelor, a somewhat controversial book that is nonetheless regarded as a minor classic in many American Buddhist circles.

WHAT DOES BUDDHISM SAY ABOUT WOMEN?

Women have had to struggle with oppression and inequality in Asia for millennia. Buddhism often offered women increased independence and comfort, at least in their spiritual lives, but at the same time it was hardly a feminist revolution. The Buddha created an order of nuns—the first of its kind in recorded history—who were held in great respect, but at the same time were required to show complete deference to the monks.

Buddhist views of women have differed depending on the time period and dominant culture that Buddhism found itself in. Some believed that women represented a lower form of rebirth than men, that they were somehow "unclean," and that they had less success in following a religious life. Others stressed that femininity and masculinity are merely illusory concepts created by the unenlightened mind, and that women's potentials are no less than men's. Regardless of their status, or lack thereof, women have always been regarded by Buddhism as capable of achieving complete enlightenment.

Historically, there have been many more male Buddhist sages than women, or at least their legends have survived more often to come down to us today. That said, the history of Buddhism is full of amazing and enlightened women, starting with the Buddha's own foster mother. Buddhist women have been great meditators, leaders, teachers, and philosophers. Buddhist tantra, one of Buddhism's highest developments, is regarded by many as having been invented by women. Buddhism is full of iconic female role models, including deities, saints, and Kwan-Yin, the embodiment of compassion.

In America women took a prominent leadership role from the start, and today there are many Buddhist groups led by women (not to mention the fact that there are more female American Buddhists than male). In New York City there are a good number of centers led by women, such as Fire Lotus Temple (see page 127) and Manhattan Won Buddhism (see page 63).

The intersection of Buddhism and feminism has proved quite fertile, and there are many books available on women's issues in Buddhism. Two good selections are *Turning the Wheel* by Sandy Boucher and *Buddhism after Patriarchy* by Rita Gross.

WHAT DOES BUDDHISM SAY ABOUT HOMOSEXUALITY?

Homosexuality isn't traditionally an issue in Buddhism. It received no attention from the Buddha and wasn't a subject of much interest to the many philosophers and sages who followed in his footsteps. The truth is that premodern Buddhist Asia lacked a widespread concept of people as homosexuals with a basic orientation toward their own gender. In a few texts it's spoken of as a negative action, which is probably the overall attitude of most Asian Buddhists. Buddhists with such attitudes don't normally view it as an evil act, just an inappropriate one, far less serious than killing or stealing. Buddhist philosophy itself isn't as proscriptive about behavior as Westerners expect religion to be—sexual activity is considered a secular act, and homosexual intercourse, like heterosexual, is not good or evil. It's just another worldly attachment.

In the modern Western world of identity politics and gay liberation, American Buddhists have largely, though not unanimously, taken the stance that homosexuals are not any different in terms of morality than their straight counterparts. There is resistance to "uncloseted" gays and lesbians in some circles and complete acceptance in others. Across the country there are several prominent gay Buddhist groups, and there are even gay and lesbian Zen masters, including Pat O'Hara of the Village Zendo (see page 102). A prominent New York City gay Buddhist organization is Maitri Dorje (see page 92).

For gay Buddhist theory, one good resource is the two-volume anthology *Queer Dharma* edited by Winston Leyland.

WHAT DOES BUDDHISM SAY ABOUT ABORTION?

Buddhism neither strictly accepts nor condemns abortion. Traditionally, Buddhists believe that life begins at conception, and abortion is an act of violence that violates the first precept—do not harm living things. Although it's not a particularly prominent topic of discussion, when it is focused on, abortion is discouraged for moral reasons. Like all harmful acts, it's seen as having potentially detrimental karmic effects on the current or future lives of both the mother and the doctor. However, it's not seen as an especially negative act in the way that conservative Christianity labels it a great sin.

In Japan priests perform annual services for aborted fetuses at the mothers' request. Thus while it's officially frowned upon, the religious authorities also recognize abortion as a part of women's lives and offer spiritual solutions to the pain caused to both the mother and the fetus. One book that explores this phenomenon further is William LaFleur's *Liquid Life*.

WHO IS THE DALAI LAMA?

The Dalai Lama, or more specifically His Holiness Tenzin Gyatso, the Fourteenth Dalai Lama, is a prominent teacher of the Gelugpa school of Tibetan Buddhism. He is also regarded as a spiritual leader by most of the other Tibetan Buddhist schools, as well as traditionally being Tibet's highest political authority. Outside of Tibetan Buddhism, he holds no authority, though he is almost universally regarded by other Buddhists with respect and admiration.

The Dalai Lama is believed to reincarnate life after life in order to guide the Tibetan people, both spiritually and politically. He is also seen as an incarnation of Chenrezig (Avalokiteshvara), the bodhisattva of infinite compassion.

The current Dalai Lama was chosen as a toddler by a mysterious process involving an oracle and other methods of divination. He was a teenager when China invaded his country and he remained for ten years championing his people's cause, but when it became apparent that his efforts inside China were bearing little fruit and that his life might be in danger, he fled to India, setting off a massive emigration movement that continues today. In Dharamsala, India, the Dalai Lama set up the Tibetan government-in-exile. He was awarded the Nobel Peace Prize in 1989 for his decades of seeking a nonviolent solution to the Chinese occupation of Tibet. He now spends much of his time traveling the world teaching about Buddhism, promoting peace, and gathering support for Tibetans both within Tibet and in exile.

The Dalai Lama has visited New York City many times. In 1999 he gave a public teaching in Central Park that was attended by tens of thousands. That year he also had two books that stayed on the *New York Times* best-seller list for months. People interested in his life should check out *Freedom in Exile,* his very readable autobiography; those interested in his teachings should try *The Art of Happiness* and *The Dalai Lama—A Policy of Kindness.*

WHAT RELIGIOUS RULES DO BUDDHISTS FOLLOW?

Buddhism isn't a religion of rules and laws—one should follow its precepts because the behaviors they recommend will naturally bring more happiness and peace, not because one will be punished by the universe for disobedience. Even the pronouncements of the Buddha are guidelines, not commandments, and must be put into effect with attention paid to the context of each particular situation.

Buddhism does contain many moral precepts—voluntarily observed guidelines that help one purify one's karma and lead a wise, compassionate life. The most basic formula is the Five Great Precepts, followed by most laypeople. They are abstention from harming others, stealing, lying, taking intoxicants that cloud the mind, and sexual misconduct, such as adultery or rape. These precepts are understood to have different applications in real-life situations. For instance, it may be necessary to kill in self-defense, or often it's taught that it's okay to drink some alcohol as long as you don't get so plastered that you're a danger to yourself or others.

A lot of New Yorkers think that Buddhists have to be vegetarians. The Buddha wasn't a vegetarian, and most schools don't require their followers to stick to tofu and veggies. Some do, however, particularly some Chinese forms of Buddhism, and most recommend that if it's possible for one to practice vegetarianism in one's economic and cultural environment, it's a good idea. Animals are worthy of our compassion (indeed, according to Buddhist teachings, all living beings have been our mothers at some point) and vegetarianism represents one useful way of observing nonviolence. Regardless of whether one ultimately chooses to eat Big Macs or not, enlightenment can be reached by carnivores, omnivores, and herbivores alike.

A BRIEF OVERVIEW OF THE DIFFERENT SCHOOLS OF BUDDHISM

Just how many kinds of Buddhism are there? Everybody's heard of Zen, but what the heck is Rissho Kosei Kai? Does it really matter what kind of Buddhism you choose? In this section you'll take a quick trip through the different types of Buddhism represented in the New York City area. Since virtually every major Buddhist group around the world has some sort of presence here in the city, this book can't delve into all of them in depth. But an overview should help you determine whether you'd be most attracted to Tibetan Gelugpa, Burmese Theravada, or Japanese Pure Land Buddhism.

THE WONDERFUL, WEIRD WORLD OF BUDDHISM

The variety of Buddhist groups and practices is mind-boggling: some have monks and some don't, some are vegetarian and others aren't, some meditate while others chant, some believe in the necessity of faith while other groups stress the importance of self-effort. Each group claims that its methods are effective for achieving enlightenment—so, how the heck are you supposed to figure out which one to practice?

There's a concept in Buddhism known as upaya, roughly translated as "skillful means." Upaya is the idea that the Buddha taught many different methods because there are so many different sorts of people in the world, with varying situations and needs. That means no particular school or method of Buddhism is necessarily better than another—it's all a matter of how much each method can help you, based on your personality and background. Maybe you've got the sort of temperament that's best suited to Zen meditation, or you might be better off studying Gelugpa philosophy. Perhaps you're strapped for time or have a noisy apartment building, and Pure Land chanting is the smart way to go. What matters isn't finding the "correct" kind of Buddhism in any ultimate sense, but the type that happens to be right for you.

Provided below are some short descriptions of different Buddhist traditions found in New York City. They only skim the surface of each group, but maybe something will sound interesting to you and you'll want to learn more. You can either buy a book and read some more—suggested readings are included below—or find a nearby group in whichever tradition and jump right in. The first place you try may not be the right one, so don't be discouraged—there's enough difference between each group that your second choice may be what you're looking for, or maybe your third. There's nothing wrong with visiting several centers before settling down, and in fact it's probably a good idea. You might even find that you benefit from regularly attending more than one center. There's value in each approach to Buddhism.

Another thing to keep in mind is that these descriptions are intentionally general. Some groups may differ from the brief depictions given here, and furthermore the atmosphere and practice in two separate groups that share the same tradition can sometimes be quite different. An open mind is probably the best preparation one can have for a good first-time experience at any Buddhist group.

ZEN BUDDHISM

Everything's Zen? I don't think so. Despite the fact that Zen has been dubiously linked to everything from sex to the stock market to motorcycle maintenance in recent decades, the misunderstanding of Zen Buddhism by American pop culture is almost as profound and mysterious as Zen practice itself. Zen has been tremendously popular in this country, especially since the Beat poets, writers, and musicians—such as Allen Ginsberg, Jack Kerouac, and Gary Snyder—took to it in a major way. And New York City, along with the hippie Shangri-La of the San

Francisco Bay Area, has been ground zero for the Zen fad. Today, Zen Buddhism is probably the most widely practiced form of Buddhism in both New York City and America as a whole.

If you read a popular book or two on Zen, you might get the impression that it's a freewheeling, spontaneous type of individualistic religion. But don't show up at a Zen center expecting to find an open mike and a lot of hip cats lounging around with the groove, man. Organized Zen groups revolve around intensive sitting meditation, known as zazen. Even if they incorporate other practices into their routine, expect a heavy emphasis on quiet, still meditation. You will be expected to sit cross-legged quietly and count your breaths for periods averaging thirty- to forty-five minutes, often broken up by five minutes or so of

walking meditation (basically follow-the-leader while trying to maintain a calm, focused state of mind). There may also be short (five- or ten-minute) periods of chanting in English or Japanese from a sutra book, a sermon delivered by the teacher, or even a chance to have a private interview with the teacher, called dokusan or sanzen. Some groups, particularly Korean ones, include repeated bowing as part of the practice.

Zen sitting involves paying attention to your breathing during early stages, and then the more advanced practice of shikantaza, just sitting, as your meditation ability progresses. Another type of Zen meditation involves the use of koans, illogical riddles meant to shock the mind out of its habitual patterns of reasoning. Most people are familiar with the classic koan "What is the sound of one hand clapping?" Zen students concentrate on their koans (individually assigned to them by their teacher), throwing their minds again and again against the brick wall of the puzzle, until their ordinary dualistic mind gives up and they begin to comprehend the situation on a deeper level.

Some Zen groups use a stick called the kyosaku or keisaku during sitting meditation. This is a long, flat stick that's used to jolt sleepy meditators awake during long sitting periods. Patrolling senior students will smack people on the shoulders with the kyosaku, producing a shock and loud noise, but not actually inflicting any injury. Don't be afraid of this stick—it isn't used in many groups, and in virtually all groups where it is present, it's used only upon request. Should you wish to receive a blow, you have to bow when the stick holder goes by. Misunderstanding of the kyosaku has led some people to think of Zen as violent or militaristic, two terms that certainly do not apply to Zen groups in New York.

Many Zen centers incorporate some sort of "work practice" (known as samu), a practical application of Zen that tries to demonstrate that mindfulness can be maintained during any activity. Indeed, it is bringing enlightenment into everyday activities that most typifies Zen. The Zen emphasis on concentration, freedom within discipline, and spontaneity has enabled it to make a considerable contribution to realms outside of strictly Buddhist techniques, such as poetry, painting, and the martial arts. All of this makes it attractive for laypeople, since even though Zen is traditionally a monastic discipline, there are many teachers who are applying it in creative ways to the American rat race. Maybe someday everything really will be Zen. . . .

Zen centers almost always have a formal leader, usually called a roshi or sensei, who is believed to embody the enlightenment sought by Zen Buddhists. These teachers receive permission to teach directly from their own masters once the master determines that the student has attained a suitable level of enlightenment. It's these personal relationships, as much as the sitting meditation, that convey the spirit of Zen from generation to generation. Most Zen practitioners stress the necessity of studying under a qualified Zen teacher, rather than trying to do it on your own, as the master can guide you through difficult times, offer encouragement and advice, and serve as an example of Zen enlightenment to follow. Zen leaders are the most diverse of any school—they may be celibate monastics, noncelibate, or even married with families.

If Zen practice is primarily about sitting meditation, then Zen phi-

losophy is mainly about emptiness. This concept is addressed in the famous dictum, "Form is emptiness, emptiness is form." It's understanding this emptiness, the fundamental nature of all things, that brings about mental awakening in Zen. Realizing emptiness leads to detachment from anger, greed, envy, and self-indulgence and leads to compassion for all beings, who share this nature with oneself.

Zen is a Japanese school of Buddhism, of which there are two main sects: Soto, which emphasizes shikantaza, and Rinzai, which stresses koan practice. Another lineage is the Sanbo Kyodan, which was created in the twentieth century from a mixture of both Soto and Rinzai; it has significant representation in America. In China, where it originated, Zen is known as Ch'an, and today is notable for being somewhat less sectarian than Zen and incorporating influences from the Pure Land schools of Buddhism. In Korea Zen is called Son, and includes more formal bowing practice than in other areas. Vietnamese Zen is called Thien; it is similar to Ch'an, although one Vietnamese Zen group, the Community of Mindfulness (see page 28), is large and unique enough to merit a category of its own.

In New York City, most Zen groups were founded either by a leader who specifically came to this country to teach Zen to Americans or by an American who has studied for some time under an immigrant teacher. Today many leaders may be third- and even fourth-generation teachers in these American lineages. The acceptance of Zen in mainstream American culture means that Zen groups are primarily non-Asian in membership—certainly Asians and Asian Americans are present in many groups, but local Zen groups tend to be predominantly Caucasian in makeup, with members of other racial groups also represented to varying degrees. One exception is Ch'an and Thien centers, which on the whole tend to be more oriented toward serving the needs of the Chinese- or Vietnamese-speaking population.

Local Zen groups of note include: Zen Studies Society (see page 58), Fire Lotus Temple (see page 127), and the Village Zendo (see page 102). A great Ch'an center for both Chinese and English speakers is the Ch'an Meditation Center (see page 110). The primary Korean Son group in

New York City is the Chogye International Zen Center of New York (see page 87).

The classic texts on Zen in English are by D. T. Suzuki—check out his *Manual of Zen Buddhism* or *Essays in Zen Buddhism, First Series* for a nice taste of Zen. Books by prominent American Zen teachers include Philip Kapleau's *The Three Pillars of Zen,* and Robert Aitken's *Taking the Path of Zen.* Read Sheng-Yen's *Dharma Drum* for a modern Ch'an perspective, and *Dropping Ashes on the Buddha* for Korean master Seung Sahn's approach to Zen.

COMMUNITY OF MINDFULNESS

The Community of Mindfulness is a new branch growing from the ancient tree of Zen, specifically Zen in the Vietnamese tradition. Created in 1983 by internationally renowned Vietnamese monk Thich Nhat Hanh, who was nominated for the Nobel Peace Prize by Rev. Martin Luther King, Jr., the Community of Mindfulness carries on much of the Zen tradition, but with far less emphasis on teachers and strenuous effort. It's definitely more family oriented and everyday than the more orthodox forms of Zen.

Almost all Buddhist groups form when a teacher arrives in town, sets up shop, and begins to attract disciples. But the Community of Mindfulness, while directed on a national and international level by a group of established teachers, is a firmly grassroots movement. Chapters are usually created when several people are exposed to Thich Nhat Hanh's teachings through his many books and decide to start practicing as he recommends. Then they contact the national organization and receive some assistance, but each group is firmly based on its own local community. Members gather, usually weekly, to meditate together, hold discussions, and learn about Buddhist practice through Community of Mindfulness–related books, tapes, and videos. As these are entirely lay-based groups with no firm hierarchy, there's less emphasis on formality than other Zen groups, and virtually no talk of satori, the sudden moment of breakthrough enlightenment that is the goal of most Zen students. Instead, Community of Mindfulness meetings are fairly casual, and the point is the practice itself, which is presented as a gradual reconnecting with reality in slow, moment-by-moment steps.

Community of Mindfulness practice is centered on sitting and walking meditation. As the name implies, mindfulness meditation is the practice of choice here, defined as paying attention to the breath and one's environment in a focused but detached way. It's basic Zen practice, presented in a simple way, with little esoteric doctrine. The emphasis is on practicality—how to find peace in this life, how to develop compassion, how to use the teachings to help manage relationships better, and so on. A popular technique is stopping whatever one is doing and paying attention to one's breath each time the phone rings before answering it. There are whole Community of Mindfulness books full of little verses on mindful eating, mindful dish washing, even mindful toilet functions. (Fortunately, that last one isn't demonstrated in person.)

Another aspect of the Community of Mindfulness approach is social involvement. Thich Nhat Hanh is partly responsible for the worldwide movement of Engaged Buddhism, the social action/liberation theology of Buddhist practice. Thich Nhat Hanh's conception of Engaged Buddhism is two-tiered, with engagement on the individual level with one's life through mindfulness practice, and engagement on the community or societal level through applying Buddhist insight to social problems such as war and poverty. The Community of Mindfulness groups don't tend to get involved directly in specific political or social issues, but individual members are often encouraged to take mindfulness off the cushion and work for social justice and peace.

Almost all communities gather in members' houses, rather than a special meeting space. Besides weekly meditation and discussion sessions, there are usually monthly full days of mindfulness practice, and monthly precept recitations.

In New York the Community of Mindfulness groups are mostly organized into a single large chapter, the New York Metro (see page 48). They have neighborhood groups throughout the city.

Thich Nhat Hanh's books are unusually accessible and written in simple, refreshing prose. Some good bets are *The Miracle of Mindfulness* and *Peace Is Every Step*.

THERAVADA BUDDHISM

Theravadins are the most religiously conservative branch of Buddhism, something that should be evident the moment you set foot in one of their temples. Regardless of the ethnic background of the temple or how long it's been established in New York City, you're almost certain to encounter orange or maroon-robed monks, an elaborate altar, and a beautiful golden Buddha image. While Theravada is struggling to meet the demands of fast-paced New York life, its temples present a taste of Old World charm and ritual, much more formal than some of the looser Zen or Tibetan communities.

This is old-style Buddhism, with fewer concessions to the modern world. It is fundamentalist, in the sense that it focuses on the fundamental founding tenets of Buddhism, without as much elaboration or adaptation as other schools. The Zen, Pure Land, and Tibetan schools all include veneration of many Buddhas and saints, but the Theravadins are almost solely focused on the original historical Buddha himself. It's a point of pride for them that they practice the most ancient form of Buddhism that survives to this day.

Most of the Theravadin temples are basically ethnic in character, acting as repositories of Old Country wisdom and culture for people from Sri Lanka, Thailand, Cambodia, Burma, or Laos. The monks are usually immigrants from the temple's home country, as opposed to the American-born teachers who lead many other centers in New York City. These monks usually follow stricter rules than their non-Theravadin counterparts, refusing to eat after noon, maintaining celibacy, avoiding money, and generally putting a stronger emphasis on discipline and morality than other groups. They survive entirely on donations made by the laity, who cook their meals for them, an effort that is believed to bring good fortune to the giver.

Although more Asian than some groups in New York City, many Theravadin temples have adapted to meet the needs of native New Yorkers with weekly meditation and dharma instruction in English. Theravadin meditation focuses most strongly on Vipassana, a basic technique that involves paying close attention to one's thoughts and actions, watching in a detached way as they arise and pass away. Many people find that it's similar to Zen meditation. But unlike Zen, Theravada doesn't stress the need for a one-on-one relationship with a guru. Another common Theravadin method is metta meditation, which consists of wishing happiness and peace for oneself, one's friends and enemies, and all people.

Generosity is another basic characteristic of Theravadin practice—it's considered good karma to donate food and money to support the monks, and families frequently invite groups of monks to their houses for lunch in order to generate merit and show their gratitude for receiving the teachings. This charity, known as dana, is also encouraged as a way to help other people besides the monks, and making merit through giving away money, goods, and food to those who need it is common in this school.

When visiting a Theravadin temple, be prepared to speak with monks, rather than lay representatives, and please show them deference and respect. Theravada is more dominated by the priesthood than any other form of Buddhism, and monastic renunciation of lay life is considered the most perfect way to pursue enlightenment. Many monks come from cultures that believe lay people should not sit higher than monks, so if you're asked to sit on a small stool or the floor, you risk offense by refusing. Another taboo common in these circles is touching anyone, particularly a superior, on the head.

Prominent Theravadin temples include the New York Buddhist Vihara (see page 116) and the Universal Peace Buddha Temple (see page 130). Some good books on Theravada are *Mindfulness in Plain English* by Bhante Henepola Gunaratana, and *Questions from the City, Answers from the Forest* by Ajahn Sumano Bhikkhu.

INSIGHT MEDITATION (VIPASSANA)

While Theravada Buddhism is monastically oriented, conservative, and more Asian in form and membership than most New York City groups, it's spawned a distinctly American sort of Buddhism that's in many ways its polar opposite. This new school takes its title from the meditation practice that forms its raison d'être, Vipassana—known in English as Insight Meditation.

Whereas Theravada Buddhism includes many different types of meditation, complicated liturgy, strict moral precepts, and voluminous scriptures, Insight Meditation is radically pared down, focused specifically on perfecting the practice of Vipassana as a tool for achieving nirvana. This orientation toward meditation practice, without the other ritualistic trappings of Buddhism, has resulted in a form of Buddhism that is almost entirely Western. Asian cultural norms, monks, and many other things one expects in Buddhist centers are completely absent. Even karma, reincarnation, and other staples of Buddhism are relegated to the background in favor of how-to instruction in technique.

Insight Meditation teachers are layfolk, and many have a history in Western psychology, which has a strong influence on their teaching approach and the language they use. Meetings are informal, with teachers and students alike in casual Western attire. Weekend and longer meditation retreats are a common part of this school, and participants typically take special vows, such as moral precepts or vows of silence, to enhance the quality of their practice while on retreat.

For some people, Insight Meditation's "Buddhism without Buddhism" approach is ideal, while for others it's ultimately not well rounded enough. Even some prominent teachers have taken to studying with leaders of other schools, particularly the Dzogchen lineages of Tibetan Buddhism. One way groups have sought to ease this trend is by increasing the amount of metta meditation they practice, and this has become a popular secondary technique. Insight Meditation is a new approach to Buddhism that is still evolving and finding its place in the tapestry of American dharma practice.

Currently, Insight Meditation is not as well represented in New York City as other primary forms of American Buddhism. One group to investigate is the Westbeth Vipassana Group (see page 105). The New York Insight Meditation Center (see page 67) doesn't have its own center yet. But this is a very popular school in America and will probably play an increasingly important part in New York Buddhism in the years to come. It's one to keep your eye on.

Books for further reading include Joseph Goldstein's *Insight Meditation* and Jack Kornfield's *A Path with Heart*.

TIBETAN BUDDHISM

In 1989 His Holiness the Dalai Lama won the Nobel Peace Prize, and during the 1990s Tibetan Buddhism entered the American cultural consciousness in a major way, with Hollywood movies (*Seven Years in Tibet* and *Kundun*), celebrity Buddhists (Richard Gere and Steven Seagal), and the Free Tibet political and student movement. Some of this excitement was a continuation of the Western fantasy of Shangri-La, the remote, inaccessible, spiritual land of enlightened beings untainted by decadent outside influences. Though this sort of distortion hampers real understanding of Tibetan Buddhism, the rising popularity of the Tibetan schools is slowly bringing better understanding of the Himalayan traditions to American Buddhism.

The Buddhism of Tibet, which is also practiced in Mongolia, China, Bhutan, Nepal, India, and parts of Russia, has some very unique characteristics. For one, the order of monks plays a much more active role in "secular" realms of society, often holding political as well as religious power. The monkhood itself has unique characteristics, such as the institution of tulkus, advanced Buddhist teachers who are believed to reincarnate life after life to maintain their roles as leaders and protectors. Most of the highest positions in Tibetan Buddhism are filled by these tulkus, who are chosen by mysterious means while still children and raised within the confines of the monasteries to take over their predecessors' roles.

Tibetan Buddhism is sometimes referred to as Lamaism; lamas are the Tibetan equivalent of gurus, and enlightenment is considered virtually impossible without a direct relationship with a lama. Tibetans believe that through devotion to one's lama one begins to break down the walls of ego and gain the trust necessary to absorb the higher teachings. To a degree not found in other schools, practitioners of Tibetan Buddhism venerate their personal teachers, regarding them as living Buddhas. They also worship great numbers of other Buddhas, saints, and enlightened gods and goddesses, and visualizing these spiritual beings is a major practice of the Tibetan tradition. Tibetan Buddhism sometimes draws comparisons to the Catholic Church—certainly it is the most ritualistic of all forms of Buddhism.

Another aspect of Tibetan Buddhism is tantra, a complex system of oral and written teachings and techniques that's possibly the least understood part of Buddhism among Westerners. Tantra is primarily about utilizing all aspects of life as tools to achieve enlightenment. Contrary to popular perception, Buddhist tantra is not about sex—the majority of tantric practices do not involve sexual imagery, and legitimate Buddhist groups do not use sexual tantra as a selling point. For that matter, the sexual imagery that does appear in some tantra is not about enhancing one's sex life but getting past taboos that shackle the mind and harnessing natural energies to achieve supreme wisdom. There's no boinking for Buddha: if you're looking for kinky Kama Sutra fun, you'll need to search elsewhere.

Tibetan centers tend to be much more colorful and ornate than many other groups in New York City. You'll probably find a clearly defined altar with golden images of Buddhas and saints, vivid religious paintings (called thangkas), and photographs of the prominent teachers of whichever school you visit. You will also probably meet Tibetan monks, or less frequently American ones or Buddhist nuns, though some groups are lay-led. Services usually consist of meditation and worship of some sort, often including chanting and full prostrations. Many programs will include a sermon and perhaps some textual study, though this varies from group to group. The methods of visualization and chanting of the different Tibetan schools are so elaborate that they cannot be adequately addressed here.

There are four main traditional schools of Tibetan Buddhism. The largest is the Gelugpa school, which is the sect of the Dalai Lama and the Panchen Lama, another high-level tulku with whom many Americans are familiar because of the political situation in Tibet. The Gelugpas emphasize study more than any other school of Buddhism, with many students attending monastic colleges in order to receive complete educations in Buddhist texts, history, logic, and philosophy. They also include meditation in their programs, though it's usually believed that meditation is best practiced with a firm grounding in theology and theory, and thus the higher forms of meditation tend to come as the culmination of years of prior study. All in all, Gelugpa Buddhism offers an unusually detailed, structured path to achieving enlightenment. Unlike the other schools of Tibetan Buddhism, their monks and nuns are usually strictly celibate. The Dalai Lama's books are the standard English-language Gelugpa materials; for teachings get *The Meaning of Life from a Buddhist Perspective* and *A Flash of Lightning in the Dark of Night*.

The Nyingmapas, the oldest sect of Tibetan Buddhism, take an opposite approach. They're relatively detached from politics compared to the other sects, and focus on meditation first and foremost, employing a practice known as Dzogchen, which involves penetrating directly into the spacious, naturally free nature of the enlightened mind. Guru worship is extremely important to this school, and most lamas require their students to complete strenuous devotional practices, such as doing one hundred thousand full prostrations, as preparation for the higher teachings. Many Nyingmapa lamas are not celibate, and there are prominent family lineages that have handed down the Dzogchen techniques for generations. Read Chagdud Tulku's *Gates to Buddhist Practice* and Sogyal Rinpoche's *The Tibetan Book of Living and Dying* for Nyingmapa teachings.

The Kagyupas have a strong following in the West and have displayed a high level of sophistication in bringing their teachings to American audiences. Meditation and study tend to go hand in hand in Kagyupa Buddhism, leading step by step to the realization of the empty and pure nature of mind. This school tends to put a strong emphasis on the usefulness of emotions in examining the mind, encouraging students to examine their feelings of anger and greed rather than suppress them. There is also a strong tradition of magicians in this lineage, with many shamanistic influences obvious in its teachings. It's among the Kagyupas that the tradition of discovering tulkus first arose. A great book by Kagyupa nun Pema Chödrön is *Start Where You Are*.

The fourth major school of Tibetan Buddhism is the Sakya. Like the Gelugpas, the Sakyapas greatly value scholarship and typically put off intensive tantric practice until after graduating from a monastic college. The meditation system of the Sakyapas is called the lamdre ("path and fruit"), which stresses the union of effort and achievement. Many of the teachings of this school are still strictly secret, handed down orally to select students, and thus cannot be publicized. Nevertheless, prominent Sakyapas have been active in ecumenical movements within Tibet and beyond for the last couple of centuries. *Ordinary Wisdom* by Sakya Pandita is a good place to start learning about Sakya Buddhism.

Two excellent centers for Gelugpa Buddhism are the Asian Classics Institute (see page 84) and The Tibet Center (see page 78). Nyingmapa is represented by the Padmasambhava Buddhist Center of New York (see page 71) and Palyul Changchub Dargyeling New York City (see page 72). Kagyupa Buddhism is part of the New York Shambhala Center (see page 68) program. For Sakyapa teachings try the Palden Sakya Center for Tibetan Buddhist Studies and Meditation (see page 56).

PURE LAND BUDDHISM

Although Pure Land Buddhism is the most widespread form of Buddhism worldwide and has the most adherents, it is overshadowed in America by the Zen and Tibetan schools. This is largely because it's superficially similar to Christianity in some ways, and most Western converts to Buddhist are trying to find something quite different from their Christian backgrounds. That's a shame, because Pure Land is the least elitist form of Buddhism, offering simple techniques that are designed to meet the spiritual needs of laypeople, especially those who don't have the time or the disposition to engage in rigorous silent meditation.

The various Pure Land schools are based on the story of Amitabha Buddha, the Buddha of Infinite Light and Life. Amitabha was once a king who was troubled by all the suffering in the world and vowed to become a Buddha in order to lead everyone to enlightenment and peace. Using the great store of good karma he accumulated, he created a beautiful realm of pure bliss, where there was no pain and everybody could reach enlightenment quickly without distraction. All that's required to be reborn into his pure land is to call upon Amitabha, who transfers his infinite store of good karma in order to erase all of one's bad karma. This creates a karmic link that will cause one to go to the realm of bliss after death. Thus all one needs to reach enlightenment in the Pure Land schools is faith, rather than trying to follow difficult codes of self-discipline and strenuous meditation and study, as in most other types of Buddhism.

Psychologically, the pure land is the naturally enlightened aspect of one's mind, and Amitabha is one's own Buddha nature. Infinite light represents wisdom, which illuminates the dark corners of the soul, and infinite life stands for compassion, which compels one to reach out to help other people again and again. By relying on the power of inherent enlightenment, rather than one's personal ego, one can learn to relax and let compassion and wisdom come forth on their own. The Pure Land path offers an approach to Buddhism that's steeped in humility, everyday life, faith, and sincerity. For those who find the more rigorous meditative schools of Buddhism too intimidating, it provides an easy way to live a simple, uncluttered Buddhist life.

Because Pure Land Buddhism relies on the power of Amitabha, rather than that of one's own efforts, the monastic order is less important than in other forms of Buddhism. Monks, nuns, and laypeople can equally call upon Amitabha and receive his help—in fact, one major school of Pure Land, the Jodo Shinshu, has eliminated its monks and nuns as unnecessary. In many cases, the Pure Land path is practiced by members of other schools, who continue their own practices but also call upon Amitabha to get help in their quest for enlightenment. This makes Pure Land the most ecumenical form of Buddhism, flexible enough to have made significant contributions to many different types of Buddhism, including Zen and Tibetan.

The primary practice in Pure Land Buddhism is called nembutsu. This is the act of chanting "Homage to Amitabha Buddha" ("Namo Amida Butsu" in Japanese), which depending on the circumstances can be a mantra to concentrate the mind, a cry for help, or a prayer of thanksgiving. Repeated chanting can focus the mind in a manner similar to sitting meditation. Pure Land schools do teach morality, discipline, meditation, and study to varying degrees, but they emphasize that nembutsu is all that's really necessary, with the rest being helpful methods to enhance mindfulness and compassion in this life before being reborn in the pure land in the next. From the Pure Land perspective, the techniques of the other schools of Buddhism can also work to reach enlightenment, but they're the hard way, while nembutsu is a convenient short cut.

There is still significant interest in Pure Land Buddhism among Asian immigrants and their descendants, and Pure Land Buddhism is well represented in New York City. But in the non-Asian community it has made only modest inroads so far, as Westerners tend to see it as too similar to having faith in Jesus Christ in order to go to heaven, instead of understanding Pure Land's two-thousand-year-old tradition within the Buddhist teachings. There are significant differences between Pure Land Buddhism and Christianity, including that Amitabha is not a judging figure and cannot damn anyone to hell, and the point of being born in the pure land is to become a Buddha and return to this world in order to help other people. Only time will tell if Americans will learn to look past the seemingly familiar aspects of this religion and discover the unique richness of the Pure Land path.

New York City centers in the Pure Land tradition include the New York Buddhist Church (see page 51), the Guan Kwong Temple of America (see page 90), and the New York Amitabha Society (see page 94). Pure Land teachings can also be found in virtually all Chinese and Vietnamese temples and groups, as well as many Korean ones.

Two excellent books on Pure Land Buddhism—both from a Jodo Shinshu perspective—are readily available in bookstores: *River of Fire, River of Water* by Taitetsu Unno, and *Ocean* by Kenneth Tanaka.

NICHIREN BUDDHISM

Nichiren Buddhism is another school that tends to eschew traditional sitting meditation in favor of chanting. Nichiren was a radical reformer in medieval Japan, who believed that the different forms of Buddhism had become decadent and lost their power to ferry people to enlightenment. He recommended studying a single text, the Lotus Sutra, believing that it contained the highest teachings of the Buddha. He was so impressed by this book that he advocated chanting "Homage to the Lotus Sutra" ("Namu Myoho Renge Kyo" in Japanese, a practice known as daimoku) as the true way to achieve enlightenment. This mantra is supposed to activate one's Buddha nature and create good karma.

Nichirenism had an unusually contentious history in Japan, and it was often more sectarian than most other forms of Buddhism. Some Nichirenists believed that their school alone was correct, and some even claimed that Nichiren was the only real Buddha. At the same time, other schools of Nichirenism took the upaya teachings of the Lotus Sutra to heart and were willing to live in peace with other Buddhists.

Historically, Nichirenism was a minor sect of Buddhism, but in the latter part of the twentieth century it experienced tremendous growth. Though it has a fairly low profile in New York City, with only a handful of official temples or centers, there is actually a sizable number of people practicing Nichiren Buddhism. The reasons it fails to make an impression reflective of its size are that some of its groups tend to be religiously reclusive, avoiding contact with other sorts of Buddhists, and it is a form of practice fundamentally oriented toward practicing at home rather than in public at a sacred temple.

Nichiren Buddhists pray before an image created by Nichiren, known as the gohonzan ("enlightened object of worship"). Each household has one, which means that trips to the temple aren't necessary.

When Nichirenists do gather, they usually do so at someone's house. Group services include vigorous chanting and discussion, with members offering their own experience and insight to help each other improve their lives and understand the teachings of Nichiren.

One noteworthy aspect of Nichirenism in New York is that it has done an unusually good job of attracting African Americans and Latinos to the fold—though there are non-Asian minorities in all New York Buddhist communities, the highest percentage is definitely in the Nichiren groups.

In New York City the largest Nichiren group is the Soka Gakkai, headquartered at the SGI Culture Center (see page 75). Soka Gakkai is a fairly new form of Buddhism, completely lay-led. They used to be associated with the Nichiren Shoshu Temple sect, represented in the city by the Myosetsuji Temple (see page 114). Both of these groups tend to be exclusive in their rhetoric. On the other end of the scale is Rissho Kosei-Kai, a very liberal and also relatively new Nichiren group that is active in interfaith relief aid and dialogue. Their New York City home base is the Rissho Kosei-Kai Center for Engaged Buddhism (see page 73).

OTHER BUDDHIST GROUPS

There are plenty of Buddhist groups in New York City that don't fit into these particular categories. Some are large and ancient schools in their own countries, but have only minimal representation here in this area. Others are local homegrown groups that are forging their own identities outside the traditional Buddhist lineages. These will be treated individually in the listings for each particular center. Not being listed here is in no way a judgment of their value—there simply isn't space to sketch out every single school in the amazingly diverse world of New York City Buddhism.

PART TWO

WHERE CAN I GO TO PRACTICE BUDDHISM?

PRACTICE CENTERS AND MEDITATION GROUPS: NEW YORK CITY

MANHATTAN

Manhattan prides itself on being the center of the (New York) universe, and it's no surprise that it's also at the middle of the East Coast mandala of Buddhist groups and organizations. From Chinatown's many temples to the Upper West Side's Buddhist statue that survived an atomic bomb attack, there's an amazing wealth and diversity of resources waiting for the new Buddhist.

UPTOWN

American Buddhist Study Center
331 Riverside Drive
New York, NY 10025
Tel: 212-864-7424
Fax: 212-864-7824

http://www.americanbuddhist.org
School affiliation: Jodo Shinshu Pure Land Buddhism (Nishi-Hongwanji Branch)
Languages spoken: English, Japanese

The American Buddhist Study Center (formerly the American Buddhist Academy) is located in the New York Buddhist Church (see page 51) and is closely allied with it and other Jodo Shinshu organizations in the United States. The Study Center was active during the middle part of the century, attracting such luminaries as Dr. D. T. Suzuki, but then effectively shut down until the end of 1999. Now the Center is being restarted in an effort to further the study of Buddhism in America, and particularly in New York City.

The new Center has ambitious plans to sponsor lectures, seminars, and discussion sessions, publish its own books, and sell Buddhist tapes and religious items. One immediate asset of the Center is its staggeringly enormous library of Buddhist materials in various languages, as well as non-Buddhist religious materials collected to further the discipline of interfaith studies. The Center's particular focus is Mahayana Buddhism, and not surprisingly, Pure Land Buddhism in particular. The new plans are exciting, but don't expect too much too soon—the Center is shaking off years of inertia and it is likely to take some time before the entire program is implemented.

Carnegie Hill Zen Center

124 East 95th Street
New York, NY 10128
Tel: 212-876-8213
Fax: 212-876-8062

aaaryoko@aol.com
School affiliation: Soto Zen (White Plum lineage)
Language spoken: English

Rev. Diane Ryoko Shainberg runs this relatively new zendo out of her home. She's a dharma heir of Bernie Glassman Roshi, in the White Plum lineage. Her center is also a member of the Zen Peacemaker Order (see page 246) and carries out ZPO activities.

The Carnegie Hill Zen Center's primary activity is Wednesday night services, held every week. From 7:00–10:00 P.M. the participants sit for two periods of meditation, listen to a sermon from Diane, and hold discussions with each other. Once a month there are full-day sittings, as well as another entire day a month devoted to ZPO sitting, coordinating, and Bearing Witness activities.

Activities at the center are free and open to the public, with non-Buddhists encouraged to attend. Diane also runs the Mani Center for Integral Studies out of this location, which offers classes for psychotherapists in bodywork, healing techniques, and other methods of integrating Buddhism with a wider range of activities than the specifically religious in nature.

Finally, Diane also teaches Dzogchen in the tradition of Lama Surya Das one night a month, when the Carnegie Hill Zen Center transforms into the Manhattan Dzogchen Group (see page 49). These two Buddhist groups, however, are separate and have minimal overlap in students.

Chakrasambara Manhattan Group

Alexander Robertson School
3 West 95th Street
New York, NY 10025-6753
Tel: 718-834-0210

School affiliation: Gelugpa (New
   Kadampa Tradition)
Language spoken: English

This is a Manhattan outreach class run by Kadam Morten from the Chakrasambara Buddhist Center in Brooklyn (see page 126). Classes are usually held on Thursdays, 7:00–9:00 P.M. They cost $10 each; cheaper if an entire course is taken over several weeks. Contact the Chakrasambara Buddhist Center for a schedule of upcoming classes.

Columbia Buddhist Meditation Group

At St. Paul's Chapel, Columbia University
2960 Broadway
New York, NY 10027
http://www.columbia.edu/cu/cbmg/

jah100@columbia.edu
School affiliation: eclectic
Language spoken: English

This is a student-led Buddhist meditation group that serves the Columbia University campus (though anyone is welcome to partici-

pate in their activities). Their primary practice is Vipassana (Insight Meditation). They bring in guest speakers or take trips to centers from a wide range of backgrounds, including the New York Shambhala Center (see page 68), local Zen centers, and even a Hindu ashram in Upstate New York.

The group's schedule changes as student commitments (and students) come and go; currently they meet on campus in the basement of St. Paul's Chapel two nights a week: Sunday at 8:30 P.M. in the Red Room and Tuesday night at 7:00 P.M. in the Art Gallery. They also organize formal Vipassana retreats on campus about once a year.

Community of Mindfulness—
Being with Children

New York, NY

Tel: 212-877-0355

sspsyd@aol.com

School affiliation: Community of
   Mindfulness

Language spoken: English

This is a special chapter of the Community of Mindfulness New York Metro (see page 48). Located on the Upper West Side, it was formed by a group of parents who didn't want to choose between their children and their meditation practice. It's dedicated to exploring ways for parents to practice Buddhism with their children, and to providing support for parents in their quest to raise children with a sense of mindfulness and compassion.

Understandably, the practice at Being with Children is somewhat modified from the regular Community of Mindfulness structure. The group gathers once a month on Sunday afternoons, usually with an average of four adults and five children. They take more frequent breaks, and start with a playtime for the kids. They sing Buddhist songs, tell stories, or share candid discussions on topics like friendship, love, God, holidays, peer pressure—whatever seems relevant in the lives of the children. Snacks are used to teach mindful eating, and the group ends with a modified loving-kindness meditation. Sometimes there are group arts-and-crafts projects or activities in Central Park. The kids range in age from kindergartners to preteens.

On alternate months, only the adults gather. This affords them a chance for more formal sitting meditation and to share their insights and problems with each other over their children and child raising.

First-time attendees should come to this adults-only meeting first, in order to meet the group and learn more about how to practice with their children.

The group also sometimes participates in the full Days of Mindfulness that the Community of New York Metro holds once a month.

Community of Mindfulness— New York Metro

P. O. Box 61, Planetarium Station
New York, NY 10024
Tel: 212-501-2652

School affiliation: Community of Mindfulness
Language spoken: English

The Community of Mindfulness is a form of Westernized Vietnamese Zen, lay-led, centering on the teachings of the teacher Thich Nhat Hanh (who is probably the most respected Buddhist master in America, after the Dalai Lama). Groups conduct their services in members' homes, and services usually consist of sitting and walking meditation, recitation of the five lay precepts, and often a review of Buddhist materials by Thich Nhat Hanh and a discussion. Everything is done in English, with little jargon or Asian vocabulary.

In the New York City area the local groups are loosely organized together under the banner of the Community of Mindfulness New York Metro chapter. They usually meditate separately in their own groups but often come together on the second Saturday of the month for a full Day of Mindfulness, which involves a whole day devoted to meditation and practice. Because the groups are operated out of individuals' homes, different sanghas pop up and dissolve sometimes as people move around (or out of) the city. In the wake of the Amadou Diallo shooting a socially engaged practice group was formed; there is also a Sunday study group.

Community of Mindfulness West 86th Street Sangha

West 86th Street and West End Avenue
New York, NY 10024
Tel: 212-873-3142

School affiliation: Community of Mindfulness
Language spoken: English

This Upper West Side sangha usually meets on Tuesdays, 7:30–10:00 P.M., for meditation practice and discussion, and once a month for the local Day of Mindfulness. Contact Amy Krantz for more details, and see the Community of Mindfulness New York Metro (page 48) for information on the organization.

Manhattan Dzogchen Group

123 East 95th Street
New York, NY 10128
Tel: 212-876-8213
Fax: 212-876-8062

aaaryoko@aol.com
School affiliation: Nyingmapa
Language spoken: English

When she's not running the Carnegie Hill Zen Center (see page 44) out of her home, Rev. Diane Shainberg moonlights as the local representative of popular Western teacher Lama Surya Das's tradition. The

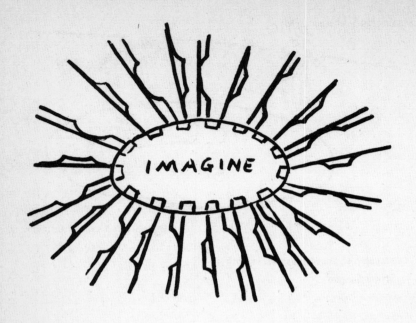

group meets on the third Thursday of the month 7:30–10:00 P.M. Meetings include meditation instruction, discussions, Dzogchen practice, and talks about Surya Das's teachings. Admission is free and many meetings include potluck dinners.

Diane's dual-tradition teaching status is something of an anomaly in New York City Buddhism. Sometimes one meets teachers trained in more than one form of Zen, or different schools of Tibetan Buddhism, but the Soto Zen of Japan and the Dzogchen Buddhism of Tibet have always been separated by enormous gulfs of geography and culture. Perhaps this is an example of how Buddhism in New York City is taking on a unique form, where practitioners from all corners of Asia can meet and influence one another. Or perhaps not—there is virtually no overlap in interest or attendance between the students of the Manhattan Dzogchen Group and the Carnegie Hill Zen Center, despite the fact that both Buddhist groups meet in the same space and have the same teacher.

Manhattan Shakubuku Group

1741 Broadway, 2nd floor
New York, NY 10019-4311

School affiliation: Nichiren Shoshu Temple
Languages spoken: English, Japanese

This is the modest outreach program of the otherwise reclusive Myosetsuji Temple (see page 114). They hold introductory meetings on Wednesdays and Fridays 7:00–9:00 P.M. This is probably the best way to get involved with orthodox Nichiren Shoshu Temple Buddhism in New York City.

Visitors should be forewarned that shakubuku translates from Japanese as "breaking and smashing false views," a proselytization technique favored by some Nichiren groups that involves systematically demolishing other people's previously held religious ideas. While physical violence certainly isn't a threat, this group is highly sectarian and believes that it holds the only true path of Buddhism.

Myosetsuji Temple Uptown Chapter

New York, NY
Tel: 718-430-9890

School affiliation: Nichiren Shoshu Temple
Language spoken: English

This is the Uptown Chapter of the Myosetsuji Temple (see page 114) in Flushing. They meet Fridays at 7:00 P.M. The contact person is Dena France, whose number is listed above. See the main Myosetsuji Temple entry for more details.

New York Buddhist Church

331-332 Riverside Drive
New York, NY 10025
Tel: 212-678-0305
Fax: 212-662-4502
http://amida.homestead.com/
   New_York_Buddhist_Church.html

jerrypev@home.com
School affiliation: Jodo Shinshu Pure Land
   Buddhism (Nishi-Hongwanji Branch)
Languages spoken: English, Japanese

People looking to get into Buddhism without the necessity of formal meditation practice should consider the New York Buddhist Church. NYBC offers an interesting hybrid of Eastern and Western influences: a Japanese liturgy, traditional Japanese arts, and a largely Japanese American congregation combined with Sunday morning services delivered in English, including a sermon by the head minister, a church school for the children (called dharma school), and an emphasis on meeting the needs of laypeople in their everyday lives. Some folks seeking an exotic oriental experience find it too close to home, while others take comfort in the familiar structure combined with Buddhist wisdom and a welcoming teaching of universal salvation.

It's hard to find Buddhists more friendly and at ease than Jodo Shinshuists. The reason is probably their teaching that rigorous meditation, ascetic monasticism, and strait-laced observance of moral codes are useless for achieving the highest spiritual goals; in fact, they believe that such actions tend to reinforce the egocentrism that's the problem to begin with. Instead, members of Jodo Shinshu groups preach a doctrine of salvation through faith in the naturally enlightened state of the mind, metaphorically represented as Amida Buddha, the Buddha of Infinite Light (Wisdom) and Life (Compassion). Their primary practice is chanting "Namo Amida Butsu" (pronounced "Na-muh Ah-mee-da Boo"— "Gratitude to the Buddha Amida"), a prayer of thanksgiving that calms the mind and reminds the chanter of the interconnectedness of all things. Whatever the reason, the openness of members of the New York Buddhist Church is disarming and sure to ease the anxieties of first-timers.

The New York Buddhist Church was founded in 1938 by Rev. Hozen Seki and his wife, Satomi, to minister to the spiritual and social needs of New York's Japanese population, and retains numerous Japanese cultural activities that are open to everyone, including calligraphy, dance, taiko drumming, and martial arts. The current minister is Rev. T. Kenjitsu Nakagaki Sensei (usually addressed as Sensei or simply T.K.), an affable young man sent from Japan to lead the church. Laypeople are also heavily involved in running the church—Nakagaki Sensei is the community's leader but by no means a guru or authoritarian figure.

NYBC has about 175–200 members, including Japanese-, European-, and African Americans.

Japanese-language services are held at 10:30 A.M. every Sunday; English services follow immediately afterward at 11:30 A.M. Old-timers will eagerly assist newcomers with the rituals and liturgy involved, and first-timers will probably be encouraged to stand and briefly give their names so that they may be greeted by the congregation. There are Japanese refreshments and social time afterward, sometimes followed by a cultural activity. No donations are required, though they are appreciated; there are also a few books for sale near the refreshment table. While you're there, look outside for the large statue of Shinran Shonin (thirteenth-century founder of Jodo Shinshu), which survived the atomic bombing of Hiroshima.

NYBC offers morning meditation sessions 6:30–7:30 A.M. on weekdays, dharma study sessions, training for lay ministers, and a quarterly three-week introductory meditation and dharma class for beginners ($30 for nonmembers), as well as other regular and seasonal activities. Most regular activities are free. Call for more information or sign up for their monthly newsletter after services. NYBC also houses the American Buddhist Study Center (see page 43).

New York City Friends of the Western Buddhist Order

P. O. Box 230316
New York, NY 10023
Tel: 212-595-3012
http://www.aryaloka.org/fwbo-nyc/
   index.html

nycfwbo@aol.com
School affiliation: Friends of the Western
   Buddhist Order
Language spoken: English

The FWBO are a new sect of Buddhism, based in England, the home country of their founder Venerable Sangharakshita. They seek to create communities that support the practice of Buddhism in the West, and have established a series of meditation centers, retreats, and Buddhist businesses to further this aim. Their presence in America is minimal, with a retreat facility in Vermont and a few scattered practice groups in cities like Boston.

The Venerable Vajramati, a British-born teacher in the FWBO tradition, has been shuttling regularly from the Boston group to offer support to followers in NYC. In mid-2000, he moved here permanently to establish a more concrete base for the group in the capital of the world. As of this writing, Vajramati did not have a center yet, and the phone listed above is a private residence where you can get more info on the group's current progress. At some point, though, he will find a permanent space and begin introducing the New York City public to this unique Buddhist hybrid, Asian in form but purely Western in expression. Vajramati plans to hold weekly meditation and study gatherings, as well as 4- to 6-week classes on meditation and Buddhism for beginners. Classes will cost around $10 each.

It should be mentioned in passing that the Friends of the Western Buddhist Order has suffered some negative press in Great Britain. Allegations of misogyny, cultlike recruiting tactics, and most bizarre of all, homosexual orgies have dogged some senior leaders of the movement. At the same time, most FWBO members are clearly committed and upright Buddhists with nothing to hide. As always, you'll want to use good judgment when studying with any group, and rely on your own observations and comfort level rather than hearsay.

New York City Karma Thegsum Choling

412 West End Avenue, #5N
New York, NY 10024
Tel: 212-580-9282
http://www.kagyu.org/centers/usa/usa-nyc.html

slrr1@aol.com
School affiliation: Kagyupa (Karma Kagyu lineage)
Languages spoken: English, Tibetan

This is the NYC affiliate of the Karma Triyana Dharmachakra (see page 153) monastery in Woodstock. It offers introductory practice instruction, as well as shamatha (concentration) meditation on Tuesdays and Wednesdays, and more advanced techniques such as Chenrezig and Amitabha practices for committed Buddhists. Contact Sandy Reese Roberts for more information about upcoming seminars and special events.

No Traces Zendo

114 West 81st Street

New York, NY 10024

Tel: 212-974-4188

nbaker@mail.slc.edu

School affiliation: Soto and Rinzai Zen

(White Plum lineage)

Language spoken: English

No Traces Zendo is led by Nancy Mujo Baker Sensei. A philosophy teacher at ultraliberal Sarah Lawrence College in Bronxville, New York, Mujo Sensei is a dharma successor of Bernie Glassman Roshi and a member of the Zen Peacemaker Order (see page 246). No Traces Zendo

meets on Thursdays at St. Ignatius Church 7:00–9:30 P.M. Their practice includes an hour of sitting meditation, followed by group sharing and discussion. They also meet once a month in the Bronx for a full day program. A $5 donation is requested. The group is quite open to newcomers, but please call ahead to confirm that you'll be coming.

Palden Sakya Center for Tibetan Buddhist Studies and Meditation

4 West 101st Street, Apt. 63
New York, NY 10025
Tel: 212-866-4339
http://www.angelfire.com/ny/Jigme/
intro1.html

sangye@aol.com
School affiliation: Sakyapa
Languages spoken: English, Tibetan

The Palden Sakya Center is one of the few groups in the area practicing in the Sakyapa tradition of Tibetan Buddhism. The center is run by Lama Pema Wangdak, a warm and unpretentious teacher who has been active in the West for fifteen years. Lama Pema has a good command of English and an excellent method of transmitting Tibetan Buddhism to Westerners without the baggage of Asian cultural traditions.

Beginners' classes are offered on Mondays at 7:30 P.M., with instruction in basic meditation and Buddhist principles. Tuesdays at 7:30 P.M. there is a study class—typically Lama Pema reads a bit of classic Buddhist text and then discusses it with the group, slowly making his way through the book. The study class requires a somewhat more sophisticated understanding of Buddhist concepts and isn't ideal for newcomers. More advanced meditations are offered on alternate weekends. No fee is charged for any activities, but a contribution is asked for if possible. It's best to call ahead before attending your first time, so that Lama Pema will be prepared to accommodate you.

Pema Nying-Thig Chokor Ling

1220 Park Avenue, #6B
New York, NY 10128
Tel: 212-794-2050

School affiliation: Nyingmapa
Languages spoken: English, Tibetan

This is a small group that practices under the guidance of Orgyen Kusum Lingpa, a Tibetan meditation master based in the San Francisco Bay Area. Kusum Lingpa visits periodically to teach in person; in the meantime, the group is led by Khandro Pema Lhamo (Chris Sarazen).

Wellness Mindfulness Group

At Wellness Center at Riverside Church
470 Riverside Drive
New York, NY 10027

Tel: 212-870-6704
School affiliation: Community of Mindfulness
Language spoken: English

Carl Smith, a practitioner with the Community of Mindfulness New York Metro (see page 48), leads a low-profile mindfulness meditation group at Riverside Church's Wellness Center. The Wellness Center is a special program of the church, designed to minister to the congregation and community in holistic ways.

The mindfulness group meets on Mondays at 6:30 P.M., and Tuesday mornings at 7:30 A.M. on the nineteenth floor of Riverside Tower. Their practice consists mostly of sitting and walking meditation. It's easygoing and well suited for beginners, without a lot of complex terminology or foreign concepts to wade through. Though organized by a Christian center, the practice is Buddhist—the Wellness Center also has Christian meditation classes for those who're interested in a more theistic meditation experience.

Occasionally this group has formal meetings with the Community of Mindfulness New York Metro, such as full Days of Mindfulness. Contact CMNYM for details about such events.

Zen Studies Society/New York Zendo
Shobo-Ji

223 East 67th Street
New York, NY 10021-6087
Tel: 212-861-3333
Fax: 212-628-6968

http://zenstudies.org/
nyzoffice@zenstudies.org
School affiliation: Rinzai Zen
Languages spoken: English, Japanese

Next to the juggernaut Fox Television studios on East 67th quietly sits New York Zendo Shobo-Ji, a three-story carriage house with a lot of New York Zen history. The Zen Studies Society was founded back in 1956 to assist the pioneering Buddhist scholar D. T. Suzuki, who taught at Columbia University and is more or less at the root of American interest in Zen. In 1965 the ZSS was placed under the control of Eido Tai Shimano Roshi, who instituted a full program of meditation and still continues today as the temple's abbot.

Zen Studies Society is probably the most rigorous Zen institution in New York City—this isn't a particularly good place for those just looking for an easygoing Buddhist experience. By making fewer concessions to the West than many teachers, Eido Roshi has sought to conserve the heart of Zen practice and insight. Newcomers should be aware that ZSS has had to deal with allegations of sexual misconduct on the part of Eido Roshi, accusations that caused large numbers of people to leave, but which the community has managed to survive.

The Shobo-Ji zendo is elegantly decorated in traditional Japanese Zen style, even including a stone garden. The Zen Studies Society also maintains Dai Bosatsu Zendo Kongo-ji (see page 147) in the Catskill Mountains of Upstate New York.

Zazen (sitting meditation) is offered Tuesdays 2:00–4:00 P.M., Wednesday through Friday 7:00–9:00 P.M., and Saturday 10:00 A.M. to 12:30 P.M. Wednesday is a member's-only gathering, while Thursday is a public night suitable for first-timers. Introduction to Zen and meditation is offered, and sometimes there is a sermon as well. You don't need a reservation, but be aware that a $15 entrance fee is strictly required (cash, no check allowed).

The zendo also offers weekend retreats several times a year. These retreats, known as sesshins, include sermons on important Zen scriptures, chanting, silent meals, lots of zazen, and dokusan (private personal dialogues with Eido Roshi). Shobo-Ji is closed for traditional periods in part of the summer and winter, so be sure to call ahead to confirm the schedule.

MIDTOWN

Aro Gar

P. O. Box 246, Chelsea Station
New York, NY 10113-0247
Tel: 212-439-4780
http://www.aroter.org/organizations/
orgs_us.htm

School affiliation: Nyingmapa (Ngakphang lineage)
Languages spoken: English, Tibetan

This small lineage is notable for being nonmonastic and for the unusually strong role of exceptional female lamas in its history. The emphasis is on using the teachings and practices in everyday life. They meet on Tuesdays for meditation in members' homes and hold retreats and workshops whenever prominent lamas of this lineage visit NYC. Though a minority within the Nyingma tradition, members of the Ngakphang lineage are unusually high-spirited. Aro Gar publishes *vision,* a quarterly magazine. See their Web site or call for more information.

Community Church of New York
Buddhist Explorers Group

At the Community Church of New York
(Unitarian-Universalist)
40 East 35th Street
New York, NY 10016

Tel: 212-683-4988
http://www.ccny.org
School affiliation: Unitarian-Universalist
Language spoken: English

The very first English translation of a Buddhist text appeared in Unitarian-affiliated Henry David Thoreau's *The Dial.* So it's natural

that Community Church, one of the city's prominent Unitarian-Universalist churches, has a study group devoted to exploring the interaction of ancient Buddhist faith with the postmodern liberalism and ecumenism of Unitarian-Universalism.

The Buddhist Explorers Group is a loose organization of individuals who are interested in the richness of Buddhism and how they can apply it to their own lives. There is no real leader, no specific doctrine, and no rules to follow. Some of the members would not describe themselves as Buddhists, but just as people who seek to learn from Buddhism. To be frank, you won't find a clear-cut path to enlightenment laid out for you by meeting with the Buddhist Explorers. Instead, you'll find some very smart and friendly people who are searching like you, who revel more in the questions than the answers, and who are both attracted to Buddhism's promise and wary of the authoritarian or antiquated ideas and structures that can be encountered in some groups.

Typical Buddhist Explorers activities include monthly meditation sessions, field trips to local Buddhist centers and art exhibits, and group discussions of popular Buddhist books or videotapes. The group is composed of Unitarian-Universalists, but open to non-UUs and non-Buddhists who are interested in joining in. Like all Unitarian-Universalist groups, there is an emphasis on the affirmation of the inherent worth and dignity of all people, creating happiness in one's daily life, promoting a healthy society, social justice, and a concern that religion be intellectually honest and free of superstition. These general Unitarian-Universalist precepts are explored within the context of Buddhism, with the group examining how, say, the notion of interconnectedness fosters a reduction in racial bias, or how the bodhisattva vow to save all sentient beings promotes an attitude of concern for human and civil rights. Also like all Unitarian-Universalist groups, there's an emphasis on being open to all genders, races, and sexual orientations. Past leaders have included a middle-aged mother and an HIV-positive gay man.

The Community Church Buddhist Explorers Group is not likely to satisfy the hard-core Buddhaphile, but it can serve as an interesting place for discovering new Buddhist ideas or discussing with an open, intelligent, and impartial group the aspects of Buddhism that you've been mulling over.

To get in touch with the group, just come to Community Church on any given Sunday. Ask around about the Buddhist Explorers Group, and eventually someone will introduce you to the right people. The Unitarian-Universalist service usually lasts from 11:00 A.M. to 12:15 P.M. or so—you can arrive afterward if you're just interested in the Buddhist angle, or come earlier for the service. One Sunday of every month there is a forty-five-minute meditation session, beginning at 12:45 P.M., which includes sitting and walking meditation, and plans are under way for a weeknight gathering as well.

First Zen Institute of America

113 East 30th Street
New York, NY 10016
Tel: 212-686-2520

School affiliation: Rinzai Zen
Languages spoken: English, Japanese

First Zen Institute of America earned its name fair and square: it was established in 1930 by Sokei-an Sasaki, the first Zen master to settle in America. It was a pioneer in other ways as well: from the start the institute was oriented toward serving the needs of non–Asian Americans, and institute member Ruth Fuller, who eventually married Sokei-an, was one of the first prominent female American Buddhist personalities.

The institute holds public meditation twice a week on Monday and Wednesday evenings, 7:30–9:30 P.M. and offers two-day meditation retreats on the second weekend of each month. Please call before attending your first session.

Gay Men's Health Crisis
Meditation Class

At The Tisch Building
119 West 24th Street
New York, NY 10011

School affiliation: Soto Zen
Language spoken: English

The Gay Men's Health Crisis is an organization that provides education, counseling, and advocacy on issues related to the AIDS epidemic. In recent years many doctors and researchers have begun to recognize the positive effects that meditation can have on those struggling with the stress and physical fatigue associated with HIV infection, and it is partly for this reason that the meditation class at GMHC was established.

The class was originally initiated by Sensei Pat Enkyo O'Hara of the Village Zendo (see page 102), who is heavily involved in social justice issues and ministering to New York City's gay and lesbian population. Sensei O'Hara is the chairperson of the AIDS National Interfaith Network. Currently the class is run by two of her students, Roberto Taiko Diaz and Michael Unzan Parsons.

Although the program is run by the Village Zendo and stresses Zen-style meditation, it is far less rigorous than the typical activities at the Zendo. The class meets 3:00–4:30 P.M. every Thursday afternoon. It begins with a sitting meditation period of about fifteen to twenty minutes, followed by a discussion. Attendance varies; if no one shows up, the leader will still meditate until the allotted time has passed. Come when you can—the class is designed so that one can attend regularly or drop in every few months. This isn't the place to get a thorough introduction to all aspects of Zen, but the class offers a method of coping with illness.

Besides the tangible benefits that meditation can bring to one's health, the GMHC meditation class is also devoted to bringing solace to suffering people's lives through the compassionate application of Buddhist concepts. The class is open to all people and does not require commitment to Buddhism or Buddhist principles.

For more information, contact the Village Zendo, not Gay Men's Health Crisis.

Kagyu Dzamling Kunchab

35 West 19th Street, 5th floor
New York, NY 10011
Tel: 212-989-5989

ccanon@aol.com
School affiliation: Kagyupa
Languages spoken: Tibetan, English

This center is part of the tradition of the late Kalu Rinpoche, a beloved lama who played an important part in bringing Tibetan Buddhism to America. It is directed by Lama Norhla of Kagyu Thubten Choling (see page 153), who visits to offer weekend seminars once a month. Weekly practice includes Chenrezig practice and sermons. The center also offers classes in Tibetan language. It was established in 1976 and has a shrine room.

Manhattan Won Buddhism

431 East 57th Street
New York, NY 10022
Tel: 212-750-2773
Fax: 212-750-2774

http://www.wonbuddhism-un.org
lee@wonbuddhism-un.org
School affiliation: Won
Languages spoken: English, Korean

Right next to the East River the Won Buddhists have set up their Manhattan headquarters in a cute little three-story gray building. When you arrive at the temple you'll be greeted at the door by a gray- or black-clad resident priest, who will ask you if you're a newcomer and show you where to leave your shoes and coat. Inside you'll find tasteful, minimalistic decor, a friendly congregation, and one of the most well-rounded programs of Buddhist study and meditation available in New York City.

The Won sect of Buddhism, founded in Korea in 1916, is one of the youngest branches of Buddhism found in New York—the Manhattan temple itself is a mere five years old. Fortunately, that freshness translates into real vigor and enthusiasm about studying and putting the practices to work in everyday life. Strongly oriented toward meeting the needs of the laity, Won Buddhism strives to identify the ineffable in the mundane and view the people in one's life as Buddhas, as expressed in a popular aphorism: "Buddhist truth is found in life, life itself is Buddhist truth." Thus you'll find no Buddha images in the Manhattan Won temple—the faithful feel that they can distract from the real-life Buddhas that one meets every day and the Buddha within yourself waiting to be born. Instead, the Won Buddhists venerate a perfect circle, the IrWon-Sang, as their symbol. They describe it as an abstract representation of the dharmakaya—the true nature of the universe.

Sunday services at the Manhattan Won Buddhist temple start at 11:00 A.M. Contemplative piano music plays softly as you settle onto your golden cushion, lulling you into a peaceful state. The service begins with chanting "Namu Ahmita Bul" (the Korean version of "Namo Amida Butsu"), followed by fifteen minutes of silent meditation. Various short prayers and vows are spoken by the group, and then there's a scripture reading and a sermon. The service is rounded out with a song and a little silent prayer. Then everyone goes downstairs for tea, cookies, and socializing. Typically there are fifteen to twenty people present, an even split of European Americans and Asian Americans, a sprinkling of older folks mixed in with the mostly twenty- and thirty-something crowd. Identify yourself as a newcomer, especially after services—you'll receive a packet of materials, extra attention, and someone may well give you a copy of the basic Won scripture for free.

The temple is run by Rev. Chung Lee, a very sincere and dedicated priest, with help from several junior priests. Reverend Lee's status as a female temple leader is hardly unusual—in fact, as many as 65–70 percent of Won priests are women. Female emancipation, both in the priesthood and among the laity, is a cardinal point of Won Buddhism. The temple is also welcoming to gay and lesbian members. The priests are free to marry, though customarily they tend to adopt a traditional celibate lifestyle rather than juggle both dharma and family.

Besides Sunday services, the temple holds group meditations 12:00–1:00 P.M. on Tuesdays and 6:30–7:30 P.M. on Thursdays. On the first Sunday of every month a study group is held 12:00–1:00 P.M. after services. Newcomers are advised to attend the introductory meditation class every second Sunday 2:00–3:00 P.M., where they can learn about medita-

tion, basic Won Buddhist philosophy, and ask questions. All regular activities are free and no pressure is put upon attendees to donate money; indeed, the collection box, discreetly placed by the altar, is difficult to find. Longer retreats typically cost $100 or so to cover expenses. There's no fee to become a member either, though the priests do expect one to complete a minimum course of study first and receive a Buddhist name from the head temple in South Korea.

Won Buddhism is committed to social, economic, and environmental justice as an important expression of spiritual realization. The Manhattan Won temple also houses the Won Buddhist United Nations Office—an official nongovernmental organization—led by Reverend Lee, which delivers Won's message of social justice and environmental responsibility to the U.N. Reverend Lee also spearheads the local Won interfaith activities: Won Buddhists believe that all religions come from the same source of truth and that cooperation between different religious and ethnic groups is the only way that universal human happiness can be achieved.

In keeping with the emphasis on lay practice, the temple teaches many practical methods for bringing Buddhism into your daily life. One unique method is keeping a "dharma journal," wherein one tallies one's Buddhist achievements of the day. Family and community are venerated as opportune relationships in which to practice Buddhist compassion and mindfulness. The laity also have a strong say in the running of the temple and its activities.

McBurney YMCA Meditation and Stress Reduction Class

215 West 23rd Avenue
New York, NY 10011
Tel: 212-741-9210

School affiliation: independent (Gelugpa)
Language spoken: English

Mary Martin Niepold, former executive editor of *Tricycle: The Buddhist Review* (see page 243), leads this informal meditation group for members of the McBurney Y in Chelsea. They meet for thirty minutes on Tuesdays for basic meditation, sitting and counting breaths. Though the group is nonsectarian, Niepold practices at Tibet Center (see page 78) and brings an overall Gelugpa perspective to the sitting. The sessions are free and open to members of McBurney YMCA.

New York Agon Shu

416 East 59th Street
New York, NY 10022
Tel: 212-754-0757

School affiliation: Agon Shu
Languages spoken: English, Japanese

Agon Shu is a very new form of Buddhism, created by a Japanese monk who combined the oldest teachings of Buddhism—the Agon (Agama in Sanskrit) Sutras—with esoteric Tibetan rituals and Japanese Mahayana sentiments. There's also lots of Shinto, the native shamanism of Japan, in the Agon Shu mix. The sect is well known in Japan, where it conducts enormous, televised outdoor fire purification ceremonies, but is just beginning to establish ties in America. They do not yet have an East Coast temple or regular activities. The address above is primarily for public relations, as the newly forming group begins to organize, look for more settled space, and invite teachers from Japan. Currently their activities are confined to irregular public purification ceremonies—purification of negative karma left over from previous generations is the primary practice of Agon Shu practice, an act that they believe will eventually help to bring about world peace.

The Agon Shu New York also operates an art gallery, the Agama Gallery, which they use to display spiritually influenced works. Call or write to get on the group's mailing list and find out about their activities; as they become more established in New York City they will eventually offer regular meditation, yoga, astrology, and purification programs.

New York Diamond Way Buddhist Center

22 West 34th Street, 5th floor
New York, NY 10001

School affiliation: Kagyupa (Karma Kagyu lineage)

Language spoken: English

The New York Diamond Way Buddhist Center is an outreach branch of the Buddhist Center of New York (see page 124), the primary New York area group of Lama Ole Nydahl's Diamond Way lineage. Programs are offered on Thursday nights at 7:00 P.M. and are usually composed of tantric purification and visualization meditations. A $5 donation is requested from participants. There are also occasional lectures or programs by visiting teachers. Contact the Buddhist Center of New York for current events.

New York Insight Meditation Center

P. O. Box 1890, Murray Hill Station
New York, NY 10156
Tel: 917-441-0915

School affiliation: Vipassana (Insight Meditation Society)

Language spoken: English

The New York Insight Meditation Center is an outgrowth of the Insight Meditation Society in Barre, Massachusetts, though officially they are separate entities. Their name is a little misleading right now, as they don't yet have their own center—they rent space from various groups around the city. Currently they offer two-hour classes, 7:00–9:00 P.M., at Sufi Books (see page 242) on Thursdays and the New York Theosophical Society (see Quest Books, page 240) on Fridays. They offer monthly Saturday introductory classes at Community Church of New York (see Community Church of New York Buddhist Explorers Group, page 59).

Classes are open to the public and teachings are technically offered free of charge, as is the Theravadin tradition; however, they do ask for a $5 donation to help cover rental fees. Call the number listed above to find out about the current schedule and to be placed on the mailing list. Though only in the very beginning stages of putting together a sangha (their address is a post office box and even their telephone is a cellular), NYIMC is a community to pay attention to—the original branch in Barre is one of the most reputable Buddhist groups in America, and Vipassana meditation's popularity is ever growing.

New York Shambhala Center and
Dharmadhatu

118 West 22nd Street, 6th floor
New York, NY 10011
Tel: 212-675-6544
Fax: 212-675-3090
http://www.shambhala.org/centers/new-
   york/

nysc@compuserv.com
School affiliation: Shambhala
   (Kagyupa/Nyingmapa)
Language spoken: English

Located in the gay-oriented neighborhood of Chelsea, New York Shambhala Center is a welcoming place for students of all sexual orientations. Established in 1970, it's one of the primary Buddhist institutions in the New York area. It has a large space with several sitting rooms, solid financial backing, gobs of programs, and a nationwide support system via the other Shambhala communities. It's certainly one of the best places for newcomers to get started in exploring Buddhism.

The Shambhala tradition was founded in the latter half of the twentieth century by Chogyam Trungpa Rinpoche, a Tibetan tulku with ties to both the Kagyu and Nyingma traditions. Trungpa Rinpoche exerted an enormous influence on the development of Buddhism in the West, particularly in America. In his various incarnations as a refugee, monk, student at Oxford, father, author, and charismatic guru figure he developed into an outstanding teacher of Westerners, as well as a controversial leader with an alcohol problem and much-gossiped-about liaisons with his female students. Chogyam Trungpa showed a continuous ability to punch holes in people's idealistic expectations of how a Buddhist should behave, an attribute that links him to the "crazy wisdom" tradition of enlightened mavericks in Tibet. Despite scandals during his teaching period and with his successors after his early death, his Shambhala community is one of the largest and most active in the West.

These days the Shambhala community is run by Trungpa Rinpoche's son, and things have settled down quite a bit from the heady earlier days of the '60s and '70s. Precisely because this community has been plagued in the past by problems with its leadership, it may now be a particularly good place for Westerners to seek teachings and support—an ongoing public dialogue over the role of the teacher, proper actions, and skillful teaching tactics has resulted in a more mature Buddhist community that can more successfully police its own and avoid the excesses that are sometimes associated with Eastern religions plunked down in the West. Leaders at the New York Shambhala Center, for instance, have shown openness and honesty in discussing the good and bad points of Trungpa's personality, and the tradition is now poised to transmit the most positive elements of his approach to the dharma.

Practice at the New York Shambhala Center is broken down into three categories: Buddhist, ecumenical "Shambhala" teachings, and contemplative arts such as Japanese archery and flower arrangement. More advanced Buddhist activities are reserved for established members, but Tuesday nights are devoted to open, public meditations and talks that provide an easygoing introduction for New Yorkers.

These Tuesday open sessions draw a crowd of about sixty or so people. The attendees are ethnically diverse (though predominantly Caucasian) and mostly in their thirties and forties, with some older and younger folks as well. They begin with thirty minutes of sitting meditation, followed by a forty-five-minute talk by one of several local lay community leaders, such as Berkeley McKeever, the center's director. The talks are usually on topics directly relevant to urban practitioners and geared toward beginners, with little Asian vocabulary. There's time at the end for questions from the audience, where concerns such as Buddhist views of abortion and vegetarianism, fitting meditation into daily life, and similar subjects often come up. Answers come from other audience members as frequently as from the teacher. Before the sitting starts the leader will ask if anyone desires private instruction in meditation, which is offered to beginners in a separate room. Afterward there's social time and refreshments.

When visiting, be sure to wear layers that you can take off and put on—the heating and air-conditioning can vary wildly from room to room. Also, try to arrive on time for the Tuesday-night open sessions, as the large number of people they draw can make it hard to find a cushion.

The Shambhala community draws its resources primarily from the Kagyu and Nyingma traditions of Tibet, both of which are strongly oriented toward formal meditation practice. Nevertheless, many whole families are involved with Shambhala, which is large enough to form a sort of subculture all its own in American Buddhism. Women play important roles within the Shambhala centers, which have been very successful in obtaining convert American members.

Nichiren Propagation Center, Daiseion-ji Temple

25 Tudor Place, #1910
New York, NY 10017
Tel: 212-599-1510
Fax: 212-599-1510

temple@i-2000.com
School affiliation: Nichiren Shu
Languages spoken: Japanese, English

This modest little Nichiren Shu temple is located in an enormous apartment building. The priest is Rev. Join Inoue. Nichiren Shu is dramatically underrepresented in New York City, considering its main-

stream status as an orthodox type of Buddhism in Japan. This school teaches enlightenment through studying and developing faith in the Lotus Sutra, said to be the highest teaching of the Buddha. Their practices include chanting the title of the Lotus Sutra and selected chapters, silent meditation, copying the Nichiren mantra to obtain merit, bodhisattva vows to save all beings, prayers for the well-being of each other and all living things, and copious amounts of study and reflection on the teachings of Nichiren and the Lotus Sutra. Unlike the more well known Nichiren Shoshu school, they do not deify Nichiren as the supreme Buddha but venerate the historical Buddha as the proper object of worship, with Nichiren regarded as his highest priest.

Padmasambhava Buddhist Center of New York

151 Lexington Avenue, Apt. 8A
New York, NY 10016
Tel: 212-683-4958
http://pbc.interliant.com/pbc/pbc.nsf

info@padmasambhava.org
School affiliation: Nyingmapa
Languages spoken: English, Tibetan

This is the main temple of Khenchen Palden Sherab Rinpoche and Khenpo Tsewang Dongyal Rinpoche, usually referred to as the Khenpos (a Tibetan title of respect for an advanced teacher). The Khenpos offer traditional Nyingma teachings and methods, including Dzogchen and all the preliminary practices. They travel extensively among their international array of connected sanghas, so they are not always in residence in New York City. Senior students lead practice in their absence.

This group is unusual in Tibetan circles because it has a homeless outreach program that offers food and clothing to the needy every Sunday.

The mailing address is different from the center's street address: P. O. Box 1533, Old Chelsea Station, New York, NY 10011.

Palyul Changchub Dargyeling
New York City

101 West 23rd Street, #2336
New York, NY 10010
http://www.well.com/user/mgp/

palyulnyc@aol.com
School affiliation: Nyingmapa
Languages spoken: English, Tibetan

Palyul doesn't maintain its own regular public space in New York. Instead, it rents a room at Sufi Books (see page 242) once a week for practice and instruction. As of this writing, the meetings are held on Mondays 7:30–10:00 P.M., but call and see what the current schedule is, as this situation is likely to change.

Palyul's methods include a focus on learning to perform important rituals and many meditation methods. The students use a practice book that can be ordered ahead of time by E-mailing the group, or picked up at your first meeting. Newcomers are always welcome at this meeting; a donation of $5 to $10 is requested. The head teacher is Lama Wangchuk.

Palyul also maintains a retreat center in Upstate New York (see page 160).

Patriarchal Zen Society in USA

43 West 33rd Street, room 403　　　http://www.worldzen.org/page3.html
New York, NY 10001　　　　　　　ptzny.kplee@att.net
Tel: 212-244-4799　　　　　　　　School affiliation: Korean Son (Zen)
Fax: 212-244-3905　　　　　　　　Languages spoken: English, Korean

The name of this Korean Zen center may rile feminists, which is ironic since it's run by a woman. It refers to the ancient line of patriarchs who transmitted Zen "mind to mind" according to tradition. The Patriarchal Zen Society was founded in Queens in 1994 by Po Hwa Sunim as part of his World Zen Fellowship, based in Virginia. It has now moved to the present Manhattan address and is led by teacher Hey-Wol, which means "Wisdom Moon," the name she is usually addressed by. The society takes an active part in Buddhist events around the city, including a leadership role at the annual Vesak celebration.

Meditation on Wednesdays at 7:00 P.M. is open to the public, followed by socializing.

Rissho Kosei-Kai New York Center for Engaged Buddhism

320 East 39th Street　　　　　　Fax: 212-697-6499
New York, NY 10016　　　　　　School affiliation: Rissho Kosei-Kai
Tel: 212-867-5677　　　　　　　Languages spoken: English, Japanese

The Rissho Kosei-Kai are a new, liberal form of Nichiren Buddhism created in the twentieth century. Unlike some more conservative forms of Nichirenism, Rissho Kosei-Kai is strongly committed to interfaith dialogue and action—they are important members of the International Association for Religious Freedom—and believe that there is value in all religious paths.

Although a major (and wealthy) sect in Japan, Rissho Kosei-Kai in New York City is represented by a single group, named the Rissho Kosei-Kai New York Center for Engaged Buddhism. As the name implies, RKK is a form of Buddhism specifically designed to meet the needs of modern laypeople, and to bring a Buddhist sense of compassion to the many political and social problems of the world. There's no ascetic monasticism or rigorous meditation practice in this tradition. Instead, members chant daimoku ("Namu Myoho Renge Kyo"—"Homage to the Lotus Sutra") and study the Lotus Sutra, their principal scripture. Another important part of RKK is reverence for one's family and ancestors.

The Rissho Kosei-Kai New York Center for Engaged Buddhism is actually located on Tunnel Approach Street, a tiny feeder for the Manhattan entrance to the Queens Midtown Tunnel. Its facilities are lovely despite the odd location—ultramodern, with a spare, meditative quality. White space is the dominant motif, creating an uncluttered frame of mind and drawing attention to the inset altar, with its large standing Shakyamuni Buddha statue, candles, and offerings. Behind a window in the shrine room is a sound room with a music system—Rissho Kosei-Kai is one of the only groups in NYC that regularly plays music during its services.

Sunday services are generally led by Rev. Yoshitaka Hatakeyama, with assistance from lay leaders (who may lead the services when he is unavailable). They typically consist of prayers, daimoku, chanting selections from the Lotus Sutra, and a sermon. The service is usually conducted in both English and Japanese. Once a month the center holds a memorial service, where they chant for the good fortune of all the deceased and troubled members of the RKK in the eastern United States. Some services are followed by hoza, a unique form of Buddhist "group therapy" where individual members tell their troubles to each other and seek advice and support from a Buddhist perspective. Practical advice is as common in these groups as more religious chant-for-good-karma-type recommendations.

The dress at services is entirely Western and basically semiformal, with dark colors preferred. The congregation is primarily Japanese American but also well mixed; women and non-Asian minorities have visible leadership roles. Like many Nichiren groups Rissho Kosei-Kai has done a better than average job of including African Americans and Latinos.

Despite the regular services, the Rissho Kosei-Kai center is primarily an administrative institution, providing support for RKK activities in America and serving as the base for the RKK mission to the United Nations, an important part of its efforts for world peace.

SGI-USA New York Culture Center

7 East 15th Street
New York, NY 10003
Tel: 212-727-7715
Fax: 212-727-7712

School affiliation: Soka Gakkai (Nichiren Shoshu)
Languages spoken: English, Spanish, Japanese

A short distance from Union Square sits a historic YWCA building that houses the local Soka Gakkai Buddhist center. No more apt location could have been chosen by the group, for in many ways Soka Gakkai is the YMCA of Buddhism. Lay-led, enthusiastic, socially involved, and missionary, the Soka Gakkai present one of the more unusual developments of Buddhism in New York City.

Soka Gakkai International (SGI) began in Japan before World War II as an education-reform organization. Its leaders became interested in Nichiren Shoshu Buddhism, and eventually SGI became the sect's primary lay organization. SGI experienced a meteoric rise in power and membership in the second half of the twentieth century, with millions of followers throughout the world and a powerful opposition political party in the Japanese Parliament. SGI organized relief aid to refugees from war and natural disasters, lobbied the U.N. for world peace, and coordinated community-based group events for the faithful, including vigorous pep rallies featuring cheerleading sessions and acrobatic demonstrations. Then in 1990 a power dispute with the priesthood reached a climax and the entire SGI membership was excommunicated.

Today SGI has somewhat recovered from the shock of schism and is rebuilding. While they still teach and practice Nichiren Shoshu Buddhism, the doctrine and practice are clearly undergoing an evolutionary change, one which on the whole is making SGI more democratic, egalitarian, and introspective. Proselytizers no longer stand on Astor Place street corners exhorting passersby to convert from their "false religions." In fact, SGI has turned to personal relationships as their primary source of new members—the typical SGI practitioner was introduced to Buddhism by a friend or family member.

The Culture Center is at the heart of New York Soka Gakkai life. It contains a bookstore, class and shrine rooms, the SGI U.N. liaison office, and serves as the coordinating place for all of the many SGI groups and activities in the area. Admission to most of the building is open only to SGI members, who must present an official ID upon entering the center. If you are not a member but want to get involved, the best thing to do is contact the center and ask them to put you in touch with the chapter in your local area. No matter where you live in New York City, there are Soka Gakkai Buddhists living and meeting in your neighborhood. SGI has the most diverse membership, both geographically and racially, of any Buddhist group in New York. Representatives will contact you about the next neighborhood meeting, held in a nearby member's home.

Try to visit during normal business hours if you do plan to go to the Culture Center. They have staff who can take care of you more efficiently at these times. While you're there, pick up a copy of *The Winning Life: An Introduction to Buddhist Practice* in the bookstore—for only a dollar you'll get a pretty good overview of what Soka Gakkai is all about. Don't expect to learn much the first time you go to the center as a nonmember. You will not participate in any services—that will have to wait until you visit a local group in your neighborhood. Also, don't necessarily believe the depictions of other forms of Buddhism that you may hear—SGI still largely maintains the belief that it is the only true form of Buddhism. Be aware that some watchdog groups consider SGI a cult, and don't let yourself be pressured into anything you're not happy to do.

Soka Gakkai is theologically different from most other Buddhist groups in some specific ways. They believe their sect's original founder, the medieval Japanese monk Nichiren, was the True Buddha for our time, and focus on the Lotus Sutra as the true scripture of Buddhism. Rather than traditional meditation, SGI members practice daimoku, the chanting of "Namu Myoho Renge Kyo" ("Homage to the Lotus Sutra"). They believe that this practice can bring them material as well as spiritual benefits—followers may chant for a new car, a promotion, to overcome addiction, and so on, a practice derided by some other Buddhists as "chanting for dollars." At local meetings there are scriptural studies and an attempt to apply Buddhist teachings to specific everyday situations through hoza, a personal sharing session sometimes likened to group therapy.

Soka Gakkai members in New York are split up into various groups, such as the Men's Division, Women's Division, Young Men's Division, Young Women's Division, and so on. There are also other goal-oriented groups, such as the Youth Peace Committee. There are on-campus activities at Columbia University—contact Margaret Holland at mh30@columbia.edu for details.

The future of Soka Gakkai is unclear; it has been consistently dogged by accusations of having a rather cultlike mentality and organization, with minorities, non-Japanese, women, and homosexuals sometimes complaining about unofficial SGI discrimination policies. Since their excommunication from the official Nichiren Shoshu church, SGI now performs gay marriages, has some high-level female and minority leaders, and is slowly beginning to undertake interfaith relations and perhaps join the larger Buddhist and religious community in a more engaged way. The history of Nichiren Shoshu Buddhism is one of small steps toward the mainstream and dramatic pull-backs into isolated orthodoxy. It remains to be seen where this unconventional form of Buddhism will go in the twenty-first century.

Still Mind Zendo II

28 West 27th Street, #10R
New York, NY 10001-6906
Tel: 212-691-2972

rczoeller@aol.com
School affiliation: Soto Zen
Language spoken: English

Still Mind Zendo II is actually a studio that's converted into a sitting space on Tuesday nights. It's used by the community at Still Mind Zendo (see page 96), a Soto Zen sangha with a decidedly interfaith approach, for weekly zazen and full-day sitting meditation retreats. They request a donation of $3 to $5 for evening settings and full-day programs. Chairs and mats are provided—bring your own meditation bench or cushion if you prefer them. Janet Abels Sensei is the teacher; contact her at the number above to receive a brochure of activities at both locations.

The Tibet Center

107 East 31st Street, 5th floor
New York, NY 10016
Phone: 212-779-1841
http://www.thetibetcenter.org

info@thetibetcenter.org
School affiliation: Gelugpa
Languages spoken: English, Tibetan

The Tibet Center was founded in 1975 by Rev. Khyongla (pro-nounded "Chung-la") Rato Rinpoche, a Tibetan reincarnate lama and scholar, and has the distinction of being the host for the Dalai Lama's visits to NYC (as well as having ties to actor Richard Gere). The center moved to its present location in midtown in 1999 and is increasingly run by Rinpoche's heir apparent, Venerable Nicholas Vreeland (usually just called Nicky), an impressively knowledgeable and engaging Western monk, who also happens to be the grandson of the late fashion guru Diana Vreeland. The apple hasn't fallen quite as far from the tree as it might appear—Nicky has helped raise money for the Tibet Center's home monastery (Rato Dratsang) in southern India by designing and marketing a line of accessories based on the monk's maroon-colored robes.

The facilities at the new Tibet Center are larger and have some fascinating and unique features. The most striking is a man-sized (it was actually designed to the specific dimensions of the Dalai Lama) gold-plated Kalachakra image. The statue has four heads and over twenty arms that wield swords, knives, bells, ritual implements, and drums; it embraces the female consort Vishvamata, who also has a plethora of golden limbs and heads. Commissioned specifically for the Tibet Center, it is the only image of its kind outside of Tibet.

Other noteworthy things at the Tibet Center include a rare three-dimensional mandala and a reference library open to the public that includes not only English and Chinese Buddhist books, but also a complete set of the entire Tibetan Buddhist Canon. The center also sells books, malas, prayer wheels, and other items. They do not sell Buddha images though, which they consider to be a sacrilegious act.

Despite all the fancy trappings, it is the teachings that truly enliven the Tibet Center. And those teachings are compellingly delivered. Monday is the night for beginners, when Nicky gives an introductory talk for newcomers and demonstrates Buddhist meditation practice at 7:00 P.M. (All weeknight activities are at this hour.) Tuesdays are devoted to silent meditation and prayers to the Medicine Buddha. It is the Wednesday night gathering that is particularly noteworthy: Nicky leads a discussion group on important Buddhist texts. The style of the discussion is in the finest Western Socratic tradition, with Nicky participating as a guide but not an authority or judge, and laymembers energetically asking questions and commenting back and forth with each other until consensus is reached on whatever topics the text inspires. The group usually consists of about thirty people, with a majority of non-Asians, a sizable Chinese contingent, and assorted other folks. Like all regular events it is kicked off by a group recitation of a prayer about Buddhism spreading in the West and the reading of the Heart Sutra (spoken, as opposed to chanted as in most Buddhist centers). All in all it is one of the most use-

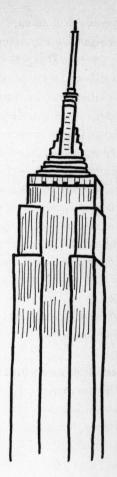

ful methods available to the layperson for directly learning Tibetan Buddhist philosophy in New York City.

Thursdays are also unusual, with non-Buddhist religious leaders often delivering lectures on their own spiritual paths. Nicky encourages even the hardcore Buddhist members to attend these talks; clearly the center's leadership feels one's focus should be on learning what spiritual methods work for oneself rather than promoting a sectarian agenda. It's hard not to be impressed with this sort of open-mindedness and egalitarian attitude.

Saturday offers a more advanced Tara meditation and Kalachakra guru yoga practice for more involved practitioners, starting at 11:00 A.M. There are also frequent seminars and guest speakers throughout the year; call for a current schedule. All of the regularly scheduled activities at the Tibet Center are free of charge and open to the public.

Feel free to approach the monks and shake their hands. You don't have to take your shoes off, but it is generally preferred. Also, bring a light sweater that you can remove easily, as the heating at the Tibet Center can be uneven, changing from one minute to the next.

World Seido Karate Organization
Headquarters

61 West 23rd Street
New York, NY 10010
Tel: 212-924-0511
Fax: 212-691-0343
http://www.seido.com/

akira@seido.com
School affiliation: Zen (Seido karate)
Languages spoken: English, Japanese, and
more

For those who like their enlightenment to be livelier than sitting around on a cushion all day, Seido karate may be the answer. Many forms of martial arts incorporate some strands from Buddhism or Taoism into their practice and philosophy. Seido karate is especially worth noting, however, because the practice of Zen meditation is a core part of Seido, which professes to be a system of spiritual cultivation, not merely a sport or type of self-defense. To this end Seido leaders teach their classes zazen, give brief instructional and inspirational dharma talks, and recommend daily schedules of meditation and proper diet.

The Zen taught in a Seido karate dojo is more spiritual than religious, a lifestyle that can be practiced by Christians, atheists, and Buddhists alike. It's meant to inform one's life by breaking down the stress-inducing dualistic thought patterns people fall into. One point that is emphasized is the unity of actor and action—the properly trained Seido karate practitioner develops freedom and flexibility by fully embodying each punch, kick, or flip, with no discursive thought or sense that "I" am kicking, punching, and so forth.

It should be understood that such freedom, like all true Zen, comes ironically from following a strict set of methods and discipline. Seido karate students must show respect to higher authorities at all times, including bowing and addressing teachers as "Osu." Karate uniforms are required in the dojo. Zazen is performed in the difficult seiza position, which involves kneeling on one's knees and feet, a position that many Westerners find excruciating. Seido karate is founded on the three pillars of respect, love, and obedience, with the expectation that the student will manifest the first and third as much as the second. But some sacrifices may well be worth it in order to get enlightened and ripped at the same time.

There are more than a dozen Seido karate dojos in the five boroughs and more in New Jersey, including special programs for adults, children, teenagers, the blind, and the hearing impaired (an extra bonus, as few centers of any type are prepared to handle those last two populations). Contact the headquarters to find out about the program nearest you.

Yeshe Nyingpo

19 West 16th Street
New York, NY 10011
Tel: 212-691-8523

School affiliation: Kagyupa (Karma Kagyu lineage)
Languages spoken: Tibetan, English

This small group is associated with the primarily West Coast community of Gyatrul Rinpoche, a reincarnate lama born in China and educated in Tibet. Their techniques include meditation and devotions to spiritual beings like Amitabha Buddha and Green Tara.

DOWNTOWN

18 Arhans Vegetarian Restaurant and Guan Gong Temple

227 Centre Street
New York, NY 10013
Tel: 212-941-8986

School affiliation: Chinese Pure Land
Languages spoken: English, Chinese

Surely one of the oddest and most interesting Buddhist establishments in New York is this little place, which serves as an excellent vegetarian restaurant and a temple devoted to a fierce warrior saint. The proprietors are Shi Jin Shi, a short, shaven-headed Buddhist nun who takes your order, and Nancy Li, a devout businesswoman.

The front part of the narrow public room is devoted to the restaurant, which seats a whopping seven people and offers a wide range of delicious Hong Kong–style Chinese vegetarian food. All dishes are $5 and larger than you expect them to be. Eighteen Arhans is a dish and also refers to a traditional collection of eighteen ancient Buddhist saints. Please note that both chopsticks and restrooms are unavailable.

Why is this establishment listed here? As if a Buddhist nun–run restaurant wasn't odd enough, the back part of the room serves as a makeshift

temple to Guan Gong, a famous Chinese general regarded by Buddhists as a saint for his heroic (and bloody) efforts to protect his homeland and fellow worshipers from invading armies. Guan Gong was a huge man with a long beard, and a replica of his wicked two-handed sword hangs on the wall (it's probably twice as tall as Shi Jin Shi)—it's no surprise that the Confucians declared him the god of war. More incongruous still, a placid statue of Kwan-Yin, the female Buddhist saint of mercy, hangs over the warlike Guan Gongs that dominate the altar space. Visitors can leave offerings before the many statues or pray for health and protection.

American Buddhist Confederation

83 Division Street
New York, NY 10002
Tel: 212-226-9027

Fax: 212-219-2817
School affiliation: Ch'an
Language spoken: Chinese

Behind the large red doors of this building you'll find not only the American Buddhist Confederation but also the Eastern Buddhist Association (not to be confused with the Eastern States Buddhist Temple), and the East Dhyana Temple. All are led by Rev. Au Ling. Practice is standard Chinese Ch'an (Zen.)

American Society of Buddhist Studies

214 Centre Street
New York, NY 10013
Tel: 212-966-1021/212-266-8985

School affiliation: Ch'an
Language spoken: Chinese

This center is easy to recognize, with its five stories painted a bright yellow. The inside is elaborately adorned with decorations, including lines of flashing Christmas lights(!). The temple is accessible from the street, and one can come in and watch the monks in their colorful yellow robes performing rituals or practicing sitting meditation. There are several large Buddha statues that you can offer incense before as well. If possible, please leave a donation in the box by the door. The leader of the American Society of Buddhist Studies is Rev. Shou Yeh.

Amitabha Foundation—
New York City branch

c/o Rande Brown
666 Greenwich Street
New York, NY 10013
Tel: 212-989-8290

rande@thorn.net
School affiliation: Nyingma and Kagyu
  (Drikung Kagyu lineage)
Languages spoken: English, Japanese

The Amitabha Foundation (see page 137) was founded by Ayang Rinpoche, the foremost master of the esoteric phowa (poh-wa) practice, to help preserve the precious culture and teachings of Tibet. This New York City branch serves as the local information clearinghouse for Rinpoche, publicizing his activities and teachings in the area. They do not have a formal public meditation group, but call to get on their mailing list and find out about upcoming NYC appearances by Ayang Rinpoche.

Asian Classics Institute

321 East Sixth Street
New York, NY 10003
Tel: 212-475-7752

http://www.world-view.org/aci.html
School affiliation: Gelugpa
Languages spoken: English, Tibetan

This is one of the real jewels of NYC Buddhism. The Asian Classics Institute offers a wide range of classes and programs, including instruction in meditation, Tibetan language and translation, Buddhist teacher training, socially engaged Buddhist work, frequent lectures, a local monastery, and even an excellent home-study correspondence course. It's run under the auspices of the Mahayana Sutra and Tantra Center in New Jersey (see page 180). ACI also runs the Three Jewels Outreach Center and Bookstore (see page 99).

ACI's head teacher is Geshe Michael Roach, the first Westerner to receive the highest degree of Gelugpa Buddhist scholasticism—a simple matter that only requires eighteen years of study and a complete command of Buddhist logic, ethics, metaphysics, philosophy, psychology, meditation, and debate. Geshe Roach is well known as a dynamic teacher and innovative interpreter of the dharma, but don't expect to see him anytime soon—in March of 2000 he began a traditional three-year-long silent retreat. In his absence the many monks, nuns, and volunteers of ACI are continuing the center's programs.

One of the more important aspects of ACI is its Asian Classics Input Project, a colossal undertaking that seeks to translate the entire Tibetan Buddhist canon into English and store it on CD-ROM to preserve its teachings for posterity. Though work has been going on for several years, the end isn't in sight—they nonchalantly estimate it could take three or four centuries.

ACI offers so many programs that a full listing can't be provided here, and the schedule is likely to change now that Geshe Roach isn't available. Programs include public lectures, language classes, meditation instruction, and even a Buddhist Alcoholics Anonymous group. The best part is that they're all free and open to the public.

The Asian Classics Institute has a different mailing address from the street location listed above: Asian Classics Institute, P. O. Box 20373, New York, NY 10009.

Buddhist Association of New York

79 Allen Street
New York, NY 10002
Tel: 212-966-7632

School affiliation: Chinese Pure Land
Language spoken: Chinese

This Chinese temple is led by Rev. Guang Xian and Rev. Xiu Jue. It's located over a busy Laundromat.

Cheng Chio Buddhist Temple

18 Allen Street, 2F
New York, NY 10002
Tel: 212-210-3833

School affiliation: Chinese Pure Land
Language spoken: Chinese

Cheng Chio is unusual in the Chinatown community because it is more or less a women's temple. It was founded in 1976 by Fa Hsing, a Buddhist nun who was invited to New York by the Eastern States Buddhist Temple (see page 88). It maintains several resident nuns who conduct services and support the laymembers, about 80 percent of whom are female.

Regular services are held on Sunday mornings, which primarily consist of chanting nien-fo: Namo O-Mi-To-Fo ("Veneration to the Buddha of Boundless Light and Life"). Afterward there is a vegetarian meal and social gathering. There are also monthly worships of the Medicine Buddha, as well as ancestor rituals, Buddhist weddings, and funeral services. Services are in Chinese.

China Buddhist Association

245 Canal Street, 2nd floor
New York, NY 10002
Tel: 212-226-8932

Fax: 212-226-9183
School affiliation: Chinese Pure Land
Languages spoken: Chinese, English

Rev. Miao Feng leads this temple, located just east of Lafayette Street. It can be recognized by a small blue plaque over the door that says "Namo Amitabha" and identifies it as the Amitabha House.

Amitabha is the Buddha of the Western Paradise, which this temple worships. Their main activity is chanting practice. Public sessions are held on weekends.

Chogye International Zen Center of New York

400 East 14th Street, #2D
New York, NY 10009
Tel: 212-353-0461
http://www1.tagonline.com/~netresul/
netresults/chogye.html

chogye@buddhist.com
School affiliation: Kwan Um Zen
Language spoken: English

The Chogye International Zen Center was founded in 1975 and is part of the Kwan Um School of Zen, an international network of Korean Zen centers founded by Seung Sahn Sunim. Zen (Ch'an) came to Korea via China, and Korean Zen has some features that distinguish it from the more familiar Japanese Zen. For one, the role of full-body prostrations is much more important—at 108 at a time, this is aerobic Zen. Korean Zen (known as Son) is also more rustic in character, less literary and refined (or elitist) than Zen in Japan.

The Chogye center's leader is Richard Shrobe, aka Zen Master Wu Kwang Soen Sa. Besides his years of Zen study he is also a psychotherapist specializing in Gestalt. Daily practice is open to all: Tuesday, Wednesday, and Thursday mornings 5:20–6:20 A.M., weekday evenings 6:30–7:40 P.M. (Wednesdays 6:00–8:00 P.M.) The Saturday session lasts from 8:00 to 10:00 A.M. and includes additional chanting and private interviews with the teacher. Sunday evenings (6:00–8:00 P.M.) include an introductory portion for newcomers, a sermon, and a question and answer period. A $5 donation is requested for all programs. There are also longer retreats offered throughout the year.

Chung Te Buddhist Association
of New York

152–154 Henry Street
New York, NY 10002

School affiliation: Chinese Pure Land
Language spoken: Chinese

This large gray building is a Chinese Pure Land temple and cultural center. They are associated with the World Buddhist Center (see page 106), located next door.

Community of Mindfulness Downtown
Manhattan Sangha

35 West 11th Street
New York, NY 10011
Tel: 212-989-0392

School affiliation: Community of Mindfulness
Language spoken: English

This downtown sangha offers a standard program of sitting and walking meditation on Wednesdays, 7:00–9:00 P.M. Meetings usually draw seven to twelve people. The group is part of the Community of Mindfulness New York Metro (see page 48) and participates in their full-length Day of Mindfulness on the second Saturday of the month. Contact Nancy Rudolph for more details.

Eastern States Buddhist Temple
of America

64 Mott Street
New York, NY 10013
Tel: 212-966-6229

School affiliation: Ch'an (Chinese Zen)
Languages spoken: Chinese, English

Eastern States Buddhist Temple is well known in New York as a common tour bus destination. The shrine room lies behind a ground-floor glass-windowed storefront overflowing with Buddhist statues, where tourists can gawk at the offerings before the elaborate altar decked with over one hundred Buddha images. People off the streets can easily come in and offer incense (or money) to the Buddhas, and for a dollar you can get your fortune told. The temple also contains a bookstore and a museum, as well as additional areas that are not open to the public.

The temple was founded by husband and wife James Ying and Jin Yu-tang, and housed the very first resident Chinese monk in New York City. Since then it has been influential in placing monks at other Chinese temples in the area. It also operates Mahayana Temple (see page 158) as a retreat center and small monastery.

Faith-Vow-Deed Buddhist Association

39 Bowery, P. O. Box 199
New York, NY 10002
Tel: 212-066-1462

Fax: 212-925-3643
School affiliation: Chinese Pure Land
Language spoken: Chinese

The Faith-Vow-Deed Buddhist Association is a Chinese Pure Land temple. The unusual name refers to having faith in the vow of Amitabha Buddha to save all sentient beings, a deed which he has accomplished by creating his Pure Land.

Fu Lai Temple

281 Broome Street
New York, NY 10002
Tel: 212-219-9647

School affiliation: Chinese Pure Land
Language spoken: Chinese

This small storefront temple has a hugely obese laughing Buddha statue just inside the door. Worshipers can offer incense before the altar.

Grace Gratitude Buddhist Temple

48 East Broadway
New York, NY 10038
Tel: 212-925-1335

School affiliation: Chinese Pure Land
Language spoken: Chinese

This building is fairly nondescript except for the red lettering of its name. Some small Buddha images watch the passing traffic from a first-floor window. It is led by Rev. Fa Yun, who also teaches at the American Buddhist Confederation (see page 83). Public services are held on Sunday afternoon around a table in the center of the room.

Guan Kwong Temple of America

94 Canal Street
New York, NY 10002
Tel: 212-219-8586

School affiliation: Chinese Pure Land
Languages spoken: Chinese, English

This Chinatown temple, operated out of a storefront, is led by Rev. Chao Fan. Services are held on Sundays, with chanting and frequent release of goldfish and turtles in local ponds to create merit (and save the lives of sentient beings otherwise destined for the stewpot). In fact, so many turtles have been released by this and other Chinatown temples that Central Park's Belvedere Lake, teeming with the cold-blooded critters, was renamed Turtle Lake by the city in 1987!

Heavenly Grace Buddhist Temple

219 Canal Street
New York, NY 10013
Tel: 212-966-6238

School affiliation: Chinese Pure Land
Language spoken: Chinese

Heavenly Grace Buddhist Temple is actually located around the corner from Canal Street, on Baxter Street. It's sandwiched between a Catholic church and a jewelry shop. This is a Chinese temple in the Pure Land tradition. All services are conducted in Chinese.

Jewel Heart Center in New York

At American Thread Building (entrance on
   St. John's Alley)
260 West Broadway
New York, NY 10013
Tel: 212-966-2807

http://www.jewelheart.org/newyork.html
newyork@jewelheart.org
School affiliation: Gelugpa
Language spoken: English

The beautifully named Jewel Heart Center is split in two—the office is in Katonah, while the group meets in New York City. This is the community of Kyabje Gelek Rinpoche, a teacher famed for his ability to make Buddhism accessible to Westerners. He was originally a monk in Tibet and holds the highest degree in Gelugpa Buddhism, but has since become a layperson in order to better serve the needs of everyday people. Gelek Rinpoche lives in Ann Arbor, Michigan, and travels to minister to his flock around the country; when he's not visiting, students usually meditate together and view videotaped teachings.

Programs in New York City are held on Thursday evenings at 7:30 P.M. The number listed above is an automated phone service that gives details on the current schedule. Further information can be obtained from the office at 33 Katonah Avenue, Katonah, NY 10536, Tel: 914-767-0024, Fax: 914-232-1398.

Mahayana Temple Buddhist Association

133 Canal Street
New York, NY 10002
Tel: 212-925-8787

School affiliation: Ch'an
Languages spoken: Chinese, English

Unlike most NYC Buddhist establishments, it's impossible to miss this temple. A faux Chinese temple facade protrudes from a golden-colored four-story building, strategically placed in the open space opposite the entrance to the Manhattan Bridge. The holy image is detracted from a bit by the gigantic billboard that looms above the building (unconnected to the temple) hawking luxury cars or other goods. It's a branch temple of the Eastern States Buddhist Temple (see page 88). Public services are held on Sundays; please heed the sign that says "Decent clothes are required in the Buddhist temple."

Maitri Dorje Society of Gay and
Lesbian Buddhists

c/o NYC Gay and Lesbian Community
    Center
One Little West 12th Street
New York, NY 10014
Tel: 212-619-4099

http://www.bigfoot.com/~potala
potala@bigfoot.com
School affiliation: Independent
Language spoken: English

Located in Greenwich Village, Maitri Dorje is an intentional community that offers a safe haven to gays and lesbians, and explores Buddhism from a queer perspective. There's a variety of traditions represented in the group—the original founders were members of the New York Shambhala Center (see page 68), and the group's spiritual advisor is Sensei Pat O'Hara of the Village Zendo (see page 102). Overall Maitri Dorje has a Zen/Tibetan emphasis, but all traditions are welcome.

The group meets at the New York Gay and Lesbian Community Center on the second Tuesday of the month 6:00–8:00 P.M. Meetings draw twenty to thirty people and include meditation and discussion. The group also maintains a Web site that has a listing of area Buddhist temples and groups considered to be particularly welcoming to homosexuals. Also check the Web site for upcoming guest speakers and occasional retreats.

Meditation Circle of Cooper Union

At Cooper Union for the Advancement of
Science and Art
New York, NY 10003
Tel: 212-982-8052
http://www.cooper.edu/organizations/
clubs/meditation/

west@cooper.edu
School affiliation: Ch'an
Language spoken: English

As its name implies, this is a loose organization of Cooper Union for the Advancement of Science and Art students who gather for group meditation. They have informal ties with the Ch'an Meditation Center (see page 110), whose teachers have been guest speakers on occasion.

Because students come and go, the schedule and contact information for this group is highly variable. Most typically, they meet for sitting meditation every Tuesday 1:00–2:00 P.M. at the Hewitt Building, room 207, Cooper Union, NY.

Myosetsuji Temple Downtown Chapter

44 Downing Street
New York, NY 10014-4354
Tel: 212-725-0030/212-627-2541

School affiliation: Nichiren Shoshu Temple
Language spoken: English

This is the Downtown Manhattan Chapter of the Myosetsuji Temple (see page 114) in Flushing. They meet on Fridays at 7:00 P.M. The contact people are Mike Fanelli and Mizan Nunes, whose numbers are listed above. Please see the Myosetsuji Temple listing for more info.

New York Amitabha Society

121 Bowery Street, 3rd floor
New York, NY 10002
Tel: 212-965-8951
Fax: 212-219-0896

School affiliation: Chinese Pure Land
(Amitabha Buddhist Society of U.S.A.)
Languages spoken: Chinese, English

This is the New York branch of the Amitabha Buddhist Society of U.S.A., based in Sunnyvale, California. The ABS was founded by Master Chin Kung in 1989 to spread the Chinese Pure Land teachings. These practices are well suited for laypeople; one of the primary techniques is the ten-recitation method: Chant "O-mi-to-fo" ("Homage to Amitabha Buddha) ten times when you wake up, at breakfast, before work, at your lunch break, at lunch, after your lunch break, when you get off work, at dinner, and at bedtime. Master Chin Kung considers this a prescription for developing peace of mind and generating good karma.

The New York Amitabha Society also offers Shaolin kung fu and tai chi martial arts training.

The One Center

10 Platt Street
New York, NY 10038
Tel: 212-809-6205

Fax: 212-809-7239
School affiliation: Ch'an
Languages spoken: Chinese, English

This is the New York branch of the Ling-Jiou Mountain Monastery in Taiwan, a temple founded by dharma master Hsin-Tao. Buddhism has always been one of the most tolerant religions in the world, but Master Hsin-Tao is taking this ecumenicism to new heights. Convinced of the need for religions to work together and support each other, he organized the construction of a major museum of world religions in Taipei, dedicated to showcasing the art and beauty of all the major spiritual paths of humankind. There will probably be a branch here in New York, too, though not for a number of years.

Ordinary Mind Zendo

33 Greenwich Avenue, #4A
New York, NY 10014
Tel: 212-691-0819
http://www.ordinarymind.com/

ordinarymind@erol.com
School affiliation: Zen
Language spoken: English

Barry Magid, a student of Charlotte Joko Beck, established the Ordinary Mind Zendo in 1996. Joko Beck, and Magid after her, is heavily involved in creating a truly American form of Zen, one shorn of Japanese hierarchy and formalism but retaining all the classic aspects of meditation, sutra and koan study, and other practices. Another primary influence on this group is psychology—Magid is a psychiatrist and psychoanalyst, and his sermons and advice are full of concepts and expressions developed in psychiatric circles. The Ordinary Mind Zendo explicitly seeks to utilize the best of both traditions to help its members wake up to their true spiritual selves.

Meditation is held in the mornings, on Tuesdays and Thursdays 7:30–8:30 A.M., and Saturdays from 10:00 to noon. The form consists of three periods of sitting meditation interspersed with two periods of walking meditation. On the first Saturday of the month a full-day retreat is held 9:00 A.M. to 5:00 P.M., which includes an opportunity for daisan (private interview with the teacher to discuss issues of practice and understanding). Silence is expected to be maintained at all times within the zendo, except during periods of chanting (performed in English). Besides chanting, sitting, and walking, the typical service contains some ritualistic bowing—just watch and do what everyone else does. All sessions are free, but donations are of course deeply appreciated. Please call ahead to let the zendo know that you will be attending before arriving your first time.

Rigpa New York

P. O. Box 513
New York, NY 10014
Tel: 212-595-3573

rigpa_ny@yahoo.com
School affiliation: Nyingmapa
Language spoken: English

Rigpa is the organization founded by Sogyal Rinpoche, a highly regarded Buddhist teacher and author of the best-selling *Tibetan Book of Living and Dying*. As the title suggests, much of his teaching includes commentary on the process of death and the bardos (in-between states), a traditional subject in Buddhism, particularly the schools of Tibet.

Rigpa New York is a study group that doesn't have its own formal headquarters. They rent space at Sufi Books (see page 242) on Wednesdays at 7:30 P.M. The program starts with thirty minutes of meditation, then a videotape of recent teachings by Sogyal Rinpoche is shown. Sogyal Rinpoche himself comes through New York City fairly frequently and offers in-person teachings; the notice for these events is often short-term, so be sure to get on Rigpa's mailing list to find out ahead of time. The regular Wednesday night program is low-key and open to the public, and beginners should find it comfortable. A $5 donation is requested to offset the cost of renting the space.

Soho Zendo

464 West Broadway, #4
New York, NY 10012
Tel: 212-460-9289

School affiliation: Rinzai Zen
Language spoken: English

Hidden on an upper floor in this trendy neighborhood below Houston Street is an unpretentious zendo. The practice is rigorous Rinzai Zen, three sitting periods' worth, five nights a week (doors close promptly at 6:25 P.M., so don't be late). Thursdays are open to first-time nonmembers, and the first Wednesday of the month is an introductory class for beginners.

Still Mind Zendo

120 Washington Place
New York, NY 10014
Tel: 212-691-2972
Fax: 212-691-2972

rczoeller@aol.com
School affiliation: Soto Zen
Language spoken: English

Still Mind Zendo is the second Soto Zen sangha in the White Plum lineage on Washington Place—just on the other side of Washington Square Park is Sensei Pat O'Hara's Village Zendo (see page 102). But while the two groups share geography and background, there are significant differences in their styles. Janet Abels Sensei, the new leader of Still Mind Zendo, received her training from Roshi Robert Kennedy, who is not only a Zen master but a Jesuit priest! Following in this vein, Still Mind Zendo, which was founded by Roshi Kennedy, is expressly interfaith, teaching Zen in a context that doesn't require belief in specifically Buddhist metaphysics. In fact, Janet (she's usually only called Sensei within the zendo itself) isn't sure that any of her students are actually Buddhists at all—some are Jewish, some Catholic or Episcopalian, some basically agnostic. The notion of non-Buddhist Zen students may be strange at first, but it seems to work for Roshi Kennedy and his students, who have found ways to engage in the practice of Zen while still maintaining ties to their childhood religious communities. And lest anyone think less of their Zen, Bernie Glassman Roshi, Roshi Kennedy's own teacher and a highly respected Zen master, is clear that he considers this new Buddhist-less Zen to still contain the important essence of the tradition.

Actually, you'd hardly know that many members of Still Mind Zendo don't consider themselves Buddhists. The practice is the same as at other White Plum Soto centers—chanting of the Heart Sutra, lots of silent sitting, walking meditation, private interviews with the teacher, koan study, and so on. Sometimes Biblical parables are used to highlight Zen philosophical ideas, but you can find that sort of eclecticism in much more conservative sanghas as well. Overall, Still Mind Zendo strives to deliver simple, accessible teachings in a way that New Yorkers can benefit from. Janet Abels Sensei is a very open person who is happy to minister to Buddhists and non-Buddhists alike, as long as they have a sincere interest in learning Zen.

Still Mind Zendo is operated out of Janet Abel's brownstone, which seats about fifteen people. There is a garden in back where private meditation can be conducted. The zendo offers introduction to Zen sessions on the first Friday or third Thursday of the month at 7:00 P.M. (a donation of $10 is requested). Meditation is held on Saturday 9:30–11:00 A.M., Monday through Friday from 7:30 A.M. to 8:30 A.M., and on Tuesday evenings at Still Mind Zendo II (see page 77), a makeshift zendo set up in a studio on West 27th Street. A donation of $3 to $5 is requested from nonmembers. The group also participates in full-day and one-week retreats. Call to receive a brochure that lists the current schedule and provides further details about the zendo.

If possible, bring your own cushion or meditation bench, as they don't always have enough to go around.

Stress Reduction Class

At Isaac T. Hopper Home
110 Second Avenue
New York, NY 10003

Tel: 212-674-1163
School Affiliation: Soto Zen
Language spoken: English

Hopper House is a residential alternative to incarceration for women, most of whom are struggling with drug-related problems. The class, which is for residents only, is led by members of the Village Zendo (see page 102). It teaches Zen meditation techniques in order to help the women deal with the difficulties of withdrawal, addiction, trauma, stress, depression, and reintegration into society. This is a good example of an outreach program through which Buddhists put the idea of compassion to work.

Sung Tak Buddhist Temple

15 Pike Street
New York, NY 10002
Tel: 212-587-5936

School affiliation: Chinese Pure Land
Language spoken: Chinese

A giant white Kwan-Yin statue, female incarnation of compassion, stands before this temple, welcoming the faithful. Rev. Hong Yo leads this congregation in the Chinese Pure Land tradition. Their main practice includes praying to the Buddha Amitabha and observing the five Buddhist precepts.

Three Jewels Outreach Center and Bookstore

211 East 5th Street
New York, NY 10003
Tel: 212-475-6650
http://www.threejewels.org

info@threejewels.org
School affiliation: Gelugpa
Languages spoken: English, Tibetan

Small isn't an adequate term to describe this tiny storefront center and bookstore, run by students (primarily monks and nuns) of the Asian Classics Institute (see page 84). Still, a surprising number of people can squeeze inside, and once there, they'll find an excellent if somewhat disorganized resource for local Buddhists. Three Jewels simultaneously offers a bookstore, lending library, meditation and teaching schedule, reading room, and many community involvement programs, including work with troubled teens, female prisoners, and drug and alcohol addicts.

Three Jewels seeks to provide a peaceful space and useful programs to the spiritually impoverished people of New York City, and indeed the center has a nicely cozy atmosphere. They have meditation in the mornings and classes in the evenings. (Please register beforehand.) The schedule varies a great deal, so drop by or call to find out what programs are currently going on. All meditations and classes are completely free of charge.

The Tara Lending Library has a nice collection of books, tapes, and videos on Tibetan Buddhism and Tibetan music. Membership requires a refundable $25 safety deposit, a nice deal since you can take out a book for two weeks at a time, and the late fee is only 25¢ a day.

Transworld Buddhist Association Buddha Virtue Temple

7 East Broadway
New York, NY 10038
Tel: 212-962-1223

School affiliation: Chinese Pure Land
Language spoken: Chinese

This building can be located fairly easily by the red-and-gold signs adorning its outside. The interior is similarly colored, with deep red cushions and candles accenting the three large Buddha images at the altar. The congregation is led by Rev. Chao Fan, as is the Guan Kwong Temple of America (see page 90). They meet for group chanting on Sunday afternoons.

True Buddha Diamond Temple

105 Washington Street
New York, NY 10006
Tel: 212-732-5264
Fax: 212-732-8478

School affiliation: True Buddha School
(Chinese Vajrayana)
Language spoken: Chinese

This is the primary New York City temple for the True Buddha School, a new lineage of Chinese Vajrayana Buddhism. The True Buddha School was founded and is led by Grand Master Sheng-yen Lu (no relation to Master Sheng-Yen of the Ch'an Meditation Center), and is known by his followers as the True Buddha Lian-shen. Grand Master Sheng-yen Lu is originally from Taiwan and studied Taoism and Christianity before becoming involved in Tantric Buddhism; currently he lives near Seattle. His teaching heavily emphasizes miracles and supernatural events that the master has witnessed or performed—enthusiastic students are fond of mailing potential converts pictures of Sheng-yen Lu with amorphous blobs of light floating near his head. While the True Buddha School takes guru worship to new heights—and the photos more often than not look like the results of film overexposure—the teaching is more or less the same as other mainline Chinese tantric schools.

The True Buddha Diamond Temple is led by Master Hui-Chun. Teachings and ceremonies are in Chinese.

True Buddha Temple of Compassionate Grace

28 Forsyth Street
New York, NY 10002-6001
Tel: 212-226-8630
Fax: 212-226-7281

School affiliation: True Buddha School
  (Chinese Vajrayana)
Language spoken: Chinese

This small branch of the tantric True Buddha Diamond Temple (see page 100), decorated with Chinese and Tibetan motifs, sits in the shadow of the Manhattan Bridge. Activities are conducted in Chinese.

U.S.A. Shaolin Temple

678 Broadway, 3rd floor
New York, NY 10012
Tel: 212-358-7876
http://www.shaolintemple.com/
  home.html

School affiliation: Ch'an
Languages spoken: English, Chinese

So, grasshopper, you want to learn about Buddha? Listen first to the story of Sifu (Master) Shi Yan-Ming. His biography reads like the exploits in some wacky Chinese martial arts movie (and in fact he starred in several before his arrival in America): Left at the temple as a child by his parents, he became a top kung fu master in the ancient Shaolin tradition. On a tour in America he defected in the middle of the night by hopping into a cab and trying to communicate with hand signals, luckily ending up in Chinatown. Now with a temple of his own in the Shaolin style, his students include notorious gangsta rappers from the Wu-Tang Clan (named after the Wu-Tang Buddhist Temple in China) and Michelle Forbes, who played an alien on *Star Trek*.

Shi Yan-Ming's U.S.A. Shaolin Temple teaches the fifteen-hundred-year-old form of original Zen, preserved in its Chinese birthplace by warrior monks who used kung fu to protect the teachings of the Buddha from marauders. Though most people come to him for study in kung fu, tai chi, and qi gong, his techniques are also excellent for learning

Buddhism as well, since his approach to martial arts is completely integrated with study and meditation in the Ch'an tradition. Martial arts students even greet and say good-bye to him by saying "Amitabha," the name of the savior Buddha, and Shi Yan-Ming expects students to demonstrate knowledge of Ch'an Buddhism and Shaolin Temple history before he'll graduate them to higher levels of practice. Meditation is required for martial arts students—this is probably the only place in the city where you can practice the peaceful art of meditation in a room filled with hand weapons of every kind! And if you don't get enlightened, at least you can always start a second career as a superhero.

The Village Zendo

15 Washington Place, #4E
New York, NY 10003
Tel: 212-674-0832
http://www.villagezendo. org

pat.ohara@nyu.edu
School affiliation: Soto Zen (White Plum lineage)
Language spoken: English

Nestled in the heart of the New York University area is an institution that simultaneously breaks all of the conventional ideas about Buddhism and offers a true taste of traditional Japanese Zen. The Village Zendo, founded in 1986, is located in the apartment of Sensei Pat Enkyo O'Hara, a student of the late Maezumi Roshi and his students John Daido Loori Roshi and Bernie Glassman Roshi. Sensei O'Hara is not exactly what one usually expects in a Zen master: she's female, of Irish Catholic extraction, a former NYU professor of new media, and a lesbian. These atypical attributes inform her Zen practice, but they don't prevent her from offering a traditional course in Soto Zen.

For now, getting to the Village Zendo isn't difficult, but its location is hardly obvious from the outside. The zendo is located in a red brick apartment building not far from Washington Square Park. Be sure to remember to push buzzer #4E, because the button is just listed as "O'Hara, Pat and Barbara," not the Village Zendo. Once inside take the elevator to the fourth floor; turn right, go to the end of the hall, and turn left. Leave your shoes on the rack outside the zendo door. Please don't make a lot of noise in the hall while removing your shoes—other people live in the building, too. Also, if you're late for an evening sitting, please wait until the walking meditation periods (at approximately 7:05 and 7:45 P.M.) before joining in so as not to disturb the meditators. The Village Zendo will relocate in August 2001; at the time of this writing further details were not available. Please check the Web site for more current information.

The Village Zendo occupies the greater portion of Sensei O'Hara's spartan but elegant apartment. There is little furniture other than Zen sitting mats on the wood floor and a few tables and shelves. An altar occupies the far wall, and mats with cushions line the walls. Although the limited space available has been put to ingenious use, be prepared for a somewhat more cramped Zen experience than you may be used to: the mats are placed sideways to minimize the space they occupy, resulting in a sitting space for each meditator that is about one half of the normal size. You'll inevitably bump knees with the folks next to you, but don't sweat it—it's just another aspect of the practice.

Regardless of who lets you in, Sensei O'Hara will eventually come and introduce herself and ask if you need meditation instruction. If you are new to Zen meditation, a senior student will take you into another room partway through the evening sit in order to give you instruction and answer your questions.

Evening sits are held Monday–Thursday at 6:15 P.M. They start with a traditional service, including chanting in Japanese and English, full-body prostrations, and prayers for the ill and deceased, while Sensei O'Hara performs various rituals in the center of the room before the altar. This can be strange and intimidating to first-timers, but don't worry about it too much. Instructions are found in the service book that is passed around (there are also materials hidden under each mat), and you'll do fine by just watching what everyone else does and imitating the best you can. No one is expected to get it right the first time.

After the service, the first period of sitting begins. It is at this point that first-timers leave for individual instruction. Otherwise, the sitting proceeds in complete silence with the meditators facing the walls. After about thirty minutes there is a period of walking meditation, where you trot around the zendo at a brisk pace, snaking around the support poles and trying to maintain some mindfulness while moving. Then there is a second period of sitting, more walking meditation, a third period of sitting (this time facing the center of the room), and finally a closing ceremony. The whole affair usually lasts until about 8:30 P.M.

On Mondays and Tuesdays dokusan is conducted. Dokusan is a private interview with the teacher. It is entirely optional, but open to first-timers and senior students alike if one wishes to participate. Dokusan provides the student with a chance to get their pressing spiritual or practice questions answered, as well as giving the teacher an opportunity to assess the progress of the student. Dokusan occurs during the second two periods of sitting; a zendo leader will announce when it is time.

Thursday nights the third sitting period is replaced with a sermon, usually delivered by Sensei O'Hara. Morning sits are held on Tuesday, Wednesday, and Friday 7:30–8:30 A.M. One Saturday a month there is an all-day sit, known as zazenkai, that includes a ritual meal, dokusan, and a sermon; zazenkai lasts from 8:00 A.M. to 5:00 P.M. There are also four one-week retreats a year (sesshins) as well as a monthlong retreat in August, all held at other locations.

Evening sits are typically attended by about fifteen to twenty people. There's usually a newcomer or two, but most people have been there before. There are NYU professors and students, but also folks from the surrounding community as well. About 50 percent of the regular members are openly gay or lesbian. Regular sits are technically free of charge, but a donation of at least $3 is requested; there's a bowl near the door for contributions. Be sure your clothing is comfortable, because there's plenty of sitting at the zendo, and the temperature can get quite hot at times.

The Village Zendo belies the common perception of Zen as purely inwardly focused and uninvolved in worldly affairs. This is a social-activist sangha, in fact. The zendo leads programs at the Gay Men's Health Crisis (see page 62) and a residence for female convicts (see page 98), and collects Buddhist books for inmates in Fort Dix. Newsletters contain articles about charitable programs locally and abroad. Sensei O'Hara is explicitly committed to examining the intersection of Zen insight with identity and difference issues. Furthermore, Sensei O'Hara is a founding teacher of the Zen Peacemaker Order (see page 246) and its current training director; the Village Zendo serves as an official Zen Peacemaker training center. Sensei O'Hara is also the chairperson of the AIDS National Interfaith Network and the spiritual advisor of Maitri Dorje (see page 92), and gives editorial guidance to *Tricycle: The Buddhist Review* (see page 243).

Westbeth Vipassana Group

463 West Street
New York, NY 10014
Tel: 212-873-6376

School affiliation: Vipassana
Language spoken: English

This group meets in a dance studio at the largest artists' commune in the world, located in the West Village. Not surprisingly, they aren't heavy on rules and restrictions. Anyone is welcome to attend (though call first), and there's no leader or fee. Westbeth Vipassana Group meets on Tuesdays 7:30–9:30 P.M. The first Tuesday of the month is strictly sitting and walking meditation. The other meetings also emphasize sitting and walking, but have some additions to the program: the second Tuesday usually includes a group discussion and a metta (loving-kindness) meditation; the third Tuesday features an audiotaped teaching; and the fourth Tuesday includes personal practice sharing. One Saturday a month they gather for a longer program, 8:00 A.M. to 3:00 P.M., focusing purely on sitting and walking meditation (with a lunch break).

Depending on the season, attendance can fluctuate from twenty people all the way down to as few as four or so. Chairs and mats can be provided, but the number of cushions is limited, so bring a pillow if you can.

Wonderful Enlightenment Temple

99 Madison Street
New York, NY 10002
Tel: 212-964-0523

Fax: 212-964-6665
School affiliation: Ch'an
Language spoken: Chinese

This is a basic Chinatown temple, run by Rev. Shih Chen. It's oddly flanked by an Evangelical Christian church on one side and a Baptist church on the other.

World Buddhist Center

158 Henry Street
New York, NY 10002
Tel: 212-964-6813

School affiliation: Chinese Pure Land
Language spoken: Chinese

Despite its grandiose name, this is a fairly typical Chinatown temple, connected to the Chung Te Buddhist Temple (see page 88) next door. Members sit on pews before the Amitabha Buddha statue for chanting and prayers.

Youth Buddhism Communications, Inc.

11 East Broadway, suite 8B
New York, NY 10038
Tel: 212-406-5109
Fax: 212-346-0611

http://www.asiawind.com/pub/
asiancom/buddhist/ybci.htm
School affiliation: Chinese Pure Land
Languages spoken: Chinese, English

Youth Buddhism Communications is a group that tries to bring Buddhism into the life of the community through lectures, publications, tours, and special events. They have a catalog of books, tapes, and props for Buddhist ceremonies, and publish a monthly newsletter. Note that most of their materials are in Cantonese Chinese. Their mailing address differs from their street address: 39 Bowery, Box 738, New York, NY 10002.

QUEENS

Queens is second only to Manhattan in the number of Buddhist groups, most located in the flourishing Asian American communities in the Flushing area. Incidentally, queens have had a substantial impact on the spread of Buddhism around the world—the Buddhist order of nuns was founded by the Buddha's stepmother, queen of the Shakya people; the first Tibetan Buddhist king was converted by the influence of his Nepali and Chinese wives; and in China the Empress Wu was a famous patron of Buddhism.

American Sri Lanka Buddhist Association, Inc.

c/o New York Buddhist Vihara
84-32 124th Street
Kew Gardens, NY 11415

Tel: 718-849-2637
School affiliation: Theravada
Languages spoken: English, Sinhalese

The American Sri Lankan Buddhist Association was founded in 1980 by Venerable Galboda Gnanissera Thero. It administers the New York Buddhist Vihara (see page 116), the Staten Island Buddhist Vihara (see page 134), and is involved in building a larger temple in Queens to accommodate monastic quarters and community gatherings. The association also distributes free Buddhist teachings through its Dhamma Book Service.

Bangladesh Buddhist Society of America

42-31 66th Street
Woodside, NY 11377
Tel: 718-899-3667

School affiliation: Theravada
Language spoken: Bengali

This Queens temple serves the Theravada Buddhist segment of the Bangladeshi population. Traditional services and teachings provide immigrants with ties to their homeland, and children born here with a chance to connect to their ancestors' way of life.

Bo Kwang Zen Center

36-25 Union Street, #1C
Flushing, NY 11354
Tel: 718-353-2474

School affiliation: Korean Zen (Kwan Um school of Zen)
Language spoken: Korean

This is a center in the tradition of Korean Zen master Seung Sahn. It is led by Rev. Tai Fong. All services are conducted in Korean.

Bodhicitta Foundation

P. O. Box 7845

Flushing, NY 11352

Tel: 718-275-6366/718-359-5987

School affiliation: Chinese Pure Land

Languages spoken: English, Chinese

Bodhicitta is the mind of enlightenment, which must be developed before true attainment can occur. Bodhicitta is thus the foundation of enlightenment, making the name of this Chinese group a bit of a pun. Call Mr. Chiang Chi-Lu or Mr. Chen Hsiu for details about their organization.

Buddha's Light International Association
Young Adult Division—New York
Subdivision

c/o International Buddhist Progress

Society, NY

154-37 Barclay Avenue

Flushing, NY 11355-1109

Tel: 718-939-8318

Fax: 718-939-4277

http://www.geocities.com/SoHo/Lofts/

2065/youth/index.html

langsu@aol.com

School affiliation: Pure Land and Ch'an (Fo

Kuang Shan)

Languages spoken: Chinese, English

This youth group is associated with the International Buddhist Progress Society New York temple (see page 112), and is a branch of the BLIA organization based in Taiwan.

The Buddhist Association of Asia,
Tsu In Temple

143-19 Ash Avenue

Flushing, NY 11355

Tel: 718-445-1180

School affiliation: Ch'an

Language spoken: Chinese

Rev. Tee-Tung's Tsu In Temple serves the Chinese American community of Flushing. The temple is a converted three-story brick house with a nice little yard, located on a quiet, residential street. Most public gatherings are on Sundays.

Ch'an Meditation Center

90-56 Corona Avenue

Elmhust, NY 11373

Tel: 718-592-6593

Fax: 718-592-0717

http://www.chan1.org

ddmbany@aol.com

School affiliation: Ch'an (Zen)

Languages spoken: English, Chinese

The Ch'an Meditation Center is a major site on the local Buddhist map, headed by Master Sheng-Yen, perhaps the most internationally respected Buddhist teacher resident in New York City. Master Sheng-Yen is one of the few people to receive teaching sanction from both major Chinese Ch'an lineages. From this three-story brick building he runs a Chinese Zen center with a large following in both the Chinese and non-Chinese community, and Dharma Drum Communications, a publishing outlet for Sheng-Yen's more than fifty books and translations. The center started as a small group at the Temple of Great Enlightenment (see page 131) but has grown so much through the years that it has moved twice and is currently constructing additional facilities in the suburbs. It currently has more than two hundred visitors a week.

Master Sheng-Yen also has headquarters in Taiwan and devotes about half the year to each country. When he is away the community is managed by the monks and nuns who live at the center. Practice includes Zen sitting meditation, sutra recitation, chanting "Namo O-mi-to-fo," and confession. The center also offers tai chi chuan, children's programs, yoga, and retreats. There are programs virtually every day of the week, most of which are open to beginners and free of charge.

The center also offers an unusual outreach program to the terminally ill, known as Compassion for the Dying. Upon request, teams of volunteers are dispatched to comfort the dying with chanting, sermons, and companionship.

China Buddhist Association

136-12 39th Avenue

Flushing, NY 11354

Tel: 718-460-4402/718-460-4318

School affiliation: Chinese Pure Land

Language spoken: Chinese

This is one of two related temples headed by Rev. Miao Feng. The practice is standard Chinese Pure Land, consisting of chanting "Namo O-mi-to-fo" to honor Amitabha Buddha, the savior of the masses. Services are held on Sunday mornings and on the first and fifteenth days of the month. The temple houses several monks and nuns; ask for Ming Yei, if possible, who speaks English. The China Buddhist Association is building Pine Woods Monastery (see page 161) upstate.

Community of Mindfulness—Queens

Rego Park, NY 11374

Tel: 718-897-4746

School affiliation: Community of Mindfulness

Language spoken: English

This is the Queens chapter of the Community of Mindfulness New York Metro (see page 48). They practice a very casual, Western style of lay-oriented Zen, in the Vietnamese tradition of Thich Nhat Hanh. The group goes through periods of growth and contraction; currently it's going through a small phase. They meet in members' homes on Thursdays at 7:30 P.M. for sitting and walking meditation, chanting of the Heart Sutra (in English), and discussion. They also take part in the New York Metro Day of Mindfulness on the second Saturday of each month.

Ruth Klein, the coordinator for the Queens group, is a longtime Zen student, and even lived at the Providence Zen Center (a large group in the Korean Zen tradition) for five years. Be sure to call ahead to confirm that events are taking place, as this group's schedule can sometimes be erratic.

Diamond Sutra Recitation Group

46-39 158th Street
Flushing, NY 11358
Tel: 718-539-9108
http://www.diamondsutra.org

ysull@mindspring.com
School affiliation: Korean Mahayana
Languages spoken: Korean, English

The Diamond Sutra is a key Buddhist scripture, describing the universe as an ever-shifting realm of cause and effect, where all thing interpenetrate and support one another. It's played an important part in East Asian Buddhist philosophy for many centuries, and is the primary text venerated by this group. They gather to chant the Diamond Sutra as prescribed by Jae Woong Kim, a Korean Buddhist master. Another aspect of their practice is surrendering negative mental states to Maitreya, the future Buddha, a method very similar to Pure Land Buddhist techniques.

Daily practice is held from 3:00 to 6:00 A.M. (!) and 7:00–9:00 P.M. On Sundays there is a larger gathering with discussion, 11:00 A.M. to 2:00 P.M. Though the bulk of this group is Korean American, everyone is cheerfully invited to join in the practice. The services are held in a normal looking house indistinct from the others on its block, except for two subtle Chinese lanterns on either side of the door.

Fu Yen True Buddha Temple

4310 National Street
Flushing, NY 11368
Tel: 718-639-2456

School affiliation: True Buddha School
(Chinese Vajrayana)
Language spoken: Chinese

The True Buddha School is a form of Chinese tantric Buddhism, based on the West Coast. Its following in New York City is mainly confined to the Chinese-American population. This is the Flushing branch temple of the True Buddha Diamond Temple (see page 100).

International Buddhist Progress Society, New York

154-37 Barclay Avenue
Flushing, NY 11355
Tel: 718-939-8318
Fax: 718-939-4277
http://www.ibps.org/newyork/
   index-ny.htm

ibpsny@worldnet.att.net
School affiliation: Chinese Pure Land and
   Ch'an (Fo Kuang Shan)
Languages spoken: Chinese, English

The International Buddhist Progress Society in New York is led by Abbess Rev. Yi Hang. It is associated with the Hsi Lai Temple in Los Angeles, which was embroiled in a big campaign fund-raising scandal with Al Gore. Though the press had a field day attributing the affair to secret Communist Chinese attempts to buy favor from the vice president, the temple's actual part in the situation was by and large innocent misunderstanding of how to navigate the confusing currents of American politics. No charges against Hsi Lai resulted from the mistake and it shouldn't have a bearing on whether to attend this branch temple.

Actually, the IBPS is an excellent resource for authentic Buddhism. Not only do they offer both Pure Land and Zen teachings, but the specifically humanistic Buddhist philosophy developed by this school's head teacher, Master Hsing Yun, is very fresh and modern in expression and application. The IBPS in Flushing, located in a large four-story building at the end of a street choked with churches, includes programs in Buddhist studies, martial arts, fine arts, Chinese language and culture, and even a Cub Scout troop, Pack 754. The temple has a good-sized parking lot that can be used by visitors.

Not all of the monastics at the IBPS speak English. If you don't speak any Chinese and are worried about your first encounter, call and ask for Venerable Chueh Yang, whose English is completely fluent and will be happy to help you out in your first visit to the temple. Don't let the apparent language barrier scare you—many of the monks, nuns, and volunteers do speak English, and the center has books in English by Master Hsing Yun that are available for further study.

International Pure Land Association of U.S.A., Inc.

56-18 135th Street
Flushing, NY 11355
Tel: 718-359-0384

School affiliation: Chinese Pure Land
Language spoken: Chinese

Most Chinese Buddhists practice Pure Land Buddhism, which is designed to offer a path to enlightenment for laypeople who can't stop their busy lives and meditate all day. This particular group is led by Rev. Hong Yi, a Buddhist monk.

Kum Kang Zen Center

3520 147th Street
Flushing, NY 11354
Tel: 718-460-3920

School affiliation: Korean Zen
Language spoken: Korean

This Zen Center serves the Korean-speaking population of Flushing. It is located in a Korean-American office/apartment building off Northern Boulevard.

Myosetsuji Temple

143-63 Beech Avenue
Flushing, NY 11355-2176
Tel: 718-961-7269
Fax: 718-461-0765
http://www.nstny.org/

info@nstny.org
School affiliation: Nichiren Shoshu Temple
Languages spoken: English, Japanese,
Spanish, Korean, Chinese

The Myosetsuji Temple is the headquarters for orthodox Nichiren Shoshu Buddhism in the Northeast, including New England, New York, New Jersey, Pennsylvania, parts of Canada, and Trinidad(!) under its jurisdiction. The Chief Priest is Rev. Jisei Nagasaka.

Nichiren Shoshu is different from other forms of Buddhism in some very particular ways. For one, it venerates its founder, the thirteenth-century Japanese teacher Nichiren, as the True Buddha, relegating Shak-

yamuni Buddha to an inferior role. Second, it is not open to outsiders. Rev. Nagasaki does not welcome casual visits at his temple—he once turned away the prince and princess of Japan because they are not Shoshu followers. Only those with a commitment to learning and practicing Nichiren Shoshu Buddhism should contact the temple. This is not to say that new and interested Buddhists are unwelcome, only that one should have a specific interest in the Shoshu teachings if one plans to drop by.

The closed nature of the temple is reflected in their teachings. Nichiren Shoshu Buddhism is very strict and does not acknowledge other Buddhist groups as teaching legitimate paths to enlightenment.

Gongyo, ritual chanting of "Namu Myoho Renge Kyo" and portions of the Lotus Sutra, takes place at the temple at 9:00 A.M. and 3:00 P.M. on Sundays and 5:00 P.M. on other days. There are monthly memorial services, study sessions, and annual activities such as holiday celebrations. Language-specific meetings, including Chinese, Korean, and Spanish, are also held. Myosetsuji is a long building with a white exterior, not immediately recognizable as a temple.

Nichiren Shoshu manages to cover such a wide geographic area with only a single temple by cultivating its lay group, the Hokkeko. Nichiren

Shoshu used to also control another larger lay group, the Soka Gakkai (see page 75), but excommunicated them in 1990 after disputes over authority. The Soka Gakkai are now evolving into a separate Shoshu sect. Hokkeko has chapters and small meeting groups throughout the Northeast, including local ones in Manhattan (see pages 51, 93) and New Jersey (see page 181). One can get contact information for them by calling the temple, but usually people learn about Hokkeko through family, friends, or co-workers, as Nichiren Shoshu now prefers a low-profile proselytizing stance.

New York Buddhist Vihara

84-32 124th Street
Kew Gardens, NY 11415
Tel: 718-849-2637

School affiliation: Theravada
Languages spoken: English, Sinhalese

On a quiet residential Queens street of modest-size houses sits a quiet, modest-size house that contains a contingent of shaven-headed Sri Lankan monks. The monks themselves are rather quiet and modest as well, blending into the background of families and community life in an unassuming way. Few would guess that their group is involved in some of the most ambitious Buddhist projects undertaken in New York City.

The New York Buddhist Vihara was founded by the American Sri Lanka Buddhist Association (see page 107) in 1981; it moved to its current location in 1986. It is presently led by Venerable Kurunegoda Piyatissa Maha Thero, a Sri Lankan–born monk who has been teaching in America for many years. The monks offer instruction in dharma, meditation, and Pali (the canonical language of Theravada Buddhism), as well as serving the needs of the ethnic Sri Lankan population through Sunday children's classes and such traditional rituals as receiving meals in families' homes. Chanting sessions are held in the mornings and evenings, with Wednesday public meditation classes in English at 6:30 P.M.

The New York Buddhist Vihara is a participant in the construction of a large Theravadin temple in Queens, as yet unfinished. Ven. Piyatissa cofounded and has led the Buddhist Council of New York (see page 229) and is active in other inter-Buddhist activities via the annual Vesak ceremony (see page 245) and Change Your Mind Day (see page 232).

Visitors are quite welcome at the Vihara, but some considerations should be kept in mind. Theravada places great importance on sila, the practice of virtue and moral correctness, and the monks strive to be examples of self-control to the community. They do not eat meals after noon or permit alcohol or smoking. People are expected to observe the five precepts in the Vihara, and should show respect to the monks. One particular aspect of this is that laypeople are not supposed to sit with their heads higher than the monks, and to this end visitors may be politely asked to sit on small stools instead of the other chairs and couches scattered about the Vihara. Don't be too worried about violating their rules—they'll inform you politely if you're breaking decorum and give you a chance to correct your behavior. Despite the formality of such arrangements, the monks are actually quite personable and enthusiastic about meeting the needs of the laity.

All activities at the Vihara are free of charge—the monks are zealous about giving away their teachings in the spirit of charity and fraternity. Donations, of course, are always welcome.

The New York Buddhist Vihara is not readily accessible from the subway. Take the Q10, Q44, or Q54 bus instead. Call ahead for class times and more specific directions for getting there from your location.

New York Chogye Sah/Korean Buddhist Jo-Gei Temple

45-18 48th Avenue
Woodside, NY 11377
Tel: 718-706-1749
Fax: 718-392-3011

School affiliation: Korean Zen (Kwan Um school of Zen)
Languages spoken: English, Korean

This is a small center in the Korean Zen tradition of Seung Sahn Sunim. The practice is similar to that at all Kwan Um temples; see the Chogye International Zen Center of New York (see page 87) for more details on typical practice. The head teacher is Dae Kwang (who isn't in residence at the temple). New York Chogye Sah offers occasional re-treats—call for upcoming events.

New York Han-Ma-Um Zen Center

144-39 32nd Avenue

Flushing, NY 11354

Tel: 718-460-2019

Fax: 718-939-3974

School affiliation: Korean Zen (Chogye)

Languages spoken: Korean, English

New York Han-Ma-Um Center is an official temple of the Chogye Order of Korean Buddhism, the main orthodox school of Buddhism in modern Korea. Chogye Buddhism includes teachings from many East Asian Buddhist schools; the Han-Ma-Um Center's particular emphasis is on Zen ("Son" in Korean). It acts as a sister school to the Han-Ma-Um Zen Center in Anyang, South Korea, and monastics such as the enlightened nun Dae Haeng Sunim sometimes visit from the Korean temple to give teachings. The center's primary programs occur on Sundays.

Saddharma Cakra Buddhist Association

P. O. Box 1469

Flushing, NY 11352

Tel: 718-463-0665

School affiliation: Chinese Pure Land

Language spoken: Chinese

The Saddharma Cakra (Great Wheel of the Teaching) Buddhist Association has a Sanskrit name, but is actually Chinese, not Indian. Many people may have seen swastikas, a type of cakra, on Buddhist statues or at temples. Though unfortunately associated with the horrors of Nazism, the swastika is an ancient pagan symbol found in religious art in India, Europe, Australia, and even throughout pre-Columbian Native American art. Buddhists consider it a symbol of good luck and use it to represent their holy teachings; though they had claim to it thousands of years before the rise of Hitler, it may now be forever tainted in the Western mind.

Other than their unusual name, the Saddharma Cakra Buddhist Association is a typical Chinese Pure Land temple, with worship on Sundays.

Shaolin Temple Overseas Headquarters

133-14 41st Avenue

Flushing, New York 11355

Tel: 718-539-0872

Fax: 718-539-0872

http://www.shaolin-overseas.org

guolin@juno.com

School affiliation: Ch'an

Languages spoken: English, Chinese

Venerable Shi Guolin leads this martial arts temple in the ancient Shao-lin tradition. Descended directly from the original Shaolin Temple in China, this lineage combines highly developed physical exercises with the mind of single-pointed concentration, creating a powerful practice of meditation in movement.

The martial arts exercises are learned in a back area with a practice space surrounded by the golden figures of five hundred traditional Chinese saints, known as lohans. Each lohan has a distinct appearance and biography; Venerable Guolin can explain them to you if you ask. All age ranges are accepted for kung fu study at the temple; there are separate classes offered for children.

The front part of the building opens onto the street and houses the traditional service area of the temple. Through wide doors below a pagoda façade with hanging Chinese lanterns, the visitor is greeted by several large Buddhist statues, an altar, and cushions for parishioners. The temple moved to its current location in April of 2000; previously it was housed in a much smaller space down the street. Venerable Guolin grew up near the original Shaolin Temple and was sent here eight years ago by the abbott specifically to make the methods of this lineage available to the West.

Non-martial arts services are held in Chinese every day at 5:00 P.M., and at 10:00 A.M. on Sundays. Everyone is welcome to attend, and the service book has phonetic Chinese text that can be used by non-Chinese speakers. These services include study of the Buddhist scriptures, recitation of Pure Land mantras and the Heart Sutra, taking the three vows, and sermons on how to apply dharma to one's daily life situations. On Saturdays a special instruction in using the temple's ritual implements is offered. All services are free and include no martial arts.

Students address Venerable Guolin as "Sifu" ("Master"). When greeting or leaving someone at the temple it is polite to bow with palms touching and say "Omitofo" (the name of the Buddha of Infinite Light). Two other monks besides Venerable Guolin live at the temple.

True Buddha Temple—Elmhurst Branch

4-17 Gleane Avenue, 3rd floor
Elmhurst, NY 11373
Tel: 718-424-4047
Fax: 212-254-7178

School affiliation: True Buddha School
  (Chinese Vajrayana)
Language spoken: Chinese

This is the Elmhurst branch temple of the True Buddha Diamond Temple (see page 100). See the description of that temple for more information on this type of Buddhism.

Wat Buddha Thai Thavorn Vanaram

76-16 46th Avenue
Elmhurst, NY 11373
Tel: 718-803-9881
Fax: 718-803-3819

School affiliation: Theravada (Dhammayut
  Order)
Languages spoken: Thai, English

Founded six years ago, this Theravadin temple belongs to the Dhammayut (Forest Meditation) sect, a reformist subschool popularized in Thailand by King Mongkut of *The King and I* fame. Although to outsiders it won't seem much different from any other ethnic Theravadin temple, there is a stronger emphasis on meditation and asceticism among the monks.

More unusual still, this temple is actually a haunted house! Originally a two-story residential frame house, its former owners were frightened away by eerie noises in the night and the specter of a ghostly man. A house next door that the temple bought to use as a parsonage for the monks burned down, and it looked like the temple might be a doomed venture. But the monks have now appeased the protective apparition by building him a special spirit house in the backyard, and the temple's fortunes have subsequently improved.

The monks survive by receiving food from the laity during morning rounds of begging from house to house, a common practice in Theravadin temples. The temple offers regular services, as well as counseling to the New York City area Thai-American population. All services are provided in the Thai language, but English is spoken by many of the regular visitors and some of the resident monks.

Won Buddhism of New York

143-42 Cherry Avenue

Flushing, NY 11355

Tel: 718-762-4103

Fax: 718-353-5282

School affiliation: Won

Language spoken: Korean

Won Buddhism of New York is a large Korean American temple, emphasis on the Korean. Services are conducted entirely in Korean, and those without facility in the language will not get much out of a visit to this temple (though the members will certainly do their best to be accommodating).

Essentially, Won Buddhism of New York is a family temple, where several generations come together to worship on Sunday. The Sunday service starts at 11:00 A.M. and is quite similar to that at Manhattan Won Buddhism (see page 63). Afterward people gather informally to chat and gossip over kimchee and other refreshments. The social situation follows typical Korean mores, with all the grandmothers together in one room, the men in another, and so on. There are numerous gender- and age-specific subgroups, such as the Youth Group, Men's Group, and so forth, which carry out their own activities related to the temple and practicing the dharma. Unlike the Manhattan Won temple, which is largely frequented by individuals and couples without their children, Won Buddhism of New York offers an excellent look at the principle of gratitude toward parents—one of Won Buddhism's "Four Graces"—in this sect's practice.

Since its founding fifteen years ago, Won Buddhism of New York has become an important institution for the preservation of Korean culture in the melting pot of New York City. Besides the regular Buddhist activities, the temple runs the Won Kwang Korean School of New York, which has weekend classes in Korean language and culture for young people. The school is open to all, regardless of whether they have an interest in Buddhism or not.

If you decide to attend, wear nice clothing as if you were going to church, show respect to the older members of the congregation, and try to arrive on time so as not to disrupt meditation. But don't barge in without Korean fluency and expect to get very far. The Won Buddhists are warmhearted, but there isn't much they can offer you if you all can't communicate with each other.

BROOKLYN

Brooklyn doesn't have as many organized Buddhist centers as Manhattan or Queens, but those it does have represent a nice mix of traditions. In just a dozen or so centers you can find Theravada, Zen, Tibetan, Pure Land, Nichiren, and more, basically a very accurate microcosm of New York City Buddhism on the whole. There are groups led by Asians, Caucasians, and African Americans, ranging from the highly traditional to the extremely informal.

The American Burma Buddhist Association, Inc.

c/o Universal Peace Buddha Temple
619 Bergen Street
Brooklyn, NY 11238
Tel: 718-622-8019
http://www.mahasiusa.org/

School affiliation: Theravada (Mahasi Sayadaw lineage)
Languages spoken: Burmese, English

ABBA was founded in 1981 and is led by Venerable Ashin Indaka, a Pali expert and meditation teacher. It administers the Universal Peace Buddha Temple (see page 130) and the Mahasi Meditation Retreat Center (see page 180) in Englishtown, New Jersey.

Part of ABBA's mission is to preserve traditional Burmese culture and religion in the New World, and many of its activities are designed to help the ethnic Burmese American population sustain cultural forms from Burma. However, since the Mahasi Sayadaw lineage itself represents a reform movement from Southeast Asia, the association and its centers advocate a form of practice and understanding that is already more innovative than that of many more traditional temples in Burma. In fact, ABBA shares lineage ties with the ultra-Western Vipassana movement, as typified by the New York Insight Meditation Center (see page 67), and it could well serve as a sort of middle ground for Vipassana students seeking a wider exposure to Theravada forms and principles who nonetheless still aren't prepared for the more conservative approach found in most temples.

Bangladesh Buddhist Center of America

217 East 8th Street, 3rd floor
Brooklyn, NY 11218
Tel: 718-972-4473

School affiliation: Theravada
Language spoken: Bengali

Like Theravadin centers established by other ethnic groups, this temple provides a link to the ways and values of the Old Country. The Bengali Buddhists are substantially outnumbered in their homeland by

Muslims and Hindus, so ironically distant America sometimes offers a more accepting environment in which to practice their ancient religion.

Brooklyn Buddhist Association/
International Zen Dojo of Brooklyn
Sogenkai

211 Smith Street
Brooklyn, NY 11201
Tel: 718-488-9511
Fax: 718-797-1073
http://www.directmind.com

bbajskl@aol.com
School affiliation: Rinzai Zen and Jodo
Shinshu Pure Land Buddhism (Higashi
Honganji branch)
Language spoken: English

This is an aikido dojo with an active Zen meditation group, based in a storefront. The group is affiliated with the International Zen Dojo Sogenkai, a network of Zen aikido centers with headquarters in Hawaii. Brooklyn Buddhist Association's leader is Shaku Joseph Jarman. Rinzai Zen and aikido are both practiced as a way to focus the mind and body. Meditation is held four times a week, with sermons and group discussions. The aikido program is somewhat separate and requires a monthly membership fee.

The Brooklyn Buddhist Association also serves as a temple in the Higashi Honganji lineage of Jodo Shinshu Pure Land Buddhism, and has the extremely rare distinction of being the only New York City Buddhist temple led by an African American couple. As if that weren't enough, this isn't just any couple: Joseph Jarman is an acclaimed jazz musician from Chicago, and his wife, Thulani Davis, is a major poet, writer, and librettist. Reverend Jarman has a band based in the dojo, where they offer public performances; they've also played hip venues like the Knitting Factory.

Buddhist Center of New York

335 Court Street, suite 137
Brooklyn, NY 11231
Tel: 718-522-5052
Fax: 212-253-1883
http://diamondway.12pt.com/

newyork@diamondway-center.org
School affiliation: Kagyupa (Karma Kagyu lineage)
Language spoken: English

It may present a peaceful facade to outsiders, but segments of Tibetan Buddhism are actually roiling with intrigue and partisanship. That's what you get when separation of church and state is nonexistent, and the less enlightened cliques of the monkhood have been battling over the riches owned by monasteries since the days of Genghis Khan.

Unfortunately, the Buddhist Center of New York is part of this volatile mix of religion and power. The Karma Kagyu teacher known as the Sixteenth Gyalwa Karmapa was the leader of his sect and a brilliant translator of Buddhism for the West. After he died, the search for his reincarnation went sour and two rival boys have been served up as the next Karmapa. Most people, including, bizarrely enough, both the Dalai Lama and his archrival the Chinese Communist government, recognize Ugyen Trinley Dorje as the Karmapa. But there are disagreements, and some people believe that Thaye Dorje is the true Karmapa. Buddhist Center New York is in this latter lineage.

Actually, this dispute shouldn't really sway anyone for or against the Buddhist Center New York. It offers practice just like that of any other Kagyu center, and its members are no less devout just because their lead lama is currently the underdog. Tasso and Lisa Kallianiotis, the center's leaders, are under the direct supervision of Lama Ole Nydahl, a European and the first Westerner to study with the previous Karmapa.

Tuesday is the main day for public sessions. Programs start at 7:00 P.M. and include textual study and guru meditation. On Thursday the center holds events at the New York Diamond Way Buddhist Center (see page 67), a small outreach branch of the Buddhist Center New York. Nonmembers are asked to please give a $5 donation when attending programs.

Chakrasambara Buddhist Center

418 Pacific Street
Brooklyn, NY 11217
Tel: 718-834-0210
http://www.chakrasambara.org

chakra@chakrasambara.org
School affiliation: Gelugpa (New
    Kadampa Tradition)
Languages spoken: English, Tibetan

This is the local outpost of the New Kadampa Tradition, a new Gel-ugpa sect created by Geshe Kelsang Gyatso. The NKT is part of an unusual power struggle within the Gelugpa school, with the Dalai Lama and his followers on one side and Gyatso Rinpoche and his New Kadampa Tradition on the other. Ostensibly, the disagreement is over the proper role of Dorje Shugden, a controversial Tibetan protector deity, whose worship the Dalai Lama opposes. The real issue is much murkier and virtually impossible for Westerners to fully understand, involving centuries-old disputes over power, lineage, and tradition. The NKT became infamous in Buddhist circles and gained some attention from the press when it picketed the Dalai Lama's 1998 U.S.A. tour with signs that read DALAI LAMA, GIVE US RELIGIOUS FREEDOM!

Other than this rather esoteric disagreement, the New Kadampa Tradition offers standard Gelugpa teachings based on Geshe Kelshang's books, which present a systematic path to enlightenment. The Chakrasambara Buddhist Center, operated out of a converted apartment in Park Slope, holds regular evening meditation classes, weekend study classes, and weekly puja (purification) ceremonies. The teachings are highly structured, with different levels of courses that lead step-by-step along the path. A $10 donation per class is generally requested; special classes and retreats are typically more.

Sadhanas, prayer sessions with accompanying meditations, are less structured and free of charge. They are held weekdays 8:00–8:45 A.M. and Saturdays at 2:00 P.M.

The center houses a small number of residential monastics and students, including Kadam Morten Clausen, the center's primary teacher, as well as a library of dharma materials and a meditation room that is open to the public.

Community of Mindfulness
Brooklyn Sangha

412 Ninth Street, #3
Brooklyn, NY 11215
Tel: 718-499-5104

School affiliation: Community of Mindfulness
Language spoken: English

This is the very active Brooklyn branch of Thich Nhat Hanh's Community of Mindfulness. They have biweekly meetings with meditation and discussion. On Sundays they perform walking meditation in a nearby park. They also have monthly full-day meditation retreats. Contact Patricia Lenore for details and see the Community of Mindfulness New York Metro (page 48).

East River Ch'an Center

98 Gold Street
Brooklyn, NY 11201
Tel: 718-522-6523

School affiliation: Ch'an (Chinese Zen)
Language spoken: Chinese

Despite the similarity in names, this group isn't officially connected to the Ch'an Meditation Center (see page 110) in Queens. The East River Ch'an Center serves as a place for monastics to meditate and laypeople to worship and receive teachings and advice. The temple's head teacher is Rev. Da Wei.

Fire Lotus Temple

500 State Street
Brooklyn, NY 11217
Tel: 212-642-1591
http://www.zen-mtn.org/zcnyc

zcnyc@zen-mtn.org
School affiliation: Soto and Rinzai Zen
(Mountains and Rivers Order)
Language spoken: English

Fire Lotus Temple is the official New York City branch of John Daido Loori's Zen Mountain Monastery (see page 171). It's run by Sensei Bonnie Myotai Treace, Daido Loori's first dharma heir. Fire Lotus Temple offers modern American Zen practices like mindful arts and environmentally conscious retreats. Practice is what informs every aspect of life at Fire Lotus, and it's taken seriously—it's one of the only NYC locations to offer the traditional intense three-month ango training period.

The Fire Lotus Temple community was located in Manhattan until June of 2000, when they moved to the new location in Brooklyn. As they put it, they "hit the ground practicing," but expect some rough edges if you arrive within a year or so of their relocation. Morning practice periods are held 7:25–8:30 A.M. on Mondays, Wednesdays, and Thursdays; evening practice is Monday to Friday, 6:20–8:00 P.M. (Wednesdays include interview with teacher, and generally run till 8:30 P.M.). Sunday practice is held 10:00 A.M. to 12:30 P.M. and includes a sermon. A $3 donation is requested for weekday programs, $5 for Sundays. Also on Sundays, there is a beginner's session at 9:15 A.M. (suggested donation is $7). Please note that your first experience at Fire Lotus Temple must be the Sunday beginner's session—even for veteran Zen practitioners, there is no admittance to other programs without first receiving this instruction. The temple also holds monthly full-day zazen intensives.

As of this writing the only phone number available for the community was the old Manhattan one, listed above. Check the Web page for more recent information.

Nipponzan Myohoji New York
Japanese Temple

8906 107th Street
Richmond Hill, NY 11418
Tel: 718-805-1015

School affiliation: Nipponzan Myohoji (Nichiren)
Languages spoken: English, Japanese

Nipponzan Myohoji is a new school of Nichiren Buddhism formed before World War II in Japan. Of all the Buddhist sects in the world, it is the one most firmly committed to working and praying for peace and the welfare of all beings. Indeed, it seems almost to have little else in the way of theology. Members, led by monks and nuns, chant for the welfare of all humankind and creatures while energetically beating on drums.

The sect also erects large peace pagodas (see the Grafton Peace Pagoda, page 148) to generate good karma around the world. Frequent activities include dramatic months-long cross-country walks to highlight a variety of social issues, such as nuclear disarmament, the history of American slavery, and prison reform.

While on a walk for the latter issue, members of the Grafton Peace Pagoda visited Rikers Island and stayed for services at the Nipponzan Myohoji New York Japanese Temple. This modest temple is run by Rev. Isshi Basshi, whose command of English is a little shaky. But the practices are basic enough that if you can chant "Namu Myoho Renge Kyo" you can participate meaningfully in their services. Another way to get involved is by taking part in one of their peace walks—contact the New York temple or the Grafton Peace Pagoda to find out about upcoming pilgrimages.

Orgyen Ling

91 Second Place #2
Brooklyn, NY 11231
Tel: 718-875-5396

dt@interport.net
School affiliation: Nyingmapa
Language spoken: English

Orgyen Ling is a small collection of about a dozen layfolk who gather to study and practice the teachings of Chagdud Tulku Rinpoche, one of the last surviving members of the generation educated entirely within Tibet. The group meets weekly, usually on Wednesdays, on a rotating basis between the different houses of its members. Red Tara Meditation, a deity practice based on the personification of compassion, is the primary method. More basic meditations are also practiced, and the meetings are open to anyone with a sincere interest in the Nyingma teachings. Call to confirm the time and location of the next meeting.

Chagdud Rinpoche used to live in northern California and has now relocated to Brazil. Orgyen Ling operates as an affiliate of his Chagdud Gonpa Foundation.

**Universal Peace Buddha Temple
of New York**

619 Bergen Street
Brooklyn, NY 11238
Tel: 718-622-8019
http://www.mahasiusa.
  org/nytemple.htm

School affiliation: Theravada (Mahasi
  Sayadaw lineage)
Languages spoken: Burmese, English

This Burmese temple, founded in 1981, is in the lineage of the late internationally known teacher Mahasi Sayadaw. The outside is somewhat run-down looking, but inside there's a brilliant golden altar and Buddha statue; rugs cover most of the floor surface. This Theravadin temple is run under the auspices of the America Burma Buddhist Association, Inc. (see page 122), which also runs the Mahasi Meditation Retreat Center (see page 177) in Englishtown, New Jersey. The head monk is Venerable Ashin Indaka, a Burmese immigrant who studied Buddhism for many years in his native land. The temple provides teachings and Burmese cultural activities to the public and is primarily frequented by Burmese American immigrants and their children. Call for a current schedule of public events.

Watt Samakki

26 Rugby Road
Brooklyn, NY 11225
Tel: 718-693-3655

School affiliation: Theravada (Maha
  Nikaya)
Language spoken: Thai

This is a small Thai temple in the national Theravadin school of Buddhism. It is run by Master Thratom Thenjjento. All services are held in the Thai language.

BRONX

Da Bronx has some important Buddhist centers, but on the whole Buddhism is underrepresented here. Those that do exist in the Bronx are

mainly Asian temples, directly serving the particular local ethnic groups that cluster in some neighborhoods. Tibetan Buddhism is noticeably absent.

The Buddhist Association of the United States/Temple of Great Enlightenment

3070 Albany Crescent
Bronx, NY 10463
Tel: 718-884-9111

bausny@aol.com
School affiliation: Ch'an
Languages spoken: Chinese, English

This is the headquarters for the Buddhist Association of the United States, a Chinese American group started by the shipping magnate and devout Buddhist layman Chia-Tsin Shen. BAUS is the biggest Chinese American Buddhist organization; it administers the Temple of Great Enlightenment and Chuang Yen Monastery (see page 142).

Master Sheng-Yen, of the Ch'an Meditation Center (see page 110), was once the head teacher at the Temple of Great Enlightenment. These days it is led by Rev. Ming Kuang. Most services for the public are held on Sundays. Temple activities include meditation, study, and sermons.

Chua Thap Puong

2222 Andrews N. Avenue
Bronx, NY 10453
Tel: 718-933-4132

School affiliation: Vietnamese Zen/Pure Land
Language spoken: Vietnamese

This Vietnamese temple is located near the CUNY Bronx Community College campus. It's led by Venerable Thich Thien Tri. The temple serves as a cultural center for Vietnamese immigrants and their children; it draws its largest crowds on traditional holidays.

Khmer Buddhist Society/Jotanaram Temple

2738 Marion Avenue
Bronx, NY 10458
Tel: 718-733-8752

School affiliation: Theravada
Language spoken: Cambodian

Established in 1985, this Cambodian American temple has been fashioned out of a rather run-down two-story home. Three resident monks

live upstairs, while the first floor has an altar with bronze Buddha images. The temple serves the religious and cultural needs of the large local Cambodian American populace, most of whom are refugees from the violence unleashed in their homeland by the Khmer Rouge. For them the Jotanaram Temple acts as a representative of positive values from the Old Country. Its activities include traditional festivals, dharma instruction, and opportunities for the laity to make good karma by donating food to the monks, who live entirely off voluntary contributions. Services are in Cambodian, but open to anyone who wants to attend them.

U.S.A. Buddhayaram Temple

2084 Anthony Avenue
Bronx, NY 10457
Tel: 718-933-8053
Fax: 718-365-7095

School affiliation: Theravada (Mahanikaya Order)
Language spoken: Thai

U.S.A. Buddhayaram Temple is a Theravadin organization belonging to the Mahanikaya Order, the predominant form of Buddhism in Thailand. It serves the religious and cultural needs of the local Thai populace.

Young Men's Buddhist Association of America

2611 Davidson Avenue
Bronx, NY 10468
Tel: 718-584-0621

School affiliation: Chinese Pure Land
Language spoken: Chinese

It's fun to chant at the YMBA, an organization that provides free resources for learning about Buddhism. Reverend Lok To, the YMBA's leader, is an accomplished translator who has made many traditional and modern Chinese texts available to English speakers. If you'd like to pick up some (or all) of these free Dharma books then just send a request to the address above, or better yet, stop by and pick some out yourself. You can also drop in to get free lessons in meditation, chanting, and other essential Buddhist practices. Despite the group's name, the Young Men's Buddhist Association freely gives teachings to all genders, ages, and religious preferences alike.

Zen Community of New York

14 Ashburton Place
Yonkers, NY 10703
Tel: 914-968-4734
Fax: 914-968-4816

School affiliation: Soto Zen (White Plum lineage)
Language spoken: English

All right, so Zen Community of New York technically isn't in New York City. Originally located in the Bronx, it was moved across the borough border by founder Bernie Glassman Roshi to the economically depressed city of Yonkers, sandwiched between the Bronx and wealthy Westchester County, in order to better minister to the community in need. But with its Bronx roots, nearby location, and many programs in the borough, ZCNY is still a part of the New York City community, geography aside.

ZCNY is too complex to be adequately described in the space available here. Socially involved action, informed by Zen Buddhist practice and insight, is the hallmark of Zen Community of New York. Under Glassman Roshi's guidance ZCNY created a homeless shelter (Greyston Family Inn), bakery (Greyston Bakery—which, incidentally, provides the brownies for Ben & Jerry's chocolate fudge brownie ice cream), health care clinic (Greyston Health Services), and community-based sewing business (Pamsula Patchwork and Sewing), as well as offering Zen retreats on the streets among the homeless population, zendo-based daily sitting and interviews, AIDS support, and special Bearing Witness retreats. ZCNY was also the birthplace of the Zen Peacemaker Order; though Glassman Roshi has now moved west, the programs continue.

All of these programs are tied together as part of the Greyston Mandala, an interconnected network named after the Greyston Mansion in the Bronx where ZCNY was originally based. And, oh, yeah, they also offer regular Zen sitting, too.

STATEN ISLAND

Staten Island doesn't have much of an overt Buddhist presence yet, despite housing an excellent collection of Tibetan art (see page 209). The groups that do exist here are more or less extensions of older, more established groups in other boroughs. But as more Asian Americans move to the island and Buddhism continues to attract ever-increasing interest from Americans of all types, expect to see the number of Staten Island Buddhist groups mushroom in the future.

Staten Island Buddhist Vihara

115 Jones Street
Staten Island, NY 10351
Tel: 718-551-2051
http://www.sibv.org/

admin@sibv.org
School affiliation: Theravada
Languages spoken: English, Sinhalese

The Staten Island Buddhist Vihara was opened in July 1999 by the American Sri Lanka Buddhist Association (see page 107). It is an outgrowth of the New York Buddhist Vihara (see page 116). The leader is Heenbunne Kondanna Thera.

The Vihara is a refurbished two-story frame house, light yellow in color and impossible to miss due to two large stone guardians flanking the front sidewalk. Inside there's an altar with a seated Buddha statue, spacious rooms for group practice, and sleeping quarters for the monks. Services are mainly in Sinhalese or Pali, but most of the monks speak good English and are happy to give instruction to whoever asks. There is a weekly meditation and discussion Thursdays at 7:30 P.M. The Vihara is family oriented and holds regular programs for children and young adults.

Zen Community of Staten Island

Staten Island, NY

Tel: 718-981-1389

http://www.peacemakercommunity.org/
    zcsi/index.

htmkbyalin@hotmail.com

School affiliation: Zen

Language spoken: English

The Zen Community of Staten Island is a small group that meets on Mondays at 6:30 P.M. for meditation. It is affiliated with the Zen Peacemaker Order (see page 246) and offers opportunities for applying Buddhist wisdom and compassion to local social action causes. Additionally, they hold a Day of Reflection on the fourth Saturday of each month, beginning at 8:30 A.M. The group is interfaith and welcomes non-Buddhists who wish to explore applying Zen practices and principles to their lives. Call Rev. Ken Tetsuji Byalin, the group's leader, for more details.

PRACTICE CENTERS AND MEDITATION GROUPS: OUTSIDE THE CITY

NEW YORK STATE

This section covers Long Island and Upstate New York, excluding New York City proper. Though obviously New York City is the jewel in the New York Buddhist crown, there are considerable resources to be found beyond the borders of the Big Apple. Upstate New York has a particularly wide range of groups; though there are fewer ethnic temples on the whole (with the major exception of Tibetan centers), Upstate New York boasts many large and beautiful retreat centers and several prominent monasteries, two types of organizations that are less successful in the crowded and expensive world of New York City.

Albany Dharma Study Group

10 McCormick Road
Slingerlands, NY 12159
Tel: 518-439-7618
http://www.angelfire.com/ny2/
    albanyshambhala/
shambhala_albany@hotmail.com

School affiliation: Shambhala (Kagyu/
    Nyingma)
Language spoken: English

This is the local Shambhala International study group. They hold evening meditation practice 7:00–8:00 P.M. in Ricketts Hall at Russell Sage College. They also gather once a month for an all-day practice program. Individual meditation instruction is available upon request.

Albany Karma Thegsum Choling

1270 Ruffner Road
Niskayuna, NY 12309
Tel: 518-374-1792
http://www.kagyu.org/centers/usa/usa-
   alba.html
rothw@global2000.net

School affiliation: Kagyupa (Karma Kagyu
   lineage)
Language spoken: English

This is an affiliate of the Karma Triyana Dharmachakra monastery in Woodstock. They meet at the home of Will Roth, who is the director of Albany Karma Thegsum Choling. They offer traditional Karma Kagyu programs, such as calm-abiding meditation, lojong (Seven-Point Mind Training), and other Vajrayana techniques.

Albany Vipassana Sangha

865 Lancaster Street
Albany, NY 12203
Tel: 518-453-6445/518-438-9102

School affiliation: Vipassana
Language spoken: English

This group holds weekly meetings consisting of reading, one hour of meditation, and refreshments with discussion. The group is informal and has no designated leader. Like most Vipassana groups, it centers on practical teachings in a modern context, devoid of Asian trappings.

Amitabha Foundation

11 S. Goodman Street
Rochester, NY 14607
Tel: 716-442-5853
Fax: 716-442-7630
http://www.amitabhafoundation.org

info@amitabhafoundation.org
School affiliation: Kagyupa (Drikung Kagyu
   lineage) and Nyingmapa
Languages spoken: English, Tibetan

Venerable K. C. Ayang Rinpoche, head teacher of the Amitabha Foundation, is one of the most respected practitioners of phowa in the world, a Tibetan ritual that provides instant enlightenment to people at the time of their death. The Amitabha Foundation isn't specifically a practice center—it acts more as a vehicle for educating Westerners about Tibet and for supporting the Tibetan exile community. Many of its activities are not religious in nature. However, they also hold weekly meditation and study classes on Sunday mornings and Wednesday evenings, as well as other regular monthly gatherings tied to the lunar calendar. There are also occasional guest teachers.

Asunam Pope Sensei

P. O. Box 362
Brewster, NY 10509-0362
Tel: 914-278-3038
http://www.asunam.com/index.html

asunam@msn.com
School affiliation: Shingon (Japanese
  Vajrayana)
Languages spoken: English, Japanese

Asunam Pope is a reiki practitioner and natural healer, who also offers esoteric Shingon Buddhist teachings from Japan. Shingon is a Japanese school of tantra, similar in some ways to Tibetan Buddhism but very distinctly East Asian. Shingon views all phenomena as emanations of Mahavairocana, the primordial Buddha essence of the universe, and thus consider all paths as representing at least partial truth and holiness. The practice is intensely ritualistic, involving mantras, mandalas, visualizations, meditation, and other techniques. Call or write for information about upcoming classes.

Blooming Lilac Sangha

260 Rosedale Street
Rochester, NY 14620
Tel: 716-442-3821

phogen@aol.com
School affiliation: Community of Mindfulness
Language spoken: English

This group practices sitting and walking meditation in the Vietnamese tradition.

Buddhist Community of Bangladesh

P. O. Box 831
Syosset, NY 11791
Tel: 516-921-5472

School affiliation: Theravada
Language spoken: Bengali

Despite its name, this group is actually based in New York. Bangladesh is primarily Muslim but retains a small yet significant percentage of Buddhists, primarily practicing in the Theravadin tradition. This group ministers to the needs of the Buddhist Bengali immigrant population. It was founded in 1989 and is led by Venerable Karunananda Thero.

Buddhist Tzu Chi Compassion Relief Foundation—Long Island office

17 Barstow Road, suite 301
Great Neck, NY 11021
Tel: 516-466-1804

Fax: 516-466-1756
School affiliation: Chinese Mahayana
Languages spoken: English, Chinese

This is the Long Island branch of a worldwide charitable relief and health care organization based in Taiwan. See Buddhist Compassion Relief Tzu Chi Foundation—New York office (page 230) for more details.

Budding Flower Sangha

77 Wells Road, R. D. 7
Newburgh, NY 12550
Tel: 914-561-0995

School affiliation: Community of Mindfulness
Language spoken: English

Budding Flower Sangha is a small Westchester branch of the Community of Mindfulness. They have meditation and discussion three times a week. Contact Patricia Hunt-Perry for further details.

Buffalo Community Center

531 Virginia Street
Buffalo, NY 14202
Tel: 716-856-2623
Fax: 716-856-5279

School affiliation: Soka Gakkai (Nichiren
Shoshu)
Language spoken: English

Soka Gakkai is a large and somewhat controversial new form of Buddhism, born in Japan but now present in a very wide range of countries. See SGI Culture Center (page 75) for more details about this group. The Buffalo Community Center serves roughly the same purpose as the Culture Center in New York City.

Buffalo Meditation Group

220 Grant Street, apt. 3
Buffalo, NY 14213
Tel: 716-884-1768
cjackson@acsu.buffalo.edu

School affiliation: Shambhala (Kagyu/
Nyingma)
Language spoken: English

This Shambhala affiliate is small and informal, with a membership partially drawn from the SUNY Buffalo campus, whose academic schedule sometimes influences that of the center. Meetings are open to the public; call for current meeting times.

Buffalo Zen Group

4056 North Freeman Road
Orchard Park, NY 14127
Tel: 716-662-2904
dhohman662@aol.com

School affiliation: Zen (loosely connected
to the Sanbo Kyodan lineage)
Language spoken: English

The Buffalo Zen Group is a rather informal collection of people interested in Zen. It isn't formally organized, and though it has connections with the Rochester Zen Center (see page 161), it's not an official branch or affiliate. Despite its minimal organizational structure, the group has existed for decades. They meet for communal sitting meditation and walking meditation on Sunday evenings at the East-West Book Store in Orchard Park for two-hour periods. They also have occasional full-day meditation retreats.

Cambodia Temple

18 Laser Street
Rochester, NY 14621
Tel: 716-266-7330

School affiliation: Theravada
Language spoken: Cambodian

Cambodia has experienced terrible violence in the past several decades, particularly under Pol Pot's murderous regime. Those who fled to relative freedom and safety in the West established temples like this one to preserve their Theravada Buddhist faith.

Catskill Zen Center

P. O. Box 233
Summitville, NY 12781
Tel: 914-888-2231

School affiliation: Korean Zen (Kwan Um
school)
Languages spoken: English, Korean

The Kwan Um school of Korean Zen has centers all over the U.S.A. and teaches a dynamic form of Zen that involves frequent bowing practice as well as the more familiar sitting meditation.

Cayuga Sangha

Ithaca, NY 14850

Tel: 607-273-5464

jweber@fcinet.com

School affiliation: Vipassana

Language spoken: English

This group practices in the Vipassana tradition, but anyone is welcome as long as they can sit for silent meditation.

Chakrasambara—Long Island

St. John's Church

Cold Spring Harbor, NY

Tel: 516-692-5608

School affiliation: Gelugpa (New
Kadampa Tradition)

Language spoken: English

This is the Long Island outreach program of the Chakrasambara Buddhist Center (see page 126) in Brooklyn. They conduct classes at St. John's Church (located behind the fish hatchery) on Mondays 7:00–9:00 P.M. The classes are highly structured and cost $10 per session, or less if an entire course is taken (usually seven to nine weeks). They are either taught by Kelsang Ganden or Kadam Morten Clausen. Call for current offerings.

Chakrasambara—Westchester

c/o White Plains Women's Club

305 Ridgeway

White Plains, NY 10605-4114

Tel: 914-949-4419

School affiliation: Gelugpa (New
Kadampa Tradition)

Language spoken: English

The Chakrasambara Buddhist Center (see page 126) conducts classes here on Wednesdays 7:30–9:30 P.M. They cost $10 each, or less for a full course, but are open to all who are interested. Call for upcoming offerings.

Chua Van Hanh

158 Genesee Street
Rochester, NY 14611
Tel: 716-235-4927/315-471-5289

School affiliation: Vietnamese Pure Land
Language spoken: Vietnamese

Chua Van Hanh is a Vietnamese Buddhist temple located next to St. Mary's Hospital.

Chuang Yen Monastery

R. D. 2, Route 301
Carmel, NY 10512
Tel: 914-225-1819
Fax: 914-225-0447

http://www.baus.org/baus/index.html
School affiliation: Ch'an and Chinese Pure
 Land
Languages spoken: Chinese, English

Chuang Yen Monastery is perhaps the most important landmark on the New York Buddhist map. Run by the Buddhist Association of the United States (see page 131), it's the product of many years of work by the Chinese American Buddhist community, particularly with help from the devout philanthropist Dr. Chia-Tsin Shen. The monastery simultaneously houses the largest Buddha in the Western hemisphere (a towering thirty-seven feet tall, surrounded by ten thousand smaller identical replicas), one of the most extensive libraries of Buddhist scriptures in America, several dormitories and residences for monks and visitors, a lake brimming over with turtles released to generate merit, and several smaller shrines and monuments. The Dalai Lama officiated at the unveiling of the Great Buddha Hall; Governor Pataki was there, too.

There are a wealth of programs and activities going on all the time at Chuang Yen Monastery. The most common time for public services is on Sundays. For specifically English-language activities contact Richard Baksa: 914-225-3285 (RJBHHH3@aol.com). The monastery has an entire building specifically for English speakers. One unique program it's offered in the past is a Buddhist summer camp for youth.

Clear Mountain Zen Center

605 Peninsula Boulevard
Hempstead, NY 11550
Tel: 516-564-9808

School affiliation: Rinzai Zen
Language spoken: English

Clear Mountain Zen Center offers an unusual blend of traditional Zen techniques, such as zazen, chanting, koan study, and sermons, with an eclectic mix of Judeo-Christian teachings and unique backpacking Zen trips through the mountains. Abbot Kendo Rich Hart's aim is to provide a thoroughly modern type of Zen that best fits the needs of typical Americans.

Sitting meditation and sermons are held three times a week, with introductory sessions for newcomers on the second Sunday of each month. The backpacking trips are held on the last weekend of the month and require prior registration. The center also offers occasional full-day retreats and longer backpacking trips—call for more information.

Community of Mindfulness—Chappaqua Sangha

49 Florence Drive
Chappaqua, NY 10514
Tel: 914-238-8296

judithdavis@aol.com
School affiliation: Community of
 Mindfulness
Language spoken: English

This group meets monthly in the home of a member for evening meditation, including sitting and walking periods. Practice is followed by potluck dinner and discussion.

Community of Mindfulness—Green Lotus Sangha

10 Gail Court
Huntington, NY 11743
Tel: 516-427-9790

tonialeon@aol.com
School affiliation: Community of Mindfulness
Language spoken: English

Like most Community of Mindfulness branches, the Green Lotus Sangha lacks a formal space and meets in various members' homes. Typically they gather two Fridays out of the month, meeting 7:30 P.M.–10:00 P.M. for sitting and walking meditation, recitation of the five precepts, and a reading with discussion. The group and its meetings are very open, informal, and ecumenical. Most meetings attract around a dozen or so folks. Unlike most Community of Mindfulness groups, they don't have a full day of mindfulness every month, offering this program only a few times a year. Instead, they take occasional field trips to the beach or canoeing. As co-coordinator Tonia Leon-Hysko puts it, "A lot of Buddhism is about working with suffering. We like to balance the suffering with a little fun."

This group is technically a part of the Community of Mindfulness New York Metro (see page 48), but operates more or less independently. Call for directions to the next meeting.

Community of Mindfulness—Valois

5801 Route 414
Valois, NY 12888
Tel: 607-277-5685

hjs@lightlink.com
School affiliation: Community of Mindfulness
Language spoken: English

This is the local branch of Thich Nhat Hanh's Community of Mindfulness, a lay-led group of practitioners. Contact Jayne Demakos for more information.

Dai Bosatsu Zendo Kongo-Ji

HCR 1, Box 171
Livingston Manor, NY 12758-9402
Tel: 914-439-4566
Fax: 914-439-3119

http://zenstudies.org/dbz2000.html
dbzoffice@zenstudies.org
School affiliation: Rinzai Zen
Languages spoken: English, Japanese

Run by the Zen Studies Society (see page 58), Dai Bosatsu is a forest retreat center and monastery located on fourteen hundred square acres of beautiful land in the Catskill Mountains, next to historic Beecher Lake. Daily practice includes chanting, zazen, samu (work practice), and formal vegetarian meals. They also observe the traditional semiannual ango three-month training periods, offer sesshins (weeklong practice intensives), weekend programs, and other activities.

Dharma Drum Retreat Center

184 Quannacut Road

Pine Bush, NY 12566

Tel: 914-744-8114

http://www.chan1.org/center.htm

School affiliation: Ch'an

Language spoken: English

This is the new retreat facility of Master Sheng-Yen's Ch'an Meditation Center (see page 110). They hold periodic retreats here in an environment that is much more suitable than the New York City rat race. Check out the Web page for upcoming events.

Dharma Song Zendo

Ossining, NY

School affiliation: Rinzai Zen

Language spoken: English

Dharma Song Zendo is located within the maximum security facility Sing Sing Prison, one of the notorious prisons in America. It is run by the Engaged Zen Foundation (see page 177). See them for more information.

Diamond Sutra Recitation Group of Syosset

11 Loretta Drive

Syosset, NY 11791

Tel: 516-921-5627

Fax: 718-875-3576

School affiliation: Korean Mahayana

Languages spoken: Korean, English

This group practices recitation of the Diamond Sutra, a short scripture that contains the essence of Mahayana Buddhist philosophy. They also chant to Maitreya, the Buddhist messiah, and follow the teachings of Master Jim Woong Kim.

Dragon Gate Sangha

Eastern New York Correctional Facility
Box 338 (Institution Road)
Napanoch, NY 12458-0338

Tel: 914-626-7374
School affiliation: Soto and Rinzai Zen
Language spoken: English

This is a Zen prison outreach group. Contact Stefano Mui Barragato for information on how to get involved.

Drikung Kagyu Enlightenment Institute

P. O. Box 25577
Rochester, NY 14625
Tel: 716-454-3844
fhoward861@aol.com

School affiliation: Kagyupa (Drikung Kagyu
    lineage)
Language spoken: English

This center was established by Venerable Ayang Rinpoche, and is run by Frank Howard. It is affiliated with the Amitabha Foundation (see page 138). The Drikung Kagyu Enlightenment Institute offers a very wide range of traditional Kagyupa practices, as well as some Nyingmapa ones. It also offers a six-week-long introductory course and public lectures.

Empty Hand Zendo

The Meeting House
624 Milton Road
Rye, NY 10580
Tel: 914-921-3327
http://www.geocities.com/HotSprings/
    8257/

susanJion@aol.com
School affiliation: Rinzai Zen
Language spoken: English

Buddhist groups in New York often have to meet in less than ideal places—converted warehouses, family homes full of toys, or cramped

apartments above noisy streets. But meditation has been taking place in Empty Hand Zendo's space since long before Buddhism came to this area. The Quakers are Christianity's counterpart to Zen, and the quiet space of the Quaker meeting house where Empty Hand Zendo gathers seems like the perfect sacred space for zazen. Never mind that they are occasionally flooded by the nearby swamp.

Meditation is held Monday, Wednesday, and Friday, 7:30–9:00 P.M. Wednesdays include a beginner's portion, and the first Monday of each month also includes a sermon. Meditation is conducted in the morning, 7:30–9:00 A.M., on Saturdays. While Empty Hand Zendo is heavily oriented toward sitting meditation, its program also includes walking meditation, chanting, and sutra study. Most activities are followed by snacks and a little socializing.

The group is led by Rev. Susan Ji-on Postal, a student of the late Maurine Stuart Roshi, who has also studied in the Tibetan Nyingma tradition and with Bernie Glassman Roshi. As one might expect from a group that meets in a Christian church, the zendo is open to people of all religious orientations, and Rev. Postal is active in Buddhist-Christian dialogue.

Grafton Peace Pagoda

87 Crandall Road
Petersburg, NY 12138
Tel: 518-658-9301
http://www.albany.net/~rusami/peace/
  gpp.html

School affiliation: Nipponzan Myohoji
Languages spoken: English, Japanese

The peace pagoda was built by Japanese Buddhists who believe it will help create world peace, the goal of the Nipponzan Myohoji school of Nichiren Buddhism. Their practice consists of chanting the mantra "Namu Myoho Renge Kyo" while banging on drums. The peace pagoda is run by Jun Yasuda, a Myohoji nun. The group puts on frequent peace walks, hikes of many weeks to raise awareness of important social problems, such as racism, police brutality, and prison conditions. The peace pagoda itself is a large, gleaming white structure in the style of ancient Asian Buddhist monuments.

Green River Meditation Group

P. O. Box 194
Hillsdale, NY 12529
Tel: 518-325-5260
vancarty@taconic.net

School affiliation: Shambhala (Kagyu/
  Nyingma)
Language spoken: English

This is a practice and study group in the Shambhala tradition, a widespread school headed by Sakyong Mipham Rinpoche. Contact group director Beth Rinzler for specific details.

Hudson Valley Kadampas

At Fellowship of Reconciliation
521 North Broadway
Nyack, NY 10960
Tel: 914-353-2696

http://www.spyral.net/skye/index.html
info@whiteconch.com
School affiliation: Gelugpa
Language spoken: English

This Gelugpa Tibetan Buddhist group meets every Wednesday 7:30–9:00 P.M. for meditation and group discussion. Their mailing address is: 312 North Highland Avenue, Nyack, NY 10960.

Hudson Valley Shambhala Meditation Group

916 Berme Road
High Falls, NY 12440
Tel: 914-687-7534
thrall@ulster.net

School affiliation: Shambhala (Kagyu and Nyingma)
Language spoken: English

The Shambhala community is composed of many centers around the world. Based on the teachings of Chogyam Trungpa Rinpoche, they are one of the most popular forms of Tibetan Buddhism in America. Contact group director Patrice Heber to learn more.

International Buddhist Progress Society, Deer Park

2005 Guymard Turnpike
Godeffroy, NY 12739-5012
Tel: 914-754-7553
Fax: 914-754-8910

http://www.ibps.org/deerpark/index.htm
School affiliation: Chinese Pure Land
Languages spoken: English, Chinese

Despite the name, this is not a petting zoo or game farm—the Deer Park was a famous place in India where the Buddha lived. This group is affiliated with the Hsi Lai Temple, infamous as the site where Al Gore received illegal campaign donations. That affair was basically a misunderstanding—don't let it keep you from visiting this group, which offers a very modern expression for the Buddha's ancient wisdom.

Ithaca Dharma Study Group

P. O. Box 4912
Ithaca, NY 14850
Tel: 607-266-8689

School affiliation: Shambhala (Kagyu/ Nyingma)
Language spoken: English

This small Shambhala group meets in the private residence of Andrew Cove. Call for details.

Ithaca Zen Center

56 Lieb Road
Spencer, NY 14883
Tel: 607-272-0694

ithacazen@aol.com
School affiliation: Rinzai Zen
Language spoken: English

This is a retreat facility run by David Yoshin Radin, a teacher in the lineage of Joshu Sasaki Roshi. The Ithaca Zen Center offers two- and seven-day-long retreats.

Kagyu Pende Kunchab

906 Annandale Road
Barrytown, NY 12507
Tel: 914-758-6549

School affiliation: Kagyupa
Language spoken: English

This is a small group in the tradition of the late meditation master Kalu Rinpoche. They are associated with Kagyu Thubten Choling (see below).

Kagyu Thubten Choling

127 Sheafe Road
Wappingers Falls, NY 12590
Tel: 914-297-2500
Fax: 914-297-5761

http://www.kagyu.com
office@kagyu.com
School affiliation: Kagyu
Languages spoken: English, Tibetan

Kagyu Thubten Choling is the East Coast monastery and retreat center for the late Kalu Rinpoche's community. It is run by Lama Norlha.

There are a limited number of private rooms available for short retreats, which may be rented by both members and nonmembers. Tibetan-language services are held every morning and evening. They offer a range of meditation and study, as well as Tibetan-language and intensive three-year-long individual retreats.

Kanzeon Zendo

80 Pauls Lane
Water Mill, NY 11976
Tel: 516-537-1163

School affiliation: Rinzai Zen (Sanbo Kyodan)
Language spoken: English

Jill Jiryu Bart has been operating this dojo out of her house in Water Mill since 1968. Public meditation consists of two half-hour sessions, conducted twice each week.

Karma Triyana Dharmachakra

352 Mead Mountain Road
Woodstock, NY 12498
Tel: 914-679-5906
Fax: 914-679-4625
http://www.kagyu.org

office@kagyu.org
School affiliation: Kagyupa (Karma Kagyupa lineage)
Languages spoken: English, Tibetan

Karma Triyana Dharmachakra is the North American headquarters of the Karmapa lama, whose dramatic escape from Chinese-controlled Tibet at the turn of the millenium made headlines around the world. The current Karmapa is a teenage boy; his predecessor, the Sixteenth Gyalwa Karmapa, was instrumental in bringing Tibetan Buddhism to the West, and the Karmapa's school is now the largest sect of Tibetan Buddhism outside of Asia. This monastery is one of the most important Buddhist institutions in the Northeast.

Karma Triyana Dharmachakra is a residential monastery built with a combination of exterior Tibetan design and modern Western architectural techniques. It houses a very large shrine room suitable for sizable public audiences, elaborately decorated with colorful Ti-

betan motifs. There are several high-ranking Tibetan lamas in residence who give teachings ranging from introductory classes for beginners to the most advanced practices of the Karma Kagyu school.

Visitors are welcome at the monastery and can receive guided tours and even accommodations with meals if reserved in advance. Some people like the monastery so much they stay for the traditional three-year-long retreat! If you're not up to such a drastic commitment, just check out their bookstore for a good book to take home.

Karuna Tendai Dharma Center

1525 Route 295
East Chatham, NY 12060
Tel: 518-392-7963
Fax: 518-392-7963

tendai1@aol.com
School affiliation: Tendai (Japanese Vajrayana)
Languages spoken: Japanese, English

This is a monastery in the Japanese Vajrayana school of Tendai, the single most influential form of Buddhism in East Asia, yet curiously absent in the West. Tendai Buddhism combines elements of many other Buddhist sects, including Zen, Pure Land, Nichiren, tantric practices and teachings similar to those of Tibet, esoteric Shingon practices, and more. Its principal scripture is the Lotus Sutra, though many other writings are also included in its enormous canon.

The Karuna Tendai Dharma Center is a large temple sitting on thirty acres of forest with a community that includes residential and nonresidential monastics and laypeople. Its many activities include public teachings, instruction in basic and advanced meditation, esoteric rituals and practices, Buddhist counseling, and monthly weekend retreats. Call or write for current schedules. The center has a bed-and-breakfast on site called the Bodhi Tree Inn that can accommodate visitors. Paul Monshin Namon is the center's abbot.

Kinpu-an

4 Providence Place
Albany, NY 12202
Tel: 518-432-4676
Fax: 518-432-4676

School affiliation: Soto and Rinzai Zen
(Mountains and Rivers Order)
Language spoken: English

Kinpu-an is the Albany lay affiliate of Zen Mountain Monastery (see page 170). It provides teaching for both residential students and visitors. Public sitting meditation is held on Tuesdays and Thursdays, 7:15–8:45 P.M. The second Saturday of the month is devoted to either a half- or full-day sitting period. Call ahead to set up an appointment for individualized instruction for beginners.

Wally Taiko Edge is the head teacher at Kinpu-an. The center has a prison outreach program with a Zen sitting group in Great Meadow Correctional Facility known as Lotus Peak Sangha (see page 157). It also maintains a library with material from Dharma Communications and other Buddhist sources.

Korean Buddhist Bul Kwang Zen
Meditation Center

434 Route 303
Tappan, NY 10983
Tel: 914-359-9516
Fax: 914-365-2370

http://www.nybulkwang.org/
School affiliation: Korean Zen (Chogye)
Languages spoken: Korean, English

This is a Korean monastery. They offer programs in both Korean and English to the public, including meditation instruction, chanting, study, and programs for children and young adults.

Long Island Zen Association

2026 Grand Avenue
Baldwin, NY 11510-2811
Tel: 516-678-7989
http://lizen.homestead.com/

sweetmeet34@yahoo.com
School affiliation: Rinzai Zen
Language spoken: English

LIZA meets on Thursday evenings 8:00–10:00 P.M. and Sunday mornings 8:00–10:00 A.M. Sevices include two periods of sitting meditation, walking meditation, chanting, a sermon, and private conversation with Rev. Kendo Rich Hart, the head teacher. Rev. Hart has been practicing Buddhism for over forty years. The association's mailing address is: P. O. Box 627, Rockville Center, NY 11570.

Long Island Zen Center

6 Brewster Court
Setauket, NY 11733-1424
Tel: 516-751-8408

edkann@aol.com
School affiliation: Rinzai Zen
Language spoken: English

Like many other small American practice centers in Joshu Sasaki Roshi's Zen lineage, this zendo is run out of a private residence. The

head teacher is Genshin Edgar Kann, an elderly monk with decades of Zen practice. He offers sitting meditation periods three times a week, sometimes followed by discussion and study. He also conducts weekend retreats several times a year.

Lotus Flower Sangha

Green Haven Correctional Facility
Drawer B, Route 216
Stormville, NY 12582

School affiliation: Soto Zen (Mountains
    and Rivers Order)
Language spoken: English

This is one of Zen Mountain Monastery's (see page 170) prison outreach affiliates. Since 1983 student volunteers from the monastery have led prisoners in meditation, chanting, and other Zen practices on Wednesday mornings and Friday evenings. They also offer dharma talks and personal discussions, as well as occasional longer retreats. Contact the monastery for further details about volunteering.

Lotus Peak Sangha

Great Meadow Correctional Facility
Comstock, NY
c/o Zen Mountain Monastery (see
    page 170)
Tel: 914-688-2228

Fax: 914-688-2415
School affiliation: Soto Zen (Mountains
    and Rivers Order)
Language spoken: English

Lotus Peak Sangha is a prison outreach program run by Kinpu-an (see page 155), the Albany affiliate of Zen Mountain Monastery (see page 170), and the monastery itself. It offers prisoners weekly instruction in Zen meditation techniques and provides counseling to inmates. It also affords Mountains and Rivers Order students a chance to test their teaching skills in an environment far more stressful than the typical zendo. Those who are interested in participating in this program should contact Zen Mountain Monastery.

Mahayana Temple

Gay Head Route, Box 307
Leeds, NY 12415
Tel: 518-622-3619

School affiliation: Ch'an
Language spoken: Chinese

This temple is affiliated with the Eastern States Buddhist Temple (see page 88) in Chinatown. Groups from that temple often visit Mahayana Temple on Sundays for special programs.

Namgyal Monastery Institute of
Tibetan Buddhist Studies

412 North Aurora Street (P. O. Box 127)
Ithaca, NY 14851
Tel: 607-273-0739
Fax: 607-256-5132

http://www.namgyal.org/
mail@namgyal.org
School affiliation: Gelugpa
Languages spoken: English, Tibetan

Namgyal Monastery in Dharamsala, India, is the personal monastery of the Dalai Lama. This branch monastery was established by the Dalai Lama specifically to educate interested Westerners about Tibetan Buddhism and art, and to provide an authentic setting for Tibetan Buddhist practice. It has a core faculty of Tibetan monks, supplemented by knowledgeable Western academics.

Public meditation is offered daily. The monastery also has classes in Tibetan language and Buddhist doctrine, and retreats. The monks are happy to meet privately with individuals—there's a sign-up sheet in the vestibule, or call to set up an appointment.

New Rochelle Vipassana Group

New Rochelle, NY
Tel: 914-636-7103

School affiliation: Vipassana
Language spoken: English

This new sangha meets in a private residence. Some members are associated with the Westbeth Vipassana Group (see page 105) and have experience with the Insight Meditation Society, but this is an independent, leaderless group. Call for more details.

Omega Institute for Holistic Studies

150 Lake Drive

Rhinebeck, New York 12572

Tel: 800-944-1001

http://www.eomega.org/

comments@eomega.org

School affiliation: non-Buddhist

Language spoken: English

Omega is the world's largest institution dedicated to "alternative education," a fuzzy category that covers psychology, cultural studies, many forms of spirituality, and New Age health techniques like massage and yoga. They offer a very diverse program of classes and workshops every year, most of which aren't Buddhist, but there's always some Buddhist stuff thrown in with the mix. Recent teachers have included Archbishop Desmond Tutu, Muslim Whirling Dervishes, actor Christopher Reeves, and Buddhist medical doctor Jon Kabat-Zinn.

Oneonta Karma Kagyu Study Group

c/o Body and Soul Lifestyle Center

175 Main Street

Oneonta, NY 13820

Tel: 607-432-6133

http://www.kagyu.org/centers/usa/usa-
one.html

bodysoul@digital-marketplace.net

School affiliation: Kagyupa

Language spoken: English

This group is very new, and their schedule is still evolving. Call to find out what current activities they are offering.

Padma Samye Ling

Route 1, P. O. Box 108P

Sidney Center, NY 13839

Tel: 607-865-8068

School affiliation: Nyingmapa

Languages spoken: English, Tibetan

This is the upstate retreat center for the Padmasambhava Buddhist Center of New York (see page 71) and its affiliated groups. Retreats are held here at least once a year, usually in midsummer.

Palden Sakya—Ancram

Ancram, NY

Tel: 518-329-3243

School affiliation: Sakyapa

Language spoken: English

The Ancram group is associated with Lama Pema Wangdak's Palden Sakya New York (see page 56) center. They meet on the last Saturday of the month. Please call for more information.

Palden Sakya—Woodstock

234 Mead Mountain Road

Woodstock, NY 12498

Tel: 914-679-4024

School affiliation: Sakyapa

Languages spoken: English, Tibetan

This group practices under the spiritual guidance of Lama Pema Wangdak. They offer Tara, Chenrezig, shamatha meditations, and dharma study on the last Sunday of each month.

Palyul Center

359 German Hollow Road

McDonough, NY 13801

Tel: 607-656-4645

http://www.palyul.org/retreatu.html

palyulctr@aol.com

School affiliation: Nyingmapa

Languages spoken: English, Tibetan

This retreat center was founded by Penor Rinpoche in 1998 in a beautiful area north of the Catskills. His community holds summer retreats on the grounds, and the center is available for individual retreats as well; one need not be specifically a part of this community to take advantage of its resources. Eventually it will offer three-year-long retreats, a key practice in the Nyingma tradition. The retreat center features a temple, dorms, dining rooms, and classrooms.

Pawling Sitting Group

Pawling, NY
Tel: 914-855-0338

School affiliation: Soto and Rinzai Zen
Language spoken: English

Amy Shoko Brown leads this Zen group, which is loosely tied to Zen Mountain Monastery's (see page 170) Mountains and Rivers Order. Contact her to find out more.

Pine Hill Zendo

49 Garlen Road
Katonah, NY 10536
Tel: 914-767-9240
http://www.pinehillzendo.org/

zazen@pinehillzendo.org
School affiliation: Rinzai Zen
Language spoken: English

Rev. Denko-San John Mortensen operates this Zen center out of his home. Meetings are held Tuesdays 7:40–9:10 P.M., Saturdays 7:00–8:00 A.M., and Sundays 7:00–10:00 A.M. Beginners should attend the Tuesday program first. There is a $15 fee per session for nonmembers.

Pine Woods Monastery

211 Crum Elbow Road
Hyde Park, NY 12538
Tel: 914-229-8365

School affiliation: Chinese Pure Land
Language spoken: Chinese

Ground was broken for this new monastery in June of 2000. Eventually it will serve as a monastery and retreat center for the China Buddhist Association (see page 111).

Plain Water Zen Practice

2997 Route 44-55
Gardiner, NY 12525
Tel: 914-255-2918

School affiliation: Soto Zen (White Plum
  lineage)
Language spoken: English

The modestly monikered Plain Water Practice is led by Helen Yohu Harkaspi Sensei, a teacher in the White Plum lineage of Maezumi Roshi.

The group meets at Harkaspi Sensei's house and the Poughkeepsie Unitarian Church, with occasional retreats at the Grail Retreat House.

Rhinebeck Insight Meditation Group

141 Lamoree Avenue

Rhinebeck, NY 12572

Tel: 914-876-7963

Fax: 914-876-6369

School affiliation: Vipassana

Language spoken: English

This group is led by Jose Reissig, a teacher from the acclaimed Insight Meditation Society in Barre, Massachusetts. They hold sitting meditation every Wednesday evening at 7:30 P.M. The service consists of forty-five minutes of Vipassana meditation, followed by a discussion period. All levels of practitioners are welcome. They also hold weekend retreats four times a year.

Rhinebeck Zen Center

10-14 East Market Street, 2nd floor

 (P. O. Box 595)

Rhinebeck, NY 12572

Tel: 914-757-3211

billdelconte@yahoo.com

School affiliation: Community of Mindfulness

Language spoken: English

This is a sitting meditation and discussion group that practices a form of highly Westernized, nonhierarchical Zen.

Rochester Zen Center

7 Arnold Park

Rochester, NY 14607

Tel: 716-473-9180

Fax: 716-473-6846

School affiliation: Zen (Sanbo Kyodan

 lineage)

Language spoken: English

Though located in relatively remote Rochester, this center has had a major impact on Zen in America. Philip Kapleau Roshi, who founded the center in 1966, is the author of *The Three Pillars of Zen,* a classic in

American Zen circles that is probably responsible for introducing more people in the States to Zen than any other single book. These days the Rochester Zen Center is led by Kapleau Roshi's successor, Sensei Bodhin Kjolhede. The center provides daily meditation sessions and monthly retreats.

Sagaponack Zendo

Bridge Lane, P. O. Box 392
Sagaponack, NY 11962
Tel: 716-473-9180

School affiliation: Soto and Rinzai Zen
(White Plum lineage)
Language spoken: English

This Zen center is led by Peter Matthiessen, the noted author of *At Play in the Fields of the Lord*, *The Snow Leopard*, and many other award-winning books. It's affiliated with the Zen Community of New York (see page 134). Call for a current schedule.

Sahng Wun Sa

244-05 Alameda Avenue
Douglaston, NY 11362
Tel: 718-631-0389

School affiliation: Chogye
Language spoken: Korean

Sahng Wun Sa is a Korean group. Call for more information.

Saratoga Center for Meditation and Mindful Living

11 Marion Place
Saratoga Springs, NY 12866
Tel: 518-587-2667

School affiliation: Community of Mindfulness
Language spoken: English

This Community of Mindfulness group meets one Sunday every month. Their program features sitting and walking meditation and recitation of the precepts. There is also a children's component available for families.

Saratoga Springs Sangha

161 Caroline Street
Saratoga Springs, NY 12866
Tel: 518-587-5806

School affiliation: Community of
   Mindfulness
Language spoken: English

Informal sitting and walking meditation in a lay environment. Call Jane Leifer for information.

Sleepy Hollow Sangha

265 Hunter Avenue
Sleepy Hollow, NY 10591
Tel: 914-631-2658
wolfie@l-2000.com

School affiliation: Community of
   Mindfulness
Language spoken: English

Buddhist teachings are nothing to be afraid of, especially in the low-key atmosphere of Community of Mindfulness meetings. They practice sitting and walking meditation and hold discussions about various aspects of practice.

Springwater Center for Meditative Inquiry and Retreats

7179 Mill Street
Springwater, NY 14560
Tel: 716-669-2141
Fax: 716-669-9573

http://www.servtech.com/~spwtrctr/
spwtrctr@servtech.com
School affiliation: Zen
Language spoken: English

This center is run by Toni Packer, a former student of Philip Kapleau Roshi, founder of Rochester Zen Center (see page 162). Toni's style of Zen is almost anti-Zen: she's opted to strip away all the usual formulations of lineage, tradition, and hierarchy, and tries instead to present a Zen that's about pure awareness of the current moment, without forms or concepts. It's a concept that worries some, but many also see it as the cutting edge of modern Zen.

Springwater is primarily a retreat center, and Toni isn't always in residence. Normally, practitioners stay at Springwater as a way to deepen their practice, paying relatively low fees for room and board (one can also volunteer to offset the cost). When Toni is present at the center, more directed programs are offered, usually on Tuesdays and Sundays, with formal meditation, talks and discussions. It's also possible to get individual attention from Toni upon request.

Still Pond Zen Center

P. O. Box 27
Old Chatham, NY 12136
Tel: 518-794-8405

School affiliation: Rinzai Zen
Language spoken: English

Still Pond Zen Center is an affiliate of Rinzai-ji Temple in Los Angeles. It is one of many American centers in the lineage of Joshu Sasaki.

Stone River Sangha

Albany, NY
Tel: 518-475-9468
http://www.geocities.com/Athens/
Rhodes/4832/stoneriver.html

School affiliation: Community of
Mindfulness
Language spoken: English

The Stone River Sangha holds meetings on Wednesdays 7:30–9:00 P.M. They consist of thirty minutes of sitting meditation and ten minutes of walking meditation, followed by either discussion, study, or precept recitation. They also have full Days of Mindfulness and other events throughout the year.

Suffolk Institute for Eastern Studies

330 Moriches Road
Saint James, NY 11780
Tel: 516-584-6085

http://www.dojos.com/eastern/
eastern1.htm
School affiliation: Independent
Language spoken: English

The Suffolk Institute for Eastern Studies is primarily a martial arts group practicing aikido, a Japanese skill heavily influenced by Zen Buddhism. They also have a weekly Vipassana meditation session on Saturday mornings. Edgar Kann, one of the institute's senior teachers, is the leader of Long Island Zen Center (see page 156).

Syracuse Dharma Study Group

218 Cambridge Street
Syracuse, NY 13210
Tel: 315-471-1527
Fax: 315-437-3430

bobtemple@earthlink.net
School affiliation: Shambhala (Kagyu and
   Nyingma)
Language spoken: English

This is a small local Shambhala group. It's directed by the appropriately named Robert Temple.

Three Cranes Zen Center

77 Bedford Road
Katonah, NY 10536
Tel: 914-234-6658

School affiliation: Zen
Language spoken: English

Call for details.

Three Hills Sangha

426 N. Titus Street
Ithaca, NY 14850-5229
Tel: 607-273-5563/607-277-3645
http://pages.hotbot.com/rel/
   3hillssangha/

School affiliation: Community of
   Mindfulness
Language spoken: English

This is the local branch of Vietnamese Zen teacher Thich Nhat Hanh's Community of Mindfulness. They hold sitting and walking meditations on the first and third Wednesdays of the month, noon to 1:00 P.M., at Tiamat Studio, 136 The Commons, Ithaca, NY. They also have full gatherings with meditation, readings, discussions, and sometimes videos on Sundays, 7:00–9:00 P.M., at the Titus Street location. Unlike most Community of Mindfulness events, some selected courses have fees, so call before attending.

Tinh Xa Minh Dang Quang

812 Wolf Street
Syracuse, NY 13208
Tel: 315-476-9541

School affiliation: Vietnamese Pure Land
Language spoken: Vietnamese

Thuong Toa Thich Buu Minh is the monk who leads this Vietnamese congregation.

Tu Vien Minh Dang Quang

191 East Frederick Street
Binghamton, NY 13904
Tel: 607-723-6861

Fax: 607-625-3255
School affiliation: Vietnamese Pure Land
Language spoken: Vietnamese

This is an ethnic Vietnamese American temple, led by Hoa Thuong Thich Giac Nhien.

Wat Vajiradhammapadip

110 Rustic Road
Centereach, NY 11720
Tel: 516-471-8006
http://www.thaitempleusa.iirt.net/
vajira@iirt.net

School affiliation: Theravada (Maha
   Nikaya)
Language spoken: Thai

A temple in the majority Maha Nikaya Thai Theravadin school. Teachings and events are usually in Thai.

Wat Vajiradhammapadip

75 California Road
Mt. Vernon, NY 10552
Tel: 914-699-5778

School affiliation: Theravada (Maha
   Nikaya)
Language spoken: Thai

A Thai temple in the Maha Nikaya school. Affiliated with the temple of the same name in Centereach.

Westchester, Rockland, and Fairfield Counties Mindfulness Group

Box 0089
Maryknoll, NY 10545
Tel: 914-762-9097

School affiliation: Community of
   Mindfulness
Language spoken: English

This wide-ranging chapter of Thich Nhat Hanh's Community of Mindfulness attempts to provide support for students throughout southern New York State. They meet one Sunday per month for a full-day program, including sitting and walking meditation, precept recitation, discussion, and potluck meals. The venue changes so be sure to contact Sally and Eric Taylor for the latest information.

White Cliff Sangha

113 East 30th Street
New Paltz, NY 11016
Tel: 914-626-7374

School affiliation: Soto and Rinzai Zen
   (White Plum lineage)
Language spoken: English

White Cliff Sangha is a member of the White Plum lineage and affiliated with the Zen Community of New York. They are led by Stefano Mui Barragato Sensei. Their zendo is actually a converted barn.

Woodstock Karma Thegsum Choling

P. O. Box 645
Shady, NY 12409
Tel: 914-679-6028
http://www.kagyu.org/centers/usa/
   usa-woo.html

dmccarthy@mhv.net
School affiliation: Kagyupa (Karma
   Kagyupa lineage)
Languages spoken: English, Tibetan

This is an affiliate of the Karmapa's Karma Triyana Dharmachakra monastery, located in Woodstock. The group takes part in many activities of the monastery, as well as hosting its own less formal gatherings in the homes of members.

World Young Men's Buddhist Association

7 Rutland Road
Great Neck, NY 11375
Tel: 516-482-7526

School affiliation: Chinese Pure Land
Languages spoken: Chinese, English

This is an activity-oriented Buddhist youth group. Contact H. Y. Lee for details.

Zen Center of Syracuse/Hoen-ji

111 Concord Place
Syracuse, NY 13210
Tel: 315-478-1253
Fax: 315-478-1253

schayat@mailbox.syr.edu
School affiliation: Rinzai Zen
Language spoken: English

Over the years Zen Center of Syracuse has transformed from a motley group of graduate students to a full-fledged zendo with an experienced teacher. Rev. Roko Sherry Chayat, originally from Dai Bosatsu Zendo (see page 146), ran the zendo out of the specially converted third floor of her home for years. Recently a separate Carriage House Zendo was opened at 266 West Seneca Turnpike. The zendo now serves the wider community as well as Syracuse students, with meditation programs offered off-site at local schools, businesses, and health centers.

Hoen-ji offers weeknight public programs, as well as semiannual three-day retreats at Alverna Heights, a Catholic nunnery (!).

Zen Dharma Community

1807 Elmwood Avenue
Buffalo, NY 14207
Tel: 716-634-1812

School affiliation: Soto Zen
Language spoken: English

Buffalo's Zen Dharma Community is well named, as they seek to offer more than just detached sitting practice. Venerable James Kozen Dodson, resident director of ZDC, encourages his students to demonstrate Buddhist compassion in action through projects that actively help other people. ZDC also offers Buddhist weddings, funerals, counseling, and other community-oriented programs. The formal practice side of Zen isn't neglected, however—ZDC holds regular sitting meditation, study classes, and retreats as well.

Zen Mountain Monastery

South Park Road, P. O. Box 197

Mt. Tremper, NY 12457

Tel: 914-688-2228

Fax: 914-688-2415

http://www1.mhv.net/~dharmacom

dharmacom@mhv.net

School affiliation: Soto and Rinzai Zen
(Mountains and Rivers Order)

Language spoken: English

Zen Mountain Monastery is one of the juggernauts of American Zen. Founded in 1980 by John Daido Loori Roshi, it serves as the head temple of the Mountains and Rivers Order. An elegant collection of buildings nestled in the beautiful forests of Catskill State Park's Mt. Tremper, ZMM is one of the most peaceful environments available to tristate Buddhists for extended retreats or residential practice.

The practice at ZMM is a combination of Old and New World styles, with much traditionalism (Daido Roshi is often referred to as a "Living Buddha") thrown in with such modern touches as Zen photography. Daido Roshi has received teaching sanction from both the Soto and Rinzai schools, the two main branches of Japanese Zen, and both forms are represented in the monastery's program. There are monthly retreats, as well as two season-long intensive training periods each year.

The resident monks and nuns are often involved in the various business/outreach programs of ZMM, including the publishing house Dharma Communications, which puts out books, a journal, audio and videotapes, meditation supplies, Buddha images, and more. Dharma Communications also offers Cybermonk, an Internet-based service whereby

folks can E-mail questions to a senior ZMM student (cybermonk@ mhv.net). Beginning in 2000, Dharma Communications plans to offer limited training and instruction directly over the Internet to practitioners around the world.

NEW JERSEY

New Jersey is a wonderfully diverse state with many Buddhist ethnic groups, including one of the few Mongolian communities on the East Coast. Though overshadowed by the Buddhist abundance in New York,

New Jersey easily holds its own as a fertile land where the dharma is growing.

Buddhist Sangha of South Jersey

164 Cheyenne Trail
Medford Lakes, NJ 08055
Tel: 609-953-8215
wslyons@voicenet.com

School affiliation: Community of
    Mindfulness
Language spoken: English

This Community of Mindfulness group meets on Sundays at 7:00 P.M. for meditation and chanting. They also have monthly meetings with audiotapes of teachings from Thich Nhat Hanh and others. Buddhist Sangha of South Jersey is somewhat less dependent on Thich Nhat Hanh materials than many other Community of Mindfulness groups, incorporating a range of teachings from a diverse Buddhist background. The actual meetings are held at 302 North Washington Street, #102, Moorestown, New Jersey.

Buddhist Study Association of Greater
New York, Inc.

P. O. Box 7115
West Orange, NJ 07052-7115
Tel: 973-736-8957
Fax: 973-736-8957 (press *51)
http://members.home.net/buddha1/
    home.html

buddha1@home.com
School affiliation: Theravada
Language spoken: English

The BSA serves primarily as a clearinghouse for all sorts of Buddhist information and resources for the general public. They provide free books, speakers, Buddhist chaplains, twenty-four-hour telephone teachings and more to Buddhist and non-Buddhist groups alike, in addition to their own regular teachings and meditation schedule. The head monk is Dhammika (Anthony) Bucci, a chaplain on call at Mountainside Hospital in Montclair, New Jersey, who frequently travels out of state to give support to Buddhist prisoners. Chaplain Dhammika is available to speak at schools, colleges, prisons, hospitals, and other appropriate places.

Buddhist Tzu Chi Compassion Relief Foundation—New Jersey branch

81 Fulton Street

Boonton, NJ 07005-1909

Tel: 973-257-1668

Fax: 973-257-9797

School affiliation: Chinese Mahayana

Languages spoken: English, Chinese

The Buddhist Tzu Chi Compassion Relief Foundation provides charitable aid to the needy around the world. This is the New Jersey office—the head office is in Taiwan, where the organization is based. See Buddhist Compassion Relief Tzu Chi Foundation—New York office (page 230) for more information.

Bul Kuk Sa Zen Temple

1286 River Road

Teaneck, NJ 07666

Tel: 201-836-0558

School affiliation: Korean Zen

Languages spoken: Korean, English

The center is named after a famous Korean Zen temple founded 1,250 years ago.

Chua Quan Am

16 St. Paul's Avenue

Jersey City, NJ 07306

Tel: 201-798-9309

School affiliation: Vietnamese Pure Land

Language spoken: Vietnamese

Chua Quan Am is led by Venerable Thich Giac Thanh. Quan Am is the Vietnamese version of the female bodhisattva of infinite compassion.

Community of Mindfulness—Central
New Jersey Sangha

37 Maple Street
Princeton, NJ 08542
Tel: 609-924-4506

Fax: 609-924-7477
School affiliation: Community of Mindfulness
Language spoken: English

This group meets for mindfulness meditation once a month. They have a full Day of Mindfulness four times a year, and occasional weekend retreats. Contact Amy Rhett LaMotte.

Community of Mindfulness—Juniper
Ridge Sangha

Kitchell Road
Convent Station, NJ 07961
Tel: 201-455-7133

alex322@concentric.net
School affiliation: Community of Mindfulness
Language spoken: English

Contact Bill Alexander. They offer regular meditations and dharma discussions, and include the twelve steps (à la Alcoholics Anonymous) as one of their primary influences.

Community of Mindfulness—
Morristown Sangha

54 Elm Street
Morristown, NJ 07960
Tel: 201-898-9368

School affiliation: Community of
   Mindfulness
Language spoken: English

This group holds their meetings at the Wholeness Center. They meet once a week for mindful practice, and offer introductory meditation classes. Once a month they meet for a Day of Mindfulness. They are connected to the Community of Mindfulness New York Metro (see page 48). Contact Sid Kemp and Kris Lindbeck.

Dhammakaya Meditation Center of New Jersey

186 East Hudson Avenue
Englewood, NJ 07631
dhammakayanj@sprintmail.com

School affiliation: Theravada (Dhammakaya)
Languages spoken: Thai, English

This center is different in significant ways from other Theravadin temples that you might encounter. It is a branch of the new dhammakaya subschool, a controversial movement in Thailand that is reshaping the way traditional Theravadin Buddhism is understood. They advocate a form of meditation that involves visualizing a crystal sphere in one's body, a practice unknown in more orthodox forms of Theravada. The group is also maligned for promising that if laypeople donate large sums of money to the head temple, they'll be reborn as millionaires. The group's detractors claim that it is a fraud, created to bilk laypeople of their money and promote their leader as a cult figure (much is made of the supposed miracles that occur in his presence). The fact that their massive main temple is shaped like a UFO certainly hasn't helped. But the many monks and believers in this school claim that they are creating a Buddhism for the modern masses, and say their critics speak out of jealousy at the movement's undeniable success.

This branch temple is run by Venerable Siddhijanno Bhikkhu, a Thai monk. The center's activities include meditation, study, social services, and programs for young people.

Dzogchen Foundation New Jersey
Sangha
Plainfield, NJ

Tel: 908-561-0462

School affiliation: Nyingmapa

Language spoken: English

This group, affiliated with popular Western teacher Lama Surya Das, meets on alternate Wednesday evenings. Call Maggy Sluyter for details.

Elberon Zen Circle
1032 Woodgate Avenue

Long Branch, NJ 07740

Tel: 732-870-9065

jhirschorn@yahoo.com

School affiliation: Soto Zen

Language spoken: English

Elberon Zen Circle offers weekly sitting meditation and instruction. They are affiliated with the Village Zendo (see page 102).

The Engaged Zen Foundation
P. O. Box 700

Ramsey, NJ 07446

http://www.engaged-zen.org

kobutsu@engaged-zen.org

School affiliation: Rinzai Zen

Language spoken: English

The toughest job you'll ever love? Rev. Kobutsu Malone's Engaged Zen Foundation is a death row advocacy group—he ministers to murderers and sexual predators in places like the infamous Sing Sing Prison. This is Zen at its rawest, most direct level. Actually, one of the Buddha's most famous disciples was a serial killer whom the Buddha taught to be an enlightened saint. Rev. Malone is practicing in a harrowing but illustrious lineage.

Flowering Dogwood Zendo
Avenel, NJ

School affiliation: Rinzai Zen

Language spoken: English

Flowering Dogwood Zendo is no ordinary Buddhist group. This zendo is located at the Adult Diagnostic and Treatment Center, an innocuous-sounding facility that's actually a special state prison for sex offenders. The Engaged Zen Foundation (see page 176) is the sponsor of this unique group—call them for details if you want to get involved.

Gaden Chophel Ling

186 West 6th Street
Howell, NJ 07731
Tel: 732-367-3940

School affiliation: Gelugpa
Languages spoken: English, Mongolian, Tibetan

This temple primarily serves the local Mongolian American community. It's headed by Venerable Yonten Gyatso, a Tibetan monk.

The Heart Circle Sangha

Ridgewood, NJ 07450
Tel: 201-444-4407/201-445-1874
joanhoberichts@compuserve.com

School affiliation: Zen
Language spoken: English

The Heart Circle Sangha is led by Rev. Joan Hoberichts. Regular programs include Zen meditation and study. Reverend Hoberichts (see page 201) also offers psychotherapy.

Island Refuge Sangha

6 Ross Drive E.
Brigantine, NJ 08203
Tel: 609-266-8281
Fax: 609-266-8281

jhintuit@aol.com
School affiliation: Community of Mindfulness
Language spoken: English

This group meets in the residence of Jules Hirsch; call for current times.

Kofuku-no-Kagaku New Jersey

2F Oak Tree Center
2024 Center Avenue
Fort Lee, NJ 07024

Tel: 201-461-7715
School affiliation: Kofuku-no-Kagaku
Languages spoken: Japanese, English

Kofuku-no-Kagaku is an extremely new form of religion, founded in 1986. Many observers believe it's a cult, and the claims of its leader, Ryuho Okawa, to be the Buddha and to know about life on Venus certainly don't do much to dispel this notion. Still, the group is popular in Japan, especially among young urban businesspeople, the group's target audience.

Kwan Chao True Buddha Temple

1612 Frontage Road
Cherryhill, NJ 08034
Tel: 609-795-3055
Fax: 609-795-2157

School affiliation: True Buddha School
(Chinese Vajrayana)
Language spoken: Chinese

This is a branch temple in Grand Master Sheng-yen Lu's True Buddha School. See the True Buddha Diamond Temple (page 100) for more details about this form of Buddhism.

The Lincroft Zen Group

c/o First Unitarian Congregation of
Monmouth County
1475 West Front Street
Lincroft, NJ 07738
Tel: 732-291-3966

Jillmcg@bellatlantic.net
School affiliation: Soto Zen (White Plum
lineage)
Language spoken: English

The Lincroft Zen Group is guided by Merle Kodo Boyd, a priest from the Zen Center of Los Angeles. The membership is largely, though not exclusively, drawn from the congregation of the Unitarian Universalist church they meet in. The group gathers at 3:00 P.M. on the second and fourth Sunday of the month for service, which includes chanting and either three thirty-minute sitting periods (interspersed with walking meditation), or meditation followed by a Buddhist sermon. They also have occasional full-day programs. The group is open to beginners and advanced practitioners. Call ahead if you're coming for the first time, and plan to arrive early at 2:30 P.M. for an introductory session. Chairs are available, but please bring your own cushion if you plan to sit on the floor.

Linh Son Buddhist Congregation

8 Church Street
Stanhope, NJ 07874
Tel: 201-347-2482/201-347-7240

School affiliation: Vietnamese Pure Land
Language spoken: Vietnamese

Auspiciously located on Church Street, this temple is headed by Dai Duc Thich Tri Dat.

The Mahasi Meditation Retreat Center

63 Gordons Corner Road
Manalapan, NJ 07726
Tel: 732-792-1484

http://www.mahasiusa.org/njtemple.htm
School affiliation: Theravada
Languages spoken: English, Burmese

This is a Burmese Theravadin temple located in a midsize frame house. It serves as a retreat center for the monks and members of the Universal Peace Buddha Temple (see page 130) in Brooklyn. There are also monks in residence here who offer teachings to the public.

Mahayana Sutra and Tantra Center

47 East Fifth Street
Howell, NJ 07731
Tel: 908-364-1824
Fax: 908-901-5940

acip@well.com
School affiliation: Gelugpa
Languages spoken: English, Tibetan

This Tibetan Gelugpa temple, housed at Rashi Gempil Ling (see page 183), was founded in 1975 by Khen Rinpoche Geshe Lobsang Tharchin, a highly honored scholar of traditional Buddhist studies. The center offers abundant dharma teachings, as well as instruction in Tibetan language, meditation, and tantric practices. It is the parent temple of the Asian Classics Institute (see page 84).

Morning Star Zendo

50 Glenwood Avenue, #309
Jersey City, NJ 07306
Tel: 201-985-1515
http://www.kennedyzen.com

rocnyc@aol.com
School affiliation: Soto Zen (White Plum lineage)
Languages spoken: English, Japanese

Roshi Robert Kennedy, who holds the highest rank available in Zen, is the leader of this sangha. He also happens to be a Jesuit Catholic priest, a fact that's sure to startle many people. Furthermore, he's a psychotherapist. Weekday sittings at the zendo take place 6:30–7:00 A.M., while weekend sittings are 9:00–11:00 A.M. The second Saturday of the month is a full-day program, 9:00 A.M. to 5:00 P.M.; a donation of $15 is requested, and bring a brown bag lunch with you. Additionally, the zendo is open to the public all day from 6:30 A.M. to 9:30 P.M., and visitors are welcome to come in and sit on their own.

Roshi Kennedy travels extensively and isn't always in residence at Morning Star Zendo, but the center's activities continue whether or not he is there.

New Jersey Community Center

60 Franklin Street
East Orange, NJ 07017
Tel: 973-395-1180
Fax: 973-395-1185

School affiliation: Soka Gakkai (Nichiren Shoshu)
Language spoken: English

This is the New Jersey headquarters of the Soka Gakkai sect, who practice a radical form of lay-led Nichiren Buddhism. See the SGI Culture Center (page 75) for more details on this unusual group.

Nichiren Shoshu New Jersey Chapter

191 Seeley Avenue
Kearny, NJ 07032-3724
Tel: 201-998-7110

School affiliation: Nichiren Shoshu Temple
Language spoken: English

This is the local meeting group of the Myosetsuji Temple (see page 114) in Flushing, NY. See the Myosetsuji Temple description for further information on this lineage.

Padmasambhava Buddhist Center of Princeton

15 Campbell Road
Kendall Park, NJ 08824
Tel: 908-821-0984

School affiliation: Nyingma
Languages spoken: English, Tibetan

This group was founded by two prominent Nyingma lamas, Khenchen Palden Sherab Rinpoche and Khenpo Tsewang Dongyal Rinpoche. The Khenpos administer a number of connected groups under the banner of the Padmasambhava Center of New York (see page 71).

Palden Sakya—Cresskill

289 Brookside Avenue
Cresskill, NJ 07626

School affiliation: Sakyapa
Language spoken: English

Lama Pema Wangdak, of the Palden Sakya New York center (see page 56), is the spiritual guide for this group. Contact the NYC group for more information about Cresskill.

Practice Community at Franklin Lakes

c/o Presbyterian Church at Franklin Lakes
730 Franklin Lakes Road
Franklin Lakes, NJ 07417
Tel: 201-891-0511
Fax: 201-891-0517

http://www.pcfl.org/medit.htm
pcfl@internexus.net
School affiliation: Community of Mindfulness
Language spoken: English

This Zen group meets in a friendly Presbyterian church, and is partially led by the church's own pastor (!). They have programs Monday 7:30–9:00 P.M., Wednesday 8:00–8:45 P.M., and Friday 7:00–8:00 A.M.

The group watches videotaped teachings of Thich Nhat Hanh, holds discussions, and practices sitting and walking meditation.

Princeton Area Zen Center

113 Commons Way
Princeton, NJ 08540-1507
Tel: 732-452-1929
http://www.princetonzen.simplenet.com/

hetty@princeton.edu
School affiliation: Zen (Sanbo Kyodan)
Language spoken: English

This democratically run zendo has meetings every Sunday 7:00–9:00 P.M. Beginners are required to attend the orientation session, which is held the first Sunday of the month at 6:30 P.M. There is a $5 fee for non-members; members pay $3 per meeting.

Princeton Friends of Tibet

42 Cuyler Road
Princeton, NJ 08540
Tel: 609-924-5243
http://www.pazona.org/friends_tibet/
    index.html

trich@aosi.com
School affiliation: Independent
Language spoken: English

This isn't a practice community, but a local organization devoted to championing the cause of Tibet's oppressed people. They meet on the second Tuesday of the month at Nassau Presbyterian Church at 7:00 P.M. Although they aren't religious in nature, they do sponsor lamas to speak in the area. Yearly membership fees are $25 ($15 for students).

Princeton Shambhala Meditation Group

144 Matthews Farm Road
Belle Mead, NJ 08502
Tel: 908-431-9617
michael_J_stephens@merck.com

School affiliation: Shambhala (Kagyu/
    Nyingma)
Language spoken: English

Michael James Stephens is the director of this local Shambhala group, which practices the Kagyu and Nyingma Tibetan Buddhist teachings of the late Chogyam Trungpa Rinpoche and his son, Sakyong Mipham Rinpoche.

Princeton Zen Society

317 Mt. Lucas Road
Princeton, NJ 08540
Tel: 609-924-0785

School affiliation: Rinzai Zen
Language spoken: English

Princeton Zen Society was founded in 1985 by Chinzan, a student of Sasaki Roshi. This zendo is located in a quiet, attractive part of Princeton. They offer weekly meditation and semiannual intensive weeklong retreats.

Rashi Gempil Ling

First Kalmuk Buddhist Temple
47 East Fifth Street
Howell, NJ 07731
Tel: 732-364-1824

School affiliation: Gelugpa
Languages spoken: English, Mongolian,
Tibetan

Rashi Gempil Ling is a Mongolian American temple, run by Tibetan Buddhists. Geshe Lobsang Tharchin, an accomplished Tibetan scholar monk, is the head teacher. Rashi Gempil is also the site of Tashi Lhunpo Monastery, a Tibetan monastery; to contact Venerable Tenzin Dakpa at the monastery call 732-363-6012.

As if two centers weren't enough, Rashi Gempil Ling also houses Khen Rinpoche's Mahayana Sutra and Tantra Center (see page 179).

Seabrook Buddhist Temple

Northville Road
Seabrook, NJ 08302
Tel: 856-451-3422

School affiliation: Japanese Pure Land
(Jodo Shinshu)
Languages spoken: English, Japanese

Seabrook Buddhist Temple is a member of the Buddhist Churches of America, a nationwide organization of Jodo Shinshu Pure Land temples. The BCA was the first large Buddhist organization in America. They preach salvation through faith alone, generated by the boundless wisdom and compassion of the Buddhist Amitabha. Followers chant "Namo Amida Butsu" to demonstrate their gratitude for the guidance of the Buddha—thankfulness and humility are the primary values of these Buddhists.

South Jersey Karma Kagyu Study Group

21 Fulton Drive

Mt. Laurel, NJ 08054

Tel: 856-222-1864

http://www.kagyu.org/centers/usa/
  usa-voo.html

junderhi@concentric.net

School affiliation: Kagyupa

Language spoken: English

This group meets on Sundays, 7:30–9:00 P.M., for sitting meditation, prayers, and study. Beginners are welcome, and individual instruction is available by appointment. They're affiliated with the Karma Triyana Dharmachakra (see page 152) monastery in Upstate New York.

Tibetan Buddhist Learning Center

93 Angen Road

Washington, NJ 07882-9767

Tel: 908-689-6080

School affiliation: Gelugpa

Languages spoken: English, Mongolian, Tibetan

This is one of the oldest centers of Tibetan Buddhist practice in America. It was founded in 1965 by Geshe Wangyal, who is actually of Mongolian extraction (Mongolia is a Buddhist nation sharing the same tradition as Tibet), and was the starting place for many of the current generation of top Buddhist academics, including Robert Thurman. The temple, situated on picturesque Montana Mountain, still houses Tibetan monastics and has public classes, meditation sessions, and prayers.

Regular services draw about twenty to thirty people, mostly Mongolian Americans. Also known as Labsum Shedrub Ling, it's one of three local Mongolian temples, each of which was founded to serve one of three Mongolian tribes. Along with the Mongolian and Tibetan presence are Joshua and Diane Cutler, who run the center and have been there since Geshe Wangyal's time.

Wildflower Zendo

P. O. Box 700
Ramsey, NJ 07446-0700
http://www.engaged-zen.org/wildflower.
    html
kobutsu@engaged-zen.org

School affiliation: Rinzai Zen
Language spoken: English

Wildflower Zen is run by Kobutsu Malone, who also heads The Engaged Zen Foundation (see page 177). Rev. Malone has open public services on Sundays, 10:30 A.M. to 1:00 P.M., which include a sermon and meditation practice. Beginners are welcome.

The Zen Society/Jizo-An Monastery

1603 Highland Avenue
Cinnaminson, NJ 08077
Tel: 609-786-4150

Fax: 609-786-2112
School affiliation: Soto Zen
Language spoken: English

Established in 1981, this Zen center is led by its founder, Seijaku Stephen Reichenbach Roshi. Despite Japanese forms such as tea service, this center is thoroughly Americanized in attitude and teaching style, with an interest in ecumenical Zen practice regardless of one's individual religious orientation—many regular members also retain their affiliations with Christian or Jewish congregations as well. They offer daily sitting meditation and dharma talks, as well as workshops and classes. The Zen Society has about thirty regular members, but as many as one thousand people participate in their classes or meditations over the course of a year. Despite the title of monastery, the training is nonresidential. The center is closed in August for retreat.

Zen Temple of Cresskill

185 Sixth Street

Cresskill, NJ 07626

Tel: 201-567-7468

Fax: 201-567-0831

School affiliation: Korean Zen

Languages spoken: English, Korean

Unlike many Korean Zen centers in America, the Zen Temple of Cresskill is not affiliated with Seung Sahn's Kwan Um school of Zen. Instead, it is a Western branch of the Yong Hwa Zen Temple in Inchun, Korea, headed by Master Songdahm. Master Songdahm's Zen teaching is unique among techniques taught in the U.S.A.: While most schools, including the Kwan Um, emphasize sitting meditation, the Zen Temple of Cresskill teaches Zen dance, a form of meditation in motion that unites the mind and body together in enlighted action. The practice isn't exactly "boogieing for Buddha"—Zen dance is highly ritualized, somewhat reminiscent of tai chi. Despite the physical nature of this meditation, one need not be a dancer to study at the temple. The resident teacher is Dr. Sun Ok Lee.

CONNECTICUT

The Nutmeg State has noticeably fewer Buddhist temples than neighboring New York and New Jersey, but considering that nearly all of them have formed in the last twenty or even ten years, Buddhism is definitely a southern New England growth industry.

Bellflower Sangha

28 Fanning Avenue

Norwich, CT 06360

Tel: 860-889-0131

george.chaput@snet.net

School affiliation: Community of Mindfulness

Language spoken: English

Like other Community of Mindfulness groups, the Bellflower Sangha meets in the homes of members for informal walking and sitting meditation.

Beth Roth Mindfulness Classes

122 Canner Street   School affiliation: independent

New Haven, CT 06511   Languages spoken: English, Spanish

Tel: 203-772-2335

Beth Roth is an independent teacher who applies ancient Buddhist meditation techniques to modern health care. She advocates using mindfulness meditation practices to reduce stress and increase relaxation in patients (though they're certainly a big help to nurses and doctors too). Her primary activity is a structured eight-week-long class, including a full-day silent retreat. It's offered at a number of area locations throughout the year, including the Community Health Care Center in Meriden, the Yale University School of Nursing (where students can receive academic credit), and the Yoga Studio of New Haven. Call to confirm upcoming classes and to receive current prices.

Buddhist Wellspring at the Universalist Church of West Hartford

433 Fern Street
West Hartford, CT 06107-2002
Tel: 660-346-6240
bertmayo@earthlink.net

School affiliation: Unitarian-Universalist (non-Buddhist)
Language: English

This is a group of Unitarian-Universalists interested in exploring the spiritual practices of Buddhism. They meet for meditation on the first and third Mondays of the month at 7:30 P.M. Introductory instruction is available for newcomers at 7:00 P.M. Contact Bert Mayo for more information.

Center for Dzogchen Studies

847 Whalley Avenue
New Haven, CT 06515
Tel: 203-387-9992

School affiliation: Nyingmapa and Kagyupa
Language spoken: English

This center is headed by residential teacher Padma Karma Rinpoche, a Caucasian Buddhist with many years of practice in the Tibetan tradition of Dzogchen. The center offers monthly daylong retreats, occasional three-day retreats, and support for longer individual retreats, as well as instruction in the practice of Dzogchen. It is located in a busy urban environment, the better to integrate its practice with hectic daily life. Call for current schedule of classes and retreats.

Chester Zen Group

Chester, CT
Tel: 860-526-1558

School affiliation: Soto and Rinzai Zen
Language spoken: English

The Chester Zen Group is loosely connected to Zen Mountain Monastery's (see page 170) Mountains and Rivers Order. Stephen Morrel is the leader of this group, which offers sitting meditation and similar activities.

Chua Hai An

255 Cherry Street
New Britain, CT 06051
Tel: 860-612-0077

School affiliation: Vietnamese Pure
    Land
Language spoken: Vietnamese

This Vietnamese temple is led by Thuong Toa Thich Tri Hoang. Services are held on Sundays.

Community of Mindfulness—
Manchester Sangha

46 Dougherty Street
Manchester, CT 06040
Tel: 203-647-0347

School affiliation: Community of
    Mindfulness
Language spoken: English

The Manchester Sangha meets once a week. Typical activities include meditation, chanting, discussion, and refreshments.

Community of Mindfulness—Storrs

86B Forest Road
Storrs, CT 06268
Tel: 860-429-1867

School affiliation: Community of
    Mindfulness
Language spoken: English

Call Annie Speiser for details about this sitting group.

Godstow

Redding, CT
Tel: 203-938-2330
http://www.world-view.org/godstow.html

School affiliation: Gelugpa
Languages spoken: English, Tibetan

This is Asian Classics Institute's (see page 84) rural retreat center. They have regular retreats here away from the hustle and bustle of New York City; individuals and other groups can also use the facilities.

Hartford Karma Thegsum Choling

157 Elizabeth Street
Hartford, CT 06105
Tel: 860-232-8366
Fax: 860-232-8722
   http://www.kagyu.org/centers/usa/
   usa-har.html

htfdktc@aol.com
School affiliation: Kagyupa
Language spoken: English

This group meets in a residential house across from Hartford's Elizabeth Park. They have evening programs on Tuesdays and Thursdays, with meditation, readings, and discussion. Newcomers to Tibetan Buddhism are welcome to come and learn about the teachings.

Hartford Shambhala Study Group

47 Dover Road
West Hartford, CT 06119
Tel: 860-571-3766
http://www.shambhala.org/centers/
   hartford/
RandyKap@aol.com

School affiliation: Shambhala (Kagyu/
   Nyingma)
Language spoken: English

This is the central Connecticut branch of the international Shambhala community. They offer Tibetan Buddhist teachings free of charge.

Hoi Phat Giao Connecticut

369 Simsbury Road
Bloomsfield, CT 06002
Tel: 203-242-8002

School affiliation: Vietnamese Pure Land
Language spoken: Vietnamese

This is a Vietnamese American temple.

Insight Meditation Practice Group

Hartford, CT

Tel: 860-232-7628/860-561-2343

rutledgecr@aol.com

School affiliation: Vipassana

Language spoken: English

This is a Vipassana group that meets every other Tuesday 7:30–9:30 P.M. Their activities include sitting meditation, sermons, readings, discussions, and occasional silent retreats.

The Living Dharma Center

P. O. Box 513

Bolton, CT 06043

Tel: 860-742-7049

School affiliation: Zen (Sanbo Kyodan)

Language spoken: English

Established in 1972, the Living Dharma Center is led by resident teacher Richard Clarke, who studied with Philip Kapleau Roshi of the Rochester Zen Center (see page 162). The center maintains a zendo and retreat facilities. The center is actually jointly based in Coventry, Connecticut, and in Amherst, Massachusetts, with the teacher shuttling back and forth between locations.

Meditation Center at St. John's-
on-the-Green

16 Church Street

Waterbury, CT 06702

Tel: 203-596-8137

Fax: 203-757-8643

School affiliation: Zen

Language spoken: English

This is a small Zen group that meets weekly for sitting meditation and discussion. Their meetings, as well as occasional full-day retreats, are free of charge and open to the public.

Mindfulness Practice Group

Hartford, CT

Tel: (203) 236-5542

School affiliation: Community of Mindfulness

Language spoken: English

This group practices mindfulness meditation but is nonsectarian in nature.

Mindfulness Sangha

255 Cherry Street

New Britain, CT 06051

Tel: 860-612-0077

robert.hoffman@snet.net

School affiliation: Community of Mindfulness

Language spoken: English

This group practices in the tradition of Vietnamese Zen master Thich Nhat Hanh, but anyone is welcome to come and meditate with them. Call for current meetings.

New Haven Shambhala Center

319 Peck Street

New Haven, CT 06513

Tel: 203-776-2331

Fax: 860-387-2913

http://dharma-haven.org/shambhala/

shambhala@dharma-haven.org

School affiliation: Shambhala (Kagyu/
   Nyingma)

Language spoken: English

Established in 1978, this is the primary Connecticut branch of the Shambhala community; see the New York Shambhala Center (see page 68) for more information about this type of Buddhism. Open to newcomers. Don't get confused and go to the nearby yoga center.

New Haven Zen Center

193 Mansfield Street

New Haven, CT 06511

Tel: 203-787-0912

nhzc@zol.com

School affiliation: Korean Zen (Kwan Um
   school)

Language spoken: English

This Korean Zen center is located next to the Yale University campus, in an old Victorian house. It was established in 1977 and is led by senior dharma teacher Paul Bloom. Open Wednesday night introductory sessions are held at 6:00 P.M. They also sometimes hold services in the Dwight Chapel on campus.

New Milford Karma Thegsum Choling

10 Vista Drive
New Milford, CT 06776
Tel: 860-350-8959
http://www.kagyu.org/centers/usa/
  usa-new.html

tomadams@snet.net
School affiliation: Kagyupa
Language spoken: English

This group meets on Thursdays at 7:30 P.M. The program includes an hour of group meditation followed by discussion. New Milford Karma Thegsum Choling meets in a private home. Please call ahead before attending the first time.

Odiyana Buddhist Center

217 S. Highland Street #3
West Hartford, CT 06119
Tel: 860-231-0157

http://www.geocities.com/odiyana
odiyana@rcn.com
School affiliation: Gelugpa (New
  Kadampa Tradition)
Language spoken: English

Gen Kelsand Sherab, an immigrant monk from England with fifteen years of Buddhist training, leads this new center. He teaches a Monday night general class at the Elmwood Community Center (1106 New Britain Avenue), and a six-week Sunday night class in Hartford (call for details).

The New Kadampa Tradition teaches a well-rounded program of Buddhist meditation, study, and devotion. In recent years the NKT has been vilified by some because of a rather esoteric sectarian dispute with the Dalai Lama, but it's best to examine their methods yourself and draw your own conclusions.

Phuoc Long Felicitous Prosperity Buddhist Temple of Connecticut

1222 Fairfield Avenue
Bridgeport, CT 06605
Tel: 203-366-3477
Fax: 203-366-3477

http://www.angelfire.com/ct/phuoclong/
phuoclong@juno.com
School affiliation: Vietnamese Pure Land
Language spoken: Vietnamese

The delightfully named Phuoc Long Felicitous Prosperity Buddhist Temple of Connecticut is a large two-story house that once served as a funeral home. It took twenty years of saving before the local community could afford to open the temple, which now serves as the center of cultural and religious life for Bridgeport's Vietnamese American Buddhists. Though services are in Vietnamese, many members speak English and everyone is welcome to attend their events, Buddhist or otherwise. Rev. Thich Minh Duc is the head monk.

Singing Bowl Sangha

10 Partridge Trail
Sherman, CT 06784
Tel: 860-350-3927

gandhi30@ix.netcom.com
School affiliation: independent
Language spoken: English

Singing Bowl Sangha is an eclectic Buddhist group that welcomes practitioners from all traditions and of all levels of skill. Their practice draws from many Buddhist traditions, including both Theravada and Mahayana resources. They meet on Mondays, 7:00 P.M., at the United Jewish Center at 141 Deer Hill Avenue in Danbury. Typical gatherings include recitation of the Heart Sutra, thirty minutes of sitting meditation, and sometimes chanting in the Pure Land style. The group is led by the auspiciously named Reverend Wisdom. Though the group is independent and mixes separate traditions, Reverend Wisdom is an ordained Buddhist priest in the combined Pure Land/Zen Vietnamese lineage.

Thepchanthararam Laotian Temple

200 Hazelwood Avenue
Bridgeport, CT 06605
Tel: 203-579-9117

School affiliation: Theravada
Language spoken: Laotian

Laotian Americans are a relatively unknown presence in American Buddhism, but their Theravadin form of Buddhism is one of the oldest and largest schools. This multisyllabic temple serves the ethnic community by giving them and their children contact with monks, who provide the moral and religious teachings in Laotian society.

Wisdom House Retreat and Conference
Center

229 East Litchfield Road
Litchfield, CT 06759-3002
Tel: 860-567-3163
Fax: 860-567-3166

http://www.wisdomhouse.org
info@wisdomhouse.org
School affiliation: independent
Language spoken: English

A more peaceful environment can hardly be found in the metropolitan New York area than Wisdom House, a former Catholic nunnery that now serves as an interfaith center for contemplative retreat. Wisdom House offers many programs and is used by many groups during the year, so it's best to ask for a current brochure of activities. One ongoing Buddhist gathering is a Community of Mindfulness (Westernized Vietnamese Zen) group that meets Tuesdays, 7:30–9:00 P.M. They request a $5 donation.

PART THREE

WHAT OTHER BUDDHIST RESOURCES ARE AVAILABLE?

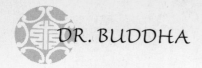

DR. BUDDHA

One of the ways that the nature of the Buddha is traditionally explained is as a doctor who diagnoses the ills of the world and offers a prescription to get well. There's even a special Medicine Buddha to whom people pray to heal their diseases. Recently there's been a fast growing interest in Buddhism among medical practitioners, who recognize the benefits that meditation can bring in relieving stress, reducing the risk of heart disease, eliminating the need for strong painkillers, and other areas. And for years now there's been a productive cross-fertilization between Buddhism, the religion of the mind, and psychology and psychotherapy, the science and medicine of the mind. There's an unusually high number of psychologists involved in Buddhist studies, especially in Zen and Vipassana practice, and many have begun exploring ways to integrate their Buddhist insights and methods with the therapy they offer their patients.

Another aspect of Asian Buddhism that has begun to attract wider attention is traditional Tibetan medicine, which recognizes the unity of the body and mind and offers holistic solutions to health problems. For people in the New York City area seeking a Buddhist alternative to Western medicine, or for people interested in psychology and who want the additional insights that a Buddhist practitioner can bring, here's a list of resources.

Affordable Psychotherapy

11th Street and Broadway

New York, NY 10003

Tel: 212-477-0253

ovid@interport.net

School affiliation: Zen

Language spoken: English

Randall Eiger, M.S.W.., C.S.W., is a psychotherapist and Zen student. He seeks to make psychotherapy affordable and accessible to all, so his fees are based on the client's ability to pay.

Shakya Dorje

Tel: 718-641-7323

Languages spoken: English, Tibetan

Shakya Dorje, a Canadian who earned a degree in Tibetan medicine, is a student of the Dalai Lama's personal physicians and teacher of Eliot Tokar (see page 206). He offers a clinic in traditional Tibetan medicine every six weeks in New York City, and is available for private consultation by appointment. Call between 10:30 A.M. and 4:00 P.M. during the week to be placed on his mailing list.

Mark Epstein

New York, NY

Language spoken: English

School affiliation: independent

Mark Epstein is a prominent author and psychologist, whose books *Thoughts without a Thinker: Psychotherapy from a Buddhist Perspective* and *Going to Pieces without Falling Apart: A Buddhist Perspective on Wholeness* are classics in the Buddhism-psychotherapy dialogue and have attracted a wide audience outside of the field. He is in private practice in downtown New York. Because he is something of a celebrity in Buddhist circles and could be swamped by inquiries from strangers at his private residence, his contact information has been excluded. Those people who are especially appropriate as potential patients may be referred to him by his colleagues.

Gay Men's Health Crisis Meditation Class

New York, NY

See Gay Men's Health Crisis Meditation Class (on page 62) for more details.

Elan Golomb, Ph.D.

New York, NY

Tel: 212-496-6003

Elan Golomb is a certified clinical psychologist, author, documentary filmmaker, and practitioner of Vipassana (Insight Meditation).

Rev. Joan Hogetsu Hoberichts, C.S.W.

Tel: 212-370-9089/201-444-9055

joanhoberichts@compuserve.com

School affiliation: Zen

Language spoken: English

Rev. Hoberichts is the leader of the Heart Circle Sangha (see page 177) in New Jersey. She offers psychotherapy for individuals, couples, and families from a Zen perspective.

Roshi Robert Kennedy

50 Glenwood Avenue, #309
Jersey City, NJ 07306
Tel: 201-985-1515
http://www.kennedyzen.com

rocnyc@aol.com
School affiliation: Soto Zen (White Plum lineage)
Languages spoken: English, Japanese

Roshi Robert Kennedy wears three surprising hats: he's a Zen master, Jesuit priest, and a psychotherapist in practice in New York City.

Barry Magid

33 Greenwich Avenue, #4A
New York, NY 10014
Tel: 212-691-0819

ordinarymind@erol.com
School affiliation: Zen
Language spoken: English

Barry Magid is the founder and head teacher of the Ordinary Mind Zendo (see page 95). A psychiatrist and psychoanalyst specializing in the field of self psychology, he's currently a faculty member and supervisor at the Postgraduate Center for Mental Health, as well as at the Institute for Contemporary Psychotherapy in New York.

Menla Center For Natural Medicine

108 Everit Street
New Haven, CT 06511
Tel: 203-562-1614
http://www.dharma-haven.org/tibetan/
menla-center-for-natural-medicine.htm

clinicmenla-clinic@dharma-haven.org
Languages spoken: English, Tibetan

This New Haven, Connecticut, center has several Tibetans and Westerners on staff and offers a wide range of services. See their Web site for extensive information on the practice of traditional Tibetan medicine.

Meridian Medical

102 East 30th Street

New York, NY 10016

Tel: 212-683-1221

Languages spoken: Tibetan, English

Meridian Medical is operated by Dr. Choeying Phuntsok.

Tenzin Namgyal

New York, NY

212-683-1221

Languages spoken: Tibetan, English

Tenzin Namgyal is a graduate of the Tibetan Medical and Astrology Institute in Dharmasala, the Indian headquarters of the Tibetan refugee population.

Barbara O'Hara

New York, NY

Barbara O'Hara, partner of Village Zendo leader Pat Enkyo O'Hara, is a longtime Zen student and psychotherapist. See The Village Zendo (on page 102) for contact information.

Beth Roth Mindfulness Classes

New Haven, CT

See Beth Roth Mindfulness Classes (on page 187) for more information.

Jeffrey Rubin, Ph.D.

66 Main Street

Bedford Hills, NY 10507

Tel: 914-242-0229

School affiliation: independent

Language spoken: English

Dr. Jeffrey Rubin has practices in both New York City and Bedford Hills. His work includes an active attempt at integration of Buddhism and psychotherapy into a total system for achieving self-understanding and peace.

Rev. Diane Ryoko Shainberg

124 East 95th Street
New York, NY 10128
Tel: 212-876-8213
Fax: 212-876-8062

aaaryoko@aol.com
School affiliation: Soto Zen (White Plum lineage)
Language spoken: English

Rev. Diane Ryoko Shainberg, Ph.D., leads the Carnegie Hill Zen Center (see page 44) and the Manhattan Dzogchen Group (see page 49). She also runs the Mani Center for Integral Studies, which offers training for psychotherapists in utilizing various Buddhist and Asian techniques in their medical practice. Diane is also available for private psychotherapy.

Richard Shrobe, A.C.S.W.

400 East 14th Street, #2D
New York, NY 10009
Tel: 212-353-0461
http://www1.tagonline.com/~netresul/ netresults/chogye.html

chogye@buddhist.com
School affiliation: Kwan Um Zen
Language spoken: English

Zen master Wu Kwang (Richard Shrobe), has a master's in social work and is a psychotherapist specializing in Gestalt psychotherapy. Gestalt is a holistic psychotherapy that combines aspects of Western and Eastern psychology. He is on the faculty of the Gestalt Associates for Psychotherapy. He was formerly the head teacher of Integral Yoga Institute and is currently head teacher of Chogye International Zen Center (see page 87).

Susan Speiler

Tel: 212-877-0355

sspsyd@aol.com

School affiliation: Community of Mindfulness

Language spoken: English

Susan Speiler, the coordinator of the Community of Mindfulness— Being with Children (see page 47), is also a psychologist in private practice on the Upper West Side. You can contact her for further information about her services.

The Stress Reduction Course at
**   Holy Name Hospital**

718 Teaneck Road

Teaneck, NJ 07666

Tel: (201) 833-7222

Fax: (201) 833-7068

mendelowitz@holyname.org

School affiliation: independent

Language spoken: English

This New Jersey Mindfulness-meditation-based stress-reduction class is unusual because it takes place in an institutionalized Western medicine setting.

Andrew Thardon, Ph.D.

85 Fifth Avenue

New York, NY 10003-3019

Tel: 212-388-8056

School affiliation: independent

Language spoken: English

Andrew Thardon is a licensed psychologist who offers meditation-based psychotherapy to his clients. Experiential study group and individual consultations are available.

Dana J. Thornley, M.S.

New York, NY

Tel: 212-777-3446

http://themindgame.com/HTML/Main/ main.htm

Dana Thornley is a New York City–based psychotherapist and Zen practitioner.

Tibetan Refugee Health

New York, NY

See Tibetan Refugee Health on page 219.

Eliot Tokar

Howard Beach, NY

Tel: 718-641-7323

http://www.tibetanmedicine.com/

etokar@aol.com

Languages spoken: English, Tibetan

Eliot Tokar offers traditional Tibetan, Chinese, and Japanese medicine, and is one of the most knowledgeable resources on Tibetan medicine in America. Please call during office hours only: Monday–Friday 10:30 A.M. to 4:00 P.M., 8:00 P.M. to 9:30 P.M., and Saturday and Sunday 11:00 A.M. to 3:00 P.M. Visit his Web site for a nicely succinct overview of Tibetan medicine.

Zen & Psychotherapy

Tel: 516-829-8081

School affiliation: Zen

Language spoken: English

Brenda Shoshanna Lukeman, Ph.D., is a certified clinical psychologist with offices in Great Neck and Manhattan. She offers therapy for individuals and groups, utilizing the principles of Zen meditation and practice to solve everyday life problems.

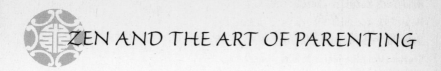

ZEN AND THE ART OF PARENTING

Sometimes it can be hard being a Buddhist parent in New York City. Meditation groups want adults who can sit still and silent for long stretches of time, and since many are in residential apartments or houses, space is limited and there's no formal staff for childcare. Heck, even the model Buddhist for many traditions is a celibate monk with no family distractions from his religious practice. And advice on raising a mindful, compassionate child with a Buddhist perspective on life can be pretty hard to find. So what can you do about your baby Buddhas?

Buddhist groups have dealt with these problems in a number of ways. Some offer programs and activities for children and youth, such as "dharma Sunday school," Buddhist summer camps, and even Buddhist Boy Scout troops. Others have sought to integrate family life and practice so that parents aren't forced to choose between their religion and their kids—teaching their children and being mindful parents become the practice itself. Here's a short list of communities who've gone out of their way to provide resources specifically for parents and/or children:

International Buddhist Progress Society—Flushing (see page 113)
New York Buddhist Church (see page 51)
New York Buddhist Vihara (see page 116)
New York Shambhala Center (see page 68)
Staten Island Buddhist Vihara (see page 135)

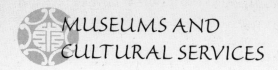

MUSEUMS AND CULTURAL SERVICES

E ver since Marco Polo, people in the West have been fascinated with the arts and culture of the East. Luckily, you don't have to travel halfway across the world to get a glimpse of the dazzling artistry of Buddhist paintings, sculptures, mandalas, and drawings. Here are some New York area resources for Buddhist and Asian art, cultural events, and lectures.

The American Museum of Natural History

Central Park West at 79th Street   Tel: 212-769-5100
New York, NY 10024   http://www.amnh.org

New Yorkers all know and love the Museum of Natural History for its incredible displays of the animal world, particularly the dinosaur exhibits. But few are aware that the museum has a modest store of Buddhist art and artifacts from various parts of the world. In the Hall of Asian Peoples there are items on permanent display from Southeast Asia, China, Japan, and Tibet. Exhibits include monks' attire, beautiful Tibetan masks and thangkas (religious paintings), and a nineteenth-century Japanese altar with a life-size seated statue of the Buddha Amida.

Upstairs in the private photo library are thousands of black-and-white pictures from Buddhist countries, particularly Tibet. This area is not normally accessible to the public, but it can be utilized by researchers.

Admission to the museum costs $9.50 for adults, $7.50 for students and seniors, and $6.00 for children; admission is free for museum members. Museum hours: Sunday to Thursday 10:00 A.M. to 5:45 P.M., Friday and Saturday 10:00 A.M. to 8:45 P.M. Be sure to bring the kids and take one of the free tours.

Asia Society
725 Park Avenue
New York, NY 10021
Tel: 212-288-6400

Fax: 212-517-8315
http://www.asiasociety.org

Asia Society offers a dizzying variety of programs from all over the continent, including film screenings, lectures, and art exhibitions. They also have a particularly good bookstore with a wide range of titles on Buddhism.

Asia Society has temporarily moved its location to 502 Park Avenue to accommodate a major overhaul of its headquarters. They will return to 725 Park Avenue in the fall of 2001. Their hours at the temporary facilities are Monday to Saturday, 10:00 A.M. to 6:00 P.M.

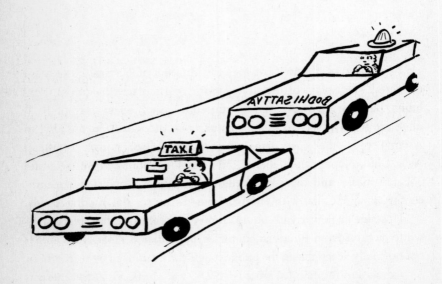

Brooklyn Museum of Art

200 Eastern Parkway
Brooklyn, NY 11238
Tel: 718-638-5000

bklynmus@echonyc.com
http://www.brooklynart.org/

While it's BMA's special exhibitions that tend to create a sensation, the museum's Asian art is still thrilling. The Chinese and Korean collections are particularly excellent, and you won't want to miss the Japanese, Nepalese, Tibetan, and Indian art either.

The Brooklyn Museum is open Wednesday through Friday 10:00 A.M. to 5:00 P.M., and 11:00 A.M. to 6:00 P.M. on weekends. The first Saturday of the month the museum stays open all the way to 11:00 P.M. Admission is $4, $2 for seniors and students.

China Institute

125 East 65th Street
New York, NY 10021
Tel: 212-744-8181

Fax: 212-628-4159
info@chinainstitute.org
http://www.chinainstitute.org

The China Institute was established in 1926 to promote an understanding and appreciation of Chinese culture, particularly its arts and history. The institute offers classes in Chinese language, calligraphy, and more, sponsors lectures and musical performances, and maintains a gallery that consistently presents dynamic and insightful exhibitions. The gallery is open Monday through Saturday 10:00 A.M. to 5:00 P.M., Tuesday and Thursday to 8:00 P.M., and Sunday 1:00 to 5:00 P.M. Admission is $3, $2 for seniors and students.

Jacques Marchais Museum of
Tibetan Art

338 Lighthouse Avenue
P. O. Box 060198
Staten Island, NY 10306-0198

Tel: 718-987-3500
Fax: 718-351-0402
http://www.tibetanmuseum.com

Appropriately, this museum of art from the roof of the world is located on the highest point on the eastern seaboard. The collection has more than just Tibetan art, including pieces from China, Nepal, Mongolia, and other Himalayan areas. It's the only museum in New York City devoted solely to Buddhist art.

The main attraction is the Tibetan altar, decked out with statues of all sizes, religious paintings, ritual implements, and other objects one would find at an altar in Tibet. It's common to see katas, white scarves used as offerings, draped over the statues by visiting Buddhists.

The museum's library is also open to the visiting public, where you can read all day about Tibet and Buddhist art. The garden and grounds are beautiful and tranquil, an ideal place to eat lunch or meditate. The museum also has a shop that sells Tibetan objects, CDs, and other similar merchandise.

The Jacques Marchais Museum of Tibetan Art is open 1:00–5:00 P.M. Wednesdays through Sundays from April to November; December through March the museum is closed on the weekends. Admission is $3 adults, $2 for students and seniors, and $1 for kids; Sunday programs usually cost an additional $3.

Japan Society

333 East 47th Street
New York, NY 10017
Tel: 212-832-1155

Fax: (212) 755-6752
http://www.jpnsoc.com/
gen@japansociety.org

Since 1907 the Japan society has tried to bring Japan and America closer together through cultural exchange and education. They have frequent lectures on all aspects of Japanese society, Japanese-language courses, film, musical and dramatic performances, a library, and even two indoor gardens and a waterfall. The gallery puts on some of the finest exhibitions in the city, many of which have had a specifically Buddhist theme.

Korea Society

950 Third Avenue, 8th floor
New York, NY 10022
Tel: 212-759-7525

Fax: 212-759-7530
http://www.koreasociety.org/
korea.ny@koreasociety.org

Like the Korean Cultural Service, The Korea Society is dedicated to fostering friendship between Korea and the U.S.A. They organize a wide range of informative events around current Korean issues, history, arts, culture, religion, and economics.

Korean Cultural Service

460 Park Avenue, 6th floor
New York, NY 10022
Tel: 212-759-9550

Fax: 212-688-8640
http://www.koreanculture.org
nykocus@koreanculture.org

Korean Cultural Service promotes understanding between Korea and the United States through cultural and academic activities. They have a multimedia lending library that includes Buddhist books, and an art gallery. KCS also produces lectures, seminars, art exhibitions, and musical performances around New York City. They're open Monday to Friday, 10:00 A.M. to 5:00 P.M.

The Metropolitan Museum of Art

1000 Fifth Avenue at 81st Street
New York, NY 10028

Tel: 212-535-7710
http://www.metmuseum.org

You could walk to the Pacific in the time it'd take to see all the wonders of the Metropolitan Museum of Art. But even if you confine yourself to just the Buddhist Asian art, you're in for a full day at the museum, if not more. With collections of Buddhist art from China, Japan, Korea, Tibet, India, Pakistan, and Southeast Asia, you can explore all the many expressions of the dharma in a wide variety of media. Some highlights: the wall covered with a giant Buddhist fresco, the towering fourteen-foot-tall bodhisattva, the Chinese philosopher's garden, and a stone

pagoda considered to be the oldest and most important piece of Chinese architecture in a Western museum. Take it all in slowly, and give yourself time to observe the connections between different pieces and how the same figures, such as the Buddha, are represented in so many strikingly various ways.

The museum is closed Mondays, open 9:30 A.M. to 5:30 P.M. Sunday, Tuesday, Wednesday, and Thursday, and open till 9:00 P.M. Friday and Saturday. Suggested donation is $10, or $5 for students and seniors.

Museum of Chinese in the Americas

70 Mulberry Street, 2nd floor   Tel: 212-619-4785
New York, NY 10013

Originally the Chinese Museum, this museum documents the history, struggles, and achievements of Chinese immigrants in the New World. Chinese prospectors and railway workers in the 1850s were the first documented Buddhists to land on American soil. The Museum of Chinese in the Americas is open Tuesday to Saturday from noon to 5:00

P.M. Admission is $3 for adults, $1 seniors and students, and free for members and children under twelve.

New York Open Center

83 Spring Street   Fax: 212-226-4056
New York, NY 10012   http://www.opencenter.org/
Tel: 212-219-2527   box@opencenter.org

The New York Open Center is an adult education center devoted to holistic and alternative spirituality subjects. Their many classes, programs, and conferences range from the dopey to the outstanding, and there's usually some Buddhism among all the tarot and feng shui activities. Often the Open Center attracts Buddhist teachers and speakers of an unusually high caliber, so it's well worth getting on their mailing list. The Open Center also has a nice gift shop, which carries Buddhist books and music.

The Newark Museum

49 Washington Street   Fax: 973-642-0459
Newark, NJ 07101   http://www.newarkmuseum.org
Tel: 973-596-6550

The greatest collection of Tibetan art outside of Tibet isn't at the Met or the British Museum, or the Tibetan museum in Staten Island, for that matter. It's here, at the Newark Museum, and it's truly something to marvel at. The centerpiece of the collection is the beautiful, brilliantly colored Tibetan Buddhist altar, consecrated by the Dalai Lama himself in 1990. The museum also has significant Chinese, Japanese, Korean, and Indian collections.

The Newark Museum is closed Mondays and Tuesdays. The rest of the week it's open noon to 5:00 P.M., plus special evening hours till 8:30 P.M. on Thursdays. Admission is free!

Nicholas Roerich Museum

319 West 107th Street

New York, NY 10025

Tel: 212-864-7752

Fax: 212-864-7704

http://www.roerich.ee/nrm/

director@roerich.org

Nicholas Roerich was born in Russian in 1874. He was an archeologist, educator, mystic, and adventurer. His artistic contributions range from collaboration on Stravinsky's *Rite of Spring* to nearly seven thousand paintings. But Buddhists will mainly be interested in him because of his travels in Tibet, China, and the Himalayas, where he eventually settled. He was profoundly influenced by Buddhism and Asian religion, and this insight and sense of spiritual understanding is magically portrayed in many of his canvases. Scenes of lamas, monasteries, Buddha images, and the towering Himalayan mountain peaks recur again and again in his metaphorical imagery. The Nicholas Roerich Museum holds about two hundred of his paintings, as well as some artifacts he collected in his Asian travels. The museum is open Tuesdays through Sundays, 2:00–5:00 P.M. They also host numerous musical and poetry events each year. Admission is free.

Tibet House

22 West 15th Street

New York, NY 10011

Tel: (212) 807-0563

Fax: (212) 807-0565

http://www.tibethouse.org

mail@tibethouse.org

In a city full of great resources for Buddhists, Tibet House stands out as one of the very best. Led by Buddhist professor Robert Thurman and with a board loaded with activists, celebrities, and philanthropists, Tibet House is the most prominent presenter of Tibetan religion and culture around. They have a library, gallery, and newsletter, host fabulous art exhibitions and sponsor many lectures, concerts, and conferences by prominent Buddhists and Tibetans.

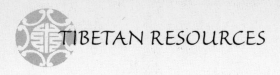

TIBETAN RESOURCES

FREE TIBET!

Much of the media attention given Buddhism in New York and elsewhere centers around the plight of the Tibetan people. In 1949 China invaded their country and annexed it, eventually killing 1.2 million Tibetans, destroying 99 percent of the country's monasteries, imprisoning and torturing thousands of monks, nuns, and laypeople, and brutally subjecting the Tibetans to a systematic campaign to destroy their religion, language, and culture. Tibet has become a nuclear-waste dumping ground, heavily deforested and held by a large force of occupying Chinese troops. Year after year, China's policies in Tibet are condemned by human rights watchdogs and international leaders.

In exile, the Dalai Lama, winner of the 1989 Nobel Peace Prize for his efforts to achieve a nonviolent resolution to his country's continuing devastation, leads the Tibetan refugee population from his home in Dharamsala, India. The Tibetan freedom cause has gone hand in hand with Tibetan Buddhism in the West—some people seek out Tibetan Buddhist masters and end up agitating for Tibetan self-rule, while others get involved to help protect human rights and turn into committed Buddhists. New York City celebrity Buddhists such as actor Richard Gere, Beastie Boy Adam Yauch, and composer Philip Glass have all contributed to the American awareness of the tragedy in Tibet. Here is a list of resources for New Yorkers who seek to get involved in the struggle for peace and freedom in this ancient Buddhist land on the roof of the world. While these organizations may not be specifically Buddhist, there is no real secular culture in Tibet, and these groups all provide ways to meet and assist Buddhists in need.

Nechung Foundation

110 First Avenue, 5th floor   Tel: 212-388-9784
New York, NY 10009

Contact Lama Pema Dorjee for details.

New York Tibetan Alliance

17 Battery Place, suite #633N   Tel: 212-898-4134
New York, NY 10004   Fax: 212-425-7240

A network of Tibetans in New York City organized to support their countrymen in exile.

Office of Tibet

241 East 32nd Street   Fax: 212-779-9245
New York, NY 10016   http://www.tibet.org/Resources/TSG/
Tel: 212-213-5010   Groups/nyc.html

The American office of the Tibetan government-in-exile.

Students for a Free Tibet

545 Eighth Avenue, 23rd floor   Fax: 212-594-6536
New York, NY 10018   http://www.tibet.org/sft
Tel: 212-594-5898   sft@i9c.org

This organization has many chapters on campuses across the country and has been instrumental in informing the younger generation about Tibetan issues.

The Tibet Fund

241 East 32nd Street

New York, NY 10016

Tel: 212-213-5011

Fax: 212-779-9245

http://www.tibetfund.org

tibetfund@tibetfund.org

The Tibet Fund is the primary fund-raising organization providing support to the Tibetan people and their culture.

Tibetan Cultural Institute

61 Grove Street, #4A

New York, NY 10014

Contact Aye Tulku for more information.

Tibetan Monastery

341 Lafayette Street, #755

New York, NY 10012

Tel: 212-898-4134

Fax: 212-717-0832

llamany@aol.com

Tibetan Monastery is a religious and cultural organization established for the preservation of Tibet's unique cultural heritage and spiritual wisdom through providing a variety of public cultural and educational programs, including lectures by prominent teachers from all four schools of Tibetan Buddhism. The monastery also supports Tibetan refugees in India.

Tibetan Refugee Health

416 West 23rd Street, suite 1D

New York, NY 10011

Tel: 212-741-2727

Fax: 212-741-2727

http://www.tibetanrefugeehealth.org/

index.html

Provides medical help for Tibetan refugees; also resources for traditional Tibetan medicine.

Tibetan Women's Association

c/o Office of Tibet
241 East 32nd Street
New York, NY 10016

Tel: 212-213-5010/718-706-9795
Fax: 212-779-9245

Tibetan women, who have suffered rape campaigns, forced steriliza-
tion, and forced abortions under Chinese rule, have taken an important
leadership role in the resistance movement.

Tibetan Youth Congress

221 East 32nd Street, #12A
New York, NY 10016

thokmey@co.gist

The Tibetan Youth Congress has recently begun to take a more mil-
itant position, in contrast to the strictly peaceful activities and views of
the Dalai Lama. Many are beginning to wonder whether Tibet can ever
be free without an armed struggle for liberation.

United States Tibet Committee

241 East 32nd Street
New York, NY 10016

Tel: 212-481-3569
Fax: 212-779-9245

The USTC is an important lobbying organization that promotes Tibetan independence by educating the public and politicians about Tibetan issues.

World Artists for Tibet

142-20 84th Drive, #7H
Briarwood, NY 11435
Tel: 718-658-0906

http://www.art4tibet1998.org/
art4tibet@aol.com

World Artists for Tibet is a nonprofit organization that coordinates
an international array of artists and musicians seeking to use art to raise
awareness of the plight of the Tibetan people. They put on a two-month

worldwide festival in 1998, with sixty-seven events in the New York City area alone, but have maintained a low profile and haven't even updated the Web page since then. Nonetheless, World Artists for Tibet is still active, working behind the scenes to preserve Tibetan culture and combat human rights abuses. Artists in any field are welcome to contribute their talents to the cause.

TIBETAN STORES

From pashmina scarves to Buddhist prayer beads, Tibetan styles have become some of the hottest trends in New York City and beyond. Whether this is a good or bad thing for Tibetan Buddhism itself remains to be seen—certainly the publicity can't hurt, but a lot of the attraction comes from fantasies of remote spiritual kingdoms that ultimately reduce Tibet and its people to stereotypes. For Buddhists, the fashion demand is a definite boon, as it's helped Tibetan stores flourish throughout the city. Besides clothes, hats, and rugs, they typically carry many specifically Buddhist items, including Buddha statues, ritual implements such as bells and vajras, malas, prayer wheels, CDs, books, and jewelry. You can even get postcards of the Buddha. There's also usually a selection of items from places outside Tibet, anywhere from Denmark to Morocco.

The following shops are overall so similar to each other that no individual descriptions are necessary. Go to any one and you're likely to find enough Himalayan goodies to max out your credit cards.

Do Kham

51 Prince Street
New York, NY 10012

Tel: 212-966-2404
Fax: 212-334-1245

Do Kham II

304 East Fifth Street
New York, NY 10003

Tel: 212-966-2404
Fax: 212-334-1245

Himalayan Crafts
2007 Broadway
New York, NY 10023
Tel: 212-787-8500

Fax: 212-787-8548
himacraft@aol.com

Himalayan Vision
1584 First Avenue
New York, NY 10028
Tel: 212-988-6573

Fax: 212-988-6573
himvision@aol.com

Himalayan Vision 2
127 Second Avenue
New York, NY 10003

Tel: 212-254-1952
Fax: 212-473-8959

Potala
9 East 36th Street
New York, NY 10016
Tel: 212-251-0360

Fax: 212-696-0431
http://www.potala.com
potala@dti.net

Shambhalla Mads
92 Thompson Street
New York, NY 10012
Tel: 212-941-6505

Fax: 212-941-6478
sohojewels@aol.com

Sharchen Imports
1309 Madison Avenue, suite 4C
New York, NY 10128

Tel: 212-860-8873

Tantra
946 Columbus Avenue
New York, NY 10025

Tel: 212-662-3316

**Tashi Delek Himalayan Gifts and
    Accessories**
210 West 80th Street
New York, NY 10024

Tel: 212-873-9884

Tibet Arts & Crafts
144 Sullivan Street
New York, NY 10012

Tel: 212-529-4344
Fax: 718-786-3258

Tibet Arts & Crafts II
197 Bleecker Street
New York, NY 10012
Tel: 212-260-5880

http://www.citysearch.com/nyc/
    tibetarts
takyab@aol.com

Tibet Bazaar

473 Amsterdam Avenue

New York, NY 10024

Tel: 212-595-8487

Fax: 212-595-8487

Tibet Carpet Center

127 Madison Avenue

New York, NY 10016

Tel: 212-686-7661

http://www.tibetcarpet.com

info@tibetcarpet.com

Tibet Himalayan Gifts & Accessories

212 West 80th Street

New York, NY 10024

Tel: 212-873-9884

Tibet Kailash

48 Greenwich Avenue

New York, NY 10011

Tel: 212-255-9572

Tibet Treasures

19 Christopher Street

New York, NY 10014

The Tibetan Village Store

49 Grove Street

New York, NY 10014

Tel: 212-727-8030

andrusurba@aol.com

Tibet West

19 Christopher Street

New York, NY 10014

Tel: 212-255-3416

Vision of Tibet

167 Thompson Street

New York, NY 10012

Tel: 212-995-9276

Fax: 212-995-9276

TIBETAN RESTAURANTS

Many folks are familiar with Putai, the Laughing Buddha, a grossly fat and jolly old Chinese fellow who acts as the Buddhist equivalent of Santa Claus. Perhaps he got so corpulent because so many Buddhists have such excellent taste buds. Though sometimes depicted as ascetics, Buddhists are just as obsessed with good food as the next person, and you've probably enjoyed dishes at Buddhist-owned Chinese, Thai, Japanese, and Korean restaurants without thinking about the religious convictions of the chefs. So why include a section on Tibetan restaurants? Basically, because they're relatively new on the cultural scene, are often overtly Buddhist and may even use their religious connections as a selling point, and because you've got a fair chance of being seated next to a party of monks when you dine at a Tibetan restaurant. Here's a quick list of places to relax once you've left the cushion.

Lhasa Restaurant

96 Second Avenue

New York, NY 10005

Tel: 212-674-5870

Tibet on Houston

136 West Houston

New York, NY 10012

Tel: 212-995-5884

Tibet Shambhala
488 Amsterdam Avenue
New York, NY 10024

Tel: 212-721-1270

Tibetan Kitchen
444 Third Avenue
New York, NY 10016

Tel: (212) 679-6286
http://www.potala.com/kitchen/

Tsampa
212 East Ninth Street
New York, NY 10003

Tel: 212-614-3226

STORES, ORGANIZATIONS, AND OTHER BUDDHIST RESOURCES IN NEW YORK

Here's all the good stuff that just didn't quite fit into the other categories in this book—Buddhist events, good places to get books, hip Buddhist zines, even a Buddhist hotline for those lonely middle-of-the-night moments when you just need to reach out and enlighten someone.

Asian Rare Books

175 West 93rd Street, #16D
New York, NY 10025
Tel: 212-316-5334

Fax: 212-316-3408
http://users.erols.com/arbs/
arbs@erols.com

Trying to find that rare, nearly impossible-to-locate Buddhist book you've always wanted? Contact Asian Rare Books. Odds are they've got it, or nobody does. They'll also take your precious scriptures off your hands at a nice price, should you be so inclined.

Barnes & Noble

Union Square
33 East 17th Street
New York, NY 10003
Tel: 212-253-0810

http://www.barnesandnoble.com
School affiliation: non-Buddhist
Language spoken: English

Why is Barnes & Noble listed in this book? Simple: these days Barnes & Noble has caught the Zen wave and begun carrying a wide selection of Buddhist books. Go to any B&N (or Borders, for that matter) and you'll find a section called "Eastern Thought" or "Eastern

Philosophy," code words for Buddhism, Hinduism, Taoism, and Sufism. Granted, the staff won't necessarily have any idea which books are good, but there's always the advantage of being able to select a book, take it to the in-store café, and read it for free while sipping your favorite latte.

Bodhiline

Tel: 212-677-9354
Fax: 212-677-9354
http://www.bodhiline.org/

webmaster@bodhiline.org
School affiliation: independent (Gelugpa)
Language spoken: English

Bodhiline is an automated phone service that provides information about current Buddhist events in New York City, a list of area Buddhist centers, and recorded Buddhist teachings and music. It is connected to the Asian Classics Institute (see page 84) but also provides news and locations for about twenty other Buddhist groups in NYC.

Let your fingers do the meditating by dialing 212-677-9354; press 12# for a list of monthly events, 13# for phone numbers of local Buddhist centers, 14# to get on their news mailing list, 15# for a list of New York City Buddhist bookshops, 16# to hear recorded Buddhist teachings on tape, 17# to hear some Buddhist music, 18# for shops that sell religious items, and 19# to receive their guide to Buddhist resources.

Bodhiline also maintains a Web site that lists this same information, plus additional teachings (all are from a Gelugpa perspective).

The Buddhist Council of New York

c/o New York Buddhist Vihara
84-32 124th Street
Kew Gardens, NY 11415
Tel: 212-781-1947

dimitrib@aol.com
School affiliation: independent
Language spoken: English

The Buddhist Council of New York was created in 1985 by several local Buddhist teachers, including Venerable Piyatissa of the New York Buddhist Vihara (see page 116), who maintains an important leadership role. The current general secretary is Dimitri Bakhroushin.

BCNY is a loose association of temples, organizations, and individuals in the tristate area. Its purpose is to foster cooperation and unity between the many different Buddhist groups in NYC. To this end it organizes an inclusive Vesak ceremony (see page 245) each year and sponsors lecture series on various Buddhist topics at Columbia

University by great modern Buddhist masters. It also holds monthly meetings, which rotate in location between member temples. Membership is open to Buddhist organizations or individuals who support the council's mission—the cost is $100 a year for centers and $50 a year for individuals.

Buddhist Peace Fellowship of NY

55 Bethune Street, #G111
New York, NY 10014
Tel: 212-691-2543

School affiliation: independent
Language spoken: English

The Buddhist Peace Fellowship is an international organization at the forefront of Engaged Buddhism, the social-action wing of Buddhist practice. The chapter in New York City is small but spunky—members have protested the Amadou Diallo shooting, commemorated the anniversary of the Hiroshima bombing, and brought in teachers to speak on contemporary social and environmental issues. Zen practitioners are more or less the majority of BPF members, though the organization includes members from all traditions and is open to all Buddhists. Overall Buddhist Peace Fellowship has a definite bias toward left-wing issues and perspectives. Contact Val DuBasky to get involved.

BPF also has contacts (a step down from full chapters) in the New York Capital area (Michael Fallarino, P.O. Box 178, Stuyvesant Falls, NY 12174) and in central New Jersey (Dodie Murphy, 2 Windingbrook Road, Bordontown, NJ 08501, Tel: 609-291-1412).

Buddhist Compassion Relief Tzu Chi
Foundation—New York Branch

41-60 Main Street, room #213
Flushing, NY 11355
Tel: 718-460-4590
Fax: 718-460-2068

tzuchiiny@aol.com
School affiliation: Chinese Mahayana
Languages spoken: Chinese, English

The Buddhist Compassion Relief Tzu Chi Foundation is a major Buddhist charity organization, founded in Taiwan in 1966 by Cheng

Yen, a Chinese Buddhist nun. From a modest beginning raising charity money by selling homemade baby booties, the organization has grown to an international network of 4 million members (sixteen thousand in the United States alone) that's collected and distributed more than $40 million on four continents. Their main activities are emergency disaster relief, health care and assistance for the poor and elderly, education, and environmental conservation. The group's commitment to providing relief wherever it is needed, regardless of the religion or nationality of the needy, has earned it worldwide respect; in 1993 Master Cheng Yen was nominated for the Nobel Peace Prize.

Women, whether Buddhist nuns or laity, play a vital part in Tzu Chi's charitable efforts. The foundation's activities grow out of a profound sense of Buddhist compassion and interconnection, though one need not be a Buddhist to get involved in their good works.

Center for Buddhist Studies

623 Kent Hall, Columbia University
New York, NY 10027
Tel: 212-854-6977
http://www.columbia.edu/cu/religion/
  cbs.html

School affiliation: independent
Languages spoken: English, Tibetan,
  Chinese, Japanese, and more

In case you find yourself with six or seven years of spare time and want to get a Ph.D. in Buddhist studies, here's where you need to go. Columbia University has had a long history with prominent Buddhist professors and teachers: D. T. Suzuki, Thich Nhat Hanh, and now Robert Thurman (father of actress Uma, and one of *People* magazine's fifty most influential people) have all taught at the college. Currently Thurman holds the Jey Tsong Khapa Professorship in Indo-Tibetan Studies. Admission requirements are steep, and graduation requirements are even harder, ensuring that you'll be the first person on your block with a genuine degree in Buddhist studies.

The center has a library and a reading area. There are many Buddhist

cultural events at Columbia throughout the year, which the center should be able to inform you about.

Change Your Mind Day

First Saturday in June
12:30–5:30 P.M.
The Great Hill in Central Park
Enter the park on Central Park West at
    106th Street

New York, NY 10025
Tel: 800-950-7008
http://www.tricycle.com
School affiliation: independent
Language spoken: English

Since 1994, the biggest annual event in New York Buddhism has been Change Your Mind Day, a sort of mini Buddhist Woodstock organized by *Tricycle* magazine (see page 243) in Central Park. The event draws about three thousand people, including folks from the different local Buddhist centers and inquisitive passersby who can't believe that several thousand New Yorkers could ever sit so still, so quietly, for so long. In 1999 the event went national, with similar CYM Days in San Francisco, Pennsylvania, and Alaska.

The event begins with the solemn tolling of a bell 108 times, as participants sit eagerly on the grass before a makeshift stage. For the next five hours they are treated to teachings from modern Buddhist masters, such as Lama Surya Das, Master Sheng-Yen, John Daido Loori Roshi, and Sensei Pat Enkyo O'Hara. The speakers are always purposely drawn from a wide variety of Buddhist schools. They lead the participants in various meditations, visualizations, and chants, offering Dharma advice and wisdom for applying Buddhism to the hectic world of the Big Apple. Usually at least 50 percent of the speakers are drawn from the New York area, offering those who attend a glimpse of what local teachers are like before visiting their centers.

Spaces between speakers are filled with musical performances from such famous Buddhist artists as Philip Glass and Jon Gibson, as well as poetry readings by well-known writers. There's usually a tai chi segment later in the day as well, to stretch out those aching muscles after sitting in the grass so long.

The day usually ends with a traditional geshe debate between monks from the Asian Classics Institute—two teams of monks square off in a battle of words (usually in Tibetan, translated for the audience), trying to trip each other up over various important Buddhist concepts. The spectacle may be a bit esoteric in nature, but the shouting and energetic hand clapping is always a treat for the crowd.

Besides the unique opportunity to attend many teachings for free in an idyllic setting, Change Your Mind Day is often worth attending simply to check out the crowd that gathers. It's only once in a great while that you can see people sunning themselves in tank tops while chanting "Om mani padme hum" or orange-robed monks vigorously chatting with passing joggers and skaters. The atmosphere is always respectful, but certainly a bit bohemian as well.

Check the weather before venturing out. CYMD does not have a rain date—if Mother Nature fails to cooperate, they just hold it anyway. So be sure to bring a towel, sunblock, and an umbrella if it looks like rain. Many people also bring food and a pad and pencil. Don't bring a lot of money. The best thing about CYMD is that's totally free. One can connect with local dharma centers, make friends, sunbathe, and enjoy the Buddha's teachings all without spending a dime. No vendors or booths are allowed, though there is a table with free material from the participating centers, and food vendors often lurk just beyond the edge of the Great Hill.

Also, even though the back of the stage is open and thus it's possible to approach the teachers, please respect their desire for privacy. Many will happily speak to you at further length, but if you had to deliver lectures in the summer sun all day while wearing a long black robe, you'd probably want a chance to rest, too.

East West Books

78 Fifth Avenue
New York, NY 10011
Phone: 212-243-5994

School affiliation: non-Buddhist
Language spoken: English

If you're looking for Buddhist books, music, or trinkets, you'll probably want to pay a visit East West Books. Just over a block from Union Square, this eclectic bookstore offers volumes on psychology, cooking, consciousness, women's spirituality, Christianity, and many other subjects, but its real strength has always been in Eastern religion.

Before the growth in popularity of Buddhism in New York, East West Books used to be *the* place to get books on Buddhism, or any other Asian religion or New Age subject, for that matter. Nowadays the large chains such as Barnes & Noble and Borders have finally realized there's a profit to be made from stocking more than just two or three Buddhist books on a shelf with Carlos Castaneda and prophecies about UFOs. Accordingly, you can now find a wide selection of Buddhist books in these stores, both new and classics of the genre, and East West has lost some of its importance. Nevertheless, East West continues to have the largest and most diverse stock of books of Buddhism available to the New York City public.

Besides books, East West also sells zafus (a type of Zen meditation cushion) and other meditation aids, malas (Buddhist rosaries, currently considered hip fashion accessories in some circles), incense, and assorted Buddhist statues and posters. They carry Buddhist and related magazines, videos, and music.

A word of caution about seeking Buddhist literature at East West Books is probably in order. Despite an impressively large stock of Buddhist items, East West is not a Buddhist bookstore, and pseudo-Buddhist materials are placed in with the more legitimate offerings—titles such as *Celtic Zen* are neither holy texts nor authoritative monographs. Buddhism and Zen are disingenuously put into two separate categories in different locations in the store. Nevertheless, feel free to ask the staff to order you a title if you don't see it on the shelf—as long as it's still in print, they'll be happy to get it for you.

Fish Drum Magazine

P. O. Box 966, Murray Hill Station
New York, NY 10156
http://www.fishdrum.com

fishdrum@earthlink.net
School affiliation: Zen
Language spoken: English

Fish Drum is a lively little literary magazine, featuring content ranging from articles by modern Zen masters to cartoons of naked monks to contemporary poetry. The Zen is often between the lines—this isn't a practice-oriented magazine, more like a stream of consciousness with an intelligently warped sense of humor. It was founded in 1988 by the late Robert Winson, and after a hiatus has been taken up again by his wife, Suzi. *Fish Drum Magazine* is perfect-bound and published somewhat irregularly; subscriptions are $24 for four issues.

In case you're wondering about the title, a fish drum is indeed a drum shaped like a fish. More specifically, it's a wooden fish-shaped instrument used in Japanese Zen temples. It's beaten during various rituals to keep time or signal the beginning or end of meditation periods.

Fong's Trading

74 Canal Street

New York, NY 10002

Tel: 212-343-0322

School affiliation: independent

Languages spoken: Chinese, English

Many Chinatown shops sell Buddhist items and implements, but for sheer variety you probably can't do better than Fong's Trading. Inside you'll find a profusion of Buddha images, incense, offering bowls, altars, scrolls, and anything else you could want.

Kim's Video

6 St. Mark's Place

New York, NY 10003

Tel: 212-505-0311

http://www.kimsvideo.com

School affiliation: non-Buddhist

Language spoken: English

For the couch potato Buddhists out there who want to relax and pop a dharmic tape in the ol' VCR, Kim's Video is probably the best place to meet your needs. Naturally they've got *Little Buddha*, *Seven Years in Tibet*, and *Kundun*, but they've also got some titles you're unlikely to find

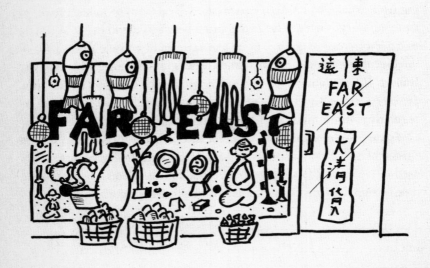

elsewhere. The Korean Zen film *Why Has Bodhidharma Left for the East?* is as profound and yet opaque as Zen itself; more accessible are the Buddhist teaching videos in their collection; and for goofy fun try a Chinese kung fu import, many of which feature Shaolin Buddhist monks kicking butt for Buddha. Kim's has four locations in downtown Manhattan, whose stock largely, but not completely, overlap.

The Learning Annex

16 East 53rd Street, 4th floor
New York, NY 10022
Phone: 212-371-0280

http://www.thelearningannex.com
School affiliation: non-Buddhist
Language spoken: English

The Seminar Center

1776 Broadway, suite 1001
New York, NY 10019
Phone: 212-655-0077
Fax: 212-655-0088

http://www.seminarcenter.com
School affiliation: non-Buddhist
Language spoken: English

With all the interest in Buddhism among New Yorkers these days, it was probably inevitable that some people would seek to capitalize on it. After all, this is the country that spawned two immortal guiding principles: "The business of America is business" and "There's a sucker born every minute." Seems there's nothing we can't sell these days, and spirituality is certainly included. Thus we come to the growing field of Buddhist lectures and seminars.

The Learning Annex and The Seminar Center are virtually identical adult education outlets, offering such classes as "Speak French in Only Three Hours," "How to Make $$ in the Adult-Entertainment Business on the Net," and "Get a Green Card and Become a Citizen!" Classes cost about $30 and usually consist of a single three-hour session.

With the increased interest in spirituality in the '90s these organizations have started offering many classes in crystals, astrology, Kabbalah, and other popular New Age trends. Both have also begun to offer an occasional seminar on Buddhism. Unfortunately, the quality of these classes varies widely, and there is an inherent limitation to the usefulness of a short lecture delivered by a stranger whose qualifications you can't be certain of. For instance, the fall 1999 catalog from The Seminar Center listed a course titled "Tibetan Healing and Time Travel" that talked about astral travel, Taoism, God force, and time travel—never mind that these things have nothing to do with Buddhism in any way, Tibetan or otherwise.

Frankly, there is no need to plunk down $30 for a mediocre course when there are so many reputable Buddhist centers and teachers in New York City whose teaching are available for free. A lecture offers virtually no advantages over an introductory session at a Buddhist center, nor is Buddhism something that is naturally conducive to being learned in a couple of hours in an impersonal setting. Such get-enlightened-quick thinking was roundly criticized as "spiritual materialism" by Chogyam Trungpa Rinpoche, one of the most influential Buddhist masters to visit the West. If you really feel the need to attend a talk on Buddhism, try the New York Open Center, whose exclusive focus on spiritual matters and higher-echelon Buddhist authorities/celebrities offer an experience that is more likely to be of worthwhile caliber.

Rafe Martin

56 Brighton Street
Rochester, New York 14607
Tel: 716-422-2826
Fax: 716-442-2709

http://www.rafemartin.com
rafem@aol.com
School affiliation: Zen
Language spoken: English

Rafe Martin, a senior member of the Rochester Zen Center, is a storyteller with a knack for updating ancient Buddhist stories. Besides performing regularly around New York, he is available for public storytelling and professional workshops. Rafe is the author of *The Hungry Tigress: Buddhist Myths, Legends, and Jataka Tales, One Hand Clapping: Zen Stories for Children of All Ages,* and others.

Myojo-Morning Star Zen Meditation Clothing

R. D. #1, Box 4
Glenford, NY 12433
Tel: 914-657-2101
http://www.myojostar.com

myojostar@netstep.net
School affiliation: Rinzai Zen
Language spoken: English

Meditate in style with Myojo-Morning Star's custom-tailored Buddhist robes. Myojo Sara Wexler offers a range of traditional Buddhist clothing, mainly Japanese in fashion.

The National Buddhist Prison Sangha

c/o Zen Mountain Monastery
South Plank Road, Box 197
Mt. Tremper, NY 12457
Tel: 914-688-2228

School affiliation: Soto and Rinzai Zen
(Mountains and Rivers Order)
Language spoken: English

Prison outreach to incarcerated Buddhists is an example of American Buddhism's emphasis on socially engaged practice. The National Buddhist Prison Sangha is one good example, run by Sensei Geoffrey Shugen Arnold out of Zen Mountain Monastery (see page 170). It offers support to inmates interested in Buddhism by matching them with local volunteers, providing dharma reading materials, and training to people who want to get involved. This is hard work, not for the squeamish or the inexperienced Buddhist practitioner.

New York Public Library

455 Fifth Avenue
New York, NY 10018
Tel: 212-340-0833

School affiliation: non-Buddhist
Languages spoken: English, Spanish, and more

Sure, this is a no-brainer, but it's still good to remember that the New York Public Library has a large section of books, and of course you don't have to pay anything. Many of the standard texts of American

Buddhism can be found in the system, as well as some obscure and fabulous gems: the reference library's Oriental section has an English translation of the Mahaparinirvana Sutra, an important Mahayana Buddhist scripture that is virtually impossible to find in English. Parting food for thought: the third-century B.C. Indian emperor Ashoka, who converted to Buddhism and spread it throughout the region, used guardian lions as his symbol.

Peaceful Dwelling Project

P. O. Box 3159
East Hampton, NY 11937-3097
Tel: 516-324-3736
Fax: 516-324-3736

peacefuldwell@hamptons.com
School affiliation: Soto Zen
Language spoken: English

The Peaceful Dwelling Project is a profound expression of the dharma in the everyday world of suffering. Rev. Madeline Ko-i Bastis, a hospital chaplain and Zen priest from the Zen Community of New York (see page 134), leads this hospice retreat program for people with serious and terminal illnesses and their caregivers. Although based on Long Island, the project's volunteers serve people throughout the metropolitan New York area on request. They provide an open weekly meditation session, weekly meditation meetings for people living with HIV and emotional difficulties, ongoing retreats for specific people and groups, and an emotional annual Obon ceremony to honor those who have passed away.

Quest Bookshop

240 East 53rd Street
New York, NY 10022
Tel: 212-758-5521
Fax: 212-758-4679
http://www.dorsai.org/~nyts/
  bookshop.html

nyts@escape.com
School affiliation: Theosophy (non-
  Buddhist)
Language spoken: English

The Quest Bookshop is a New Agey store that sells a wide range of spiritual items, including a good selection of Buddhist books. The store is run by the New York Theosophical Society; Theosophy is nineteenth-century religion that combines elements of Buddhism and many other meditative traditions. Buddhism has its own set of shelves, broken down into "Buddhism," "Tibetan Buddhism," and "Zen Buddhism." There are also random Buddhist books interspersed within other categories, such as "Consciousness" and "Death and Dying."

Quest Bookshop also sells meditation cushions and mats, incense, Buddhist posters, malas, and a very limited selection of small Buddha statues. In the back is a doorway to the New York Theosophical Society, which can also be accessed from next door. The NYTS has a space that is frequently rented by Buddhist groups, including the New York Insight Meditation Center (see page 67), which offers classes there 7:00–9:00 P.M. on Fridays. They ask for a $5.00 donation to cover costs. The Theosophical Society also offers its own classes, including a Buddhist Loving-Kindness Meditation class on Mondays, 5:30–6:00 P.M. The class is free and open to all; it is followed by a non-Buddhist hatha yoga class, which costs $8. Ask for the latest schedule to find out about upcoming speakers and classes, and don't get confused by the similarity of some aspects of Theosophy and Buddhism—they are distinct traditions.

Snow Lion Publications

P. O. Box 6483
Ithaca, NY 14851-6483
Tel: 800-950-0313/607-273-8519
Fax: 607-273-8508

http://www.snowlionpub.com/
cds@snowlionpub.com
School affiliation: Gelugpa
Languages spoken: English, Tibetan

Snow Lion is a major publisher of books on Tibet and Tibetan Buddhism, particularly the works of the Dalai Lama. But their activities also go much further: they publish a free quarterly newspaper, *Snow Lion*, which delivers news on Tibet, product reviews, and teachings (and acts as their catalog); they run a Tibetan shop in downtown Ithaca (605 West State Street) that sells many Buddhist items; and they support the preservation of Tibetan culture through their publishing and educational activities.

Sufi Books

227 West Broadway
New York, NY 10013
Tel: 212-334-5212

School affiliation: Sufi (non-Buddhist)
Languages spoken: English, Arabic

If you're in downtown Manhattan, Sufi Books is a good place to check out a nice selection of Buddhist books for sale. Although the store is, not surprisingly, run by Muslims and primarily devoted to Sufi literature and music, there is a healthy range of Buddhist books in the back under "World Mystical Traditions."

Sufi Books also serves as a rental space for local spiritual groups, including Rigpa New York (see page 95), the New York Insight Meditation Center (see page 67), and Palyul Changchub Dargyeling New York (see page 72).

Sufi Books isn't easy to find. Take the 1/9 train to Franklin or the A, C, or E to Canal Street. The store is three blocks below Canal Street, near Sixth Avenue. If you can't find it in this confusing part of Tribeca, just ask someone on the street for help. Ask for the latest schedule, as Buddhist speakers appear on a fairly regular basis and new Buddhist groups sometimes rent space for limited periods of time. But don't expect much help with Buddhist subjects—the proprietors are Muslim and can't go on at length about Buddhism.

Tibet Buddhism Merchandise Center

27 Canal Street
New York, NY 10002

School affiliation: independent
Languages spoken: English, Chinese

This modest-size shop sells a bewildering assortment of Chinese and Tibetan Buddhist objects, including incense, statues, amulets, malas, scrolls, altars, and more. Though Tibetan merchandise is included, the proprietors and many of the products are Chinese.

Tricycle: The Buddhist Review

92 Vandam Street
New York, NY 10013
Tel: 212-645-1143/800-950-7008
Fax: 212-645-1493

Subscriptions/orders: 800-873-9871
http://www.tricycle.com
editorial@tricycle.com
School affiliation: independent
Language spoken: English

Dedicated to examining the transmission of Buddhism to the West, *Tricycle: The Buddhist Review* is one of the more unusual religious publications on the newsstands. In its nine years of publication it has attracted both kudos and controversy for disseminating ancient teachings, interviewing modern Buddhist masters, and showcasing cutting-edge artists, while simultaneously examining divisive issues in American Buddhist communities that other Buddhist and New Age publications don't discuss. Contributors include the Dalai Lama, Peter Matthiessen, Philip Glass, Thich Nhat Hanh, Jack Kerouac, Pema Chödrön, Robert Aitken, Spalding Gray, and Tom Robbins. The magazine's independence from any one Buddhist school or perspective sometimes ruffles Buddhist special interest groups, but complaints haven't stopped *Tricycle* from racking up literary awards and growing into the widest-read Buddhist publication in the English language.

A typical issue of *Tricycle* includes an interview with a major Buddhist teacher, practical advice on different methods of practice, journalistic articles and magazine-style essays on Buddhism and modern issues, reviews of new books and products, and a directory of Buddhist centers across the country. The writing is intelligent but accessible, with a minimum of foreign words and Buddhist jargon. Though *Tricycle* seeks to represent itself as nonsectarian, in practice there is much more Zen and Tibetan material than other forms of Mahayana or Theravada Buddhism, something readers may wish to keep in mind. *Tricycle* does not represent the whole of Buddhism or even American Buddhism, but it does offer a consistently interesting perspective on the issues and ideas that influence many Buddhists in the United States today.

Founded in 1991, *Tricycle* is steered by editor-in-chief Helen Tworkov, a former anthropologist and longtime student of Zen and Tibetan Buddhism. The magazine is published on a quarterly basis and is available on the newsstands at Barnes & Noble, Borders, and other bookshops and magazine shops: subscriptions and single issues can be ordered at the number on page 243. *Tricycle* has also published a number of books, including *Big Sky Mind: Buddhism and the Beat Generation, Breath Sweeps Mind: A First Guide to Meditation Practice,* and *Buddha Laughing: A Tricycle Book of Cartoons.* Its Web site, the Tricycle Hub, has also won awards and is well worth visiting. Admirably, *Tricycle* is a nonprofit company and doesn't accept non-Buddhist advertising (though the necessarily hefty $7.50 price tag—$24 for a year's subscription—still gives some people plenty to grumble about).

Tricycle's editorial offices at Vandam Street are not open to the public, so don't show up expecting to chat with the editors unless you've been invited. It includes a bulletin board area where people can discuss articles in *Tricycle*, ask questions about Buddhism, and learn from each other. *Tricycle* hosts a number of Buddhist events for the public each year, including the annual Change Your Mind Day (see page 232), poetry readings, teas, and more. Call or check the Web site for more information.

Vesak ceremony

3:00–7:30 P.M.
Last Saturday in May
St. Peter's Church
619 Lexington Avenue
New York, NY 10022

Tel: 212-781-1947
School affiliation: independent
Languages spoken: English, and much
more

Vesak is the traditional Theravadin Buddhist celebration of the birth, enlightenment, and death of the Buddha. Each year since 1986 the Buddhist Council of New York (see page 229) has put on a special Vesak ceremony to bring the NYC Buddhist community closer together. As BCNY general secretary Dimitri Bakhroushin once remarked about this festival honoring the Buddha, "This is his holiday, we go all out for him!"

"Going all out" for Buddha includes a parade around the block with colorful banners, an inclusive worship service with recitation of Buddhist precepts and chants, traditional dance performances from a wide variety of Asian cultures, a sermon, a play entitled *The Buddha* put on by the Patriarchal Zen Society (see page 73), vegetarian food, book sales, and more. The event usually draws a couple thousand people from a staggering variety of ethnic and denominational backgrounds, easily making it the most diverse (and frequently chaotic) event in New York Buddhist history. This is a family affair, complete with squirming, yelling children and ancient grandmothers, shaven-head celibate monks and Indian dancers. English is the common language that the ceremonies are conducted in, but it has to compete with the din of a dozen Asian languages being whispered in the pews.

The event starts at 3:00 P.M. and last until 7:30 or so, but the pacing is uneven, and people come and go constantly, pouring green tea over a statue of the baby Buddha one moment, then chatting up a nun or watching young Korean girls dance the next. Vesak is held in May, usually on the last Saturday—call the Buddhist Council of New York for this year's schedule.

WoozleHouse

427 West 51st Street, suite 3A
New York, NY 10019
Tel: 212-489-8839
http://www.woozlehouse.com

jyoutt@woozlehouse.com
School affiliation: independent
Language spoken: English

WoozleHouse is Jene Youtt's decidedly off-kilter Buddhist photography and greeting card service. Visit the Web site to see samples and order a catalog. By the way, a woozle is a most perplexing animal that plays a role in the Winnie-the-Pooh books.

Zen Peacemaker Order

c/o the Village Zendo, 15 Washington
    Place, #4E
New York, NY 10003
Tel: 212-674-0832
http://www.peacemakercommunity.org/
    zpo/

pat.ohara@nyu.edu
School affiliation: Soto Zen
Language spoken: English

The Zen Peacemaker Order was created by Bernie Glassman Roshi and his late wife Sandra Jishu Holmes to actualize his feelings that Zen practice and social activism go hand in hand. ZPO includes both laymembers and monastics, all devoted to using Buddhism to further the goal of community and world peace, and to using service for others to deepen their Buddhist practice. Members take on special precepts, attend training sessions, take part in a wide variety of service activities (including homeless Zen retreats, meditation at former Nazi concentration camps, counseling to AIDS victims and drug addicts, and more), and participate in monthly Days of Reflection (basically a full day of Zen sitting). Sensei Pat O'Hara of the Village Zendo (see page 102) is the current head of training for the Zen Peacemaker Order. Contact her for more information about how to get involved in this unique expression of the dharma.

GLOSSARY

Abhidharma: The third part of the oldest Buddhist scriptures. It explains Buddhist psychology and metaphysics.

Amitabha Buddha: An esoteric Buddha who long ago vowed to save all those who called upon him for help, regardless of how good or evil they were. Sometimes known as Amida.

ango: A traditional three-month-long Zen training period.

Avalokiteshvara: The bodhisattva of pure compassion, who comes to the rescue of those in need.

bodhisattva: An enlightened being who vows to work forever to liberate sentient beings from their delusions and suffering.

Buddha: A fully enlightened being who teaches the path to nirvana.

Buddha nature: The inherent capacity within all living beings to become enlightened.

cakra (chakra): Nodes of psychic/spiritual energy in the body, used in esoteric rituals. Often visualized as wheels.

Ch'an: The original form of Zen, practiced in China.

Chenrezig: The Tibetan version of Avalokiteshvara.

Chogye: The mainstream Korean school of Buddhism, which combines Zen meditation, Pure Land worship, and scholasticism.

daimoku: Holy chant of the Nichiren school, believed to activate one's Buddha nature.

daisan: Another name for dokusan, a private interview with one's Zen teacher.

dana: Charity, often in the sense of giving food to monks.

dharma/dhamma: The Pali and Sanskrit terms for the Buddha's teachings.

dharmakaya/dhammakaya: The ultimate, naturally enlightened nature of the universe and all things.

Diamond Sutra: An important Mahayana Sutra that describes the empty nature of all appearances.

dokusan: A private, confidential meeting with one's Zen teacher, often used to discuss koans.

Dzogchen: The highest meditation technique of the Nyingmapa school, sometimes considered a lineage of its own.

Engaged Buddhism: The worldwide movement applying Buddhist compassion and mindfulness to issues of social justice, violence, and environmentalism.

enlightenment: The goal of Buddhist practice, the perfection of wisdom and compassion, which eliminates suffering and brings complete peace of mind.

Five Great Precepts: The basic moral guidelines for laypeople, not to kill, lie, steal, abuse alcohol, or commit sexual misdeeds.

Four Noble Truths: The foundation of Buddhist philosophy. (1) All lives entail suffering. (2) Suffering comes from unhealthy attachment. (3) There is a way to end suffering. (4) That path is a combination of morality, wisdom, and meditation.

Gelugpa: The dominant school of Tibetan Buddhism, led by the Dalai Lama.

gohonzan: The object of worship for Nichiren Buddhists, usually a scroll.

Heart Sutra: The shortest Mahayana text, and one of the most important, which describes the nature of emptiness.

Holy Eightfold Path: The Buddhist method of achieving enlightenment. See page 6.

hoza: A Nichiren Buddhist technique of group sharing, similar to group therapy.

Jodo Shinshu: A Japanese form of Pure Land Buddhism that advocates salvation through faith.

Kagyupa: The largest school of Tibetan Buddhism in the West.

karma: The Buddhist law of cause and effect, which brings about happiness or suffering based on one's good or bad deeds.

koan: A Zen teaching story, often told as a nonsensical riddle, used as a meditation device.

Kwan Um: A school of Korean Zen founded by Seung Sahn Sunim.

Kwan-Yin: The female version of Avalokiteshvara, worshiped in East Asia.

lama: A Tibetan Buddhist teacher.

Lotus Sutra: An influential Mahayana book, held to be the highest of the Buddhist scriptures by the Tendai and Nichiren schools.

Mahayana: One of the two great surviving streams of Buddhism, characterized by a more liberal approach to dogma and discipline, an abundance of nonhistorical Buddhas and saints, and a universalistic teaching meant to encompass both monastics and laypeople.

Maitreya: The prophesied Buddha of the future, who will restore Buddhism when it dies out.

mandala: An image that depicts an enlightened world, often in the form of a scroll, painting, or even two-dimensional sand sculpture.

mantra: A holy phrase that can be used as a meditation tool or spell.

metta: Loving-kindness, often used as particular meditation in the Theravada school.

monk: A general term for male Buddhist monastics, who may or may not be celibate.

Namo Amida Butsu: "Homage to Amitabha Buddha," the primary chant in Pure Land Buddhism. It is spelled and pronounced differently in different cultures.

Namu Myoho Renge Kyo: "Homage to the Lotus Sutra," the central mantra of the Nichiren school, known as daimoku.

nembutsu: Saying or chanting the name of Amitabha Buddha, the Pure Land savior.

ngondros: Preliminary practices performed by beginners in Tibetan Buddhism, often quite involved and time consuming.

Nichiren: A medieval Buddhist reformer, and the title of the school of Buddhism he founded.

Nichiren Shoshu: A conservative form of Nichiren Buddhism.

Nichiren Shu: Mainstream Nichiren Buddhism, confined primarily to Japan.

Nipponzan Myohoji: A peace-oriented school of Nichiren Buddhism.

nirvana: The extinction of pain and suffering, akin to enlightenment.

nun: A general term for ordained female Buddhist monastics.

Nyingmapa: The oldest school of Tibetan Buddhism, which emphasizes meditation over study.

Pali: The canonical language of Theravada Buddhism, related to Sanskrit.

phowa: A Tibetan practice performed at the time of death to achieve enlightenment for the dying.

Pure Land Buddhism: The largest form of Buddhism, which venerates the Buddha Amitabha.

rebirth: Also known as reincarnation, the Buddhist belief that living beings are born again and again as new creatures or people after each life.

Rinzai: One of the two main branches of Japanese Zen, which focuses on koan practice.

Rissho Kosei-Kai: A liberal, nonmonastic form of Nichiren Buddhism.

roshi: A Zen term for a respected, experienced teacher.

sadhana: Prayers and meditation techniques used as worship in Tibetan Buddhism.

Sakyapa: The smallest of the four main schools of Tibetan Buddhism.

samu: The Zen method of using everyday, secular activities as ways to practice mindfulness.

Sanbo Kyodan: A reformist Zen lineage that draws from both the Soto and Rinzai schools.

sangha: The community of Buddhists, or more specifically a certain group of practicing Buddhists.

sanzen: Another term for dokusan, a private interview with one's Zen teacher.

satori: A Zen term for the moment of enlightenment.

sensei: "Teacher," a term of respect used in Japanese-derived forms of Buddhism.

sesshin: Three- or seven-day periods of intense Zen meditation practice.

shamatha: Basic concentration meditation, often paired with Vipassana.

Shambhala: Shangri-La, the mythical Buddhist paradise. Also a school of Tibetan Buddhism founded by Chogyam Trungpa Rinpoche, that combines Kagyu and Nyingma teachings.

shastra: A Buddhist text, usually a commentary written by a saint or scholar.

shikantaza: The Zen practice of just sitting without any object of concentration for meditation, considered the highest form of meditation by the Soto school.

Shingon: Japanese esoteric Buddhism, somewhat similar to Tibetan Buddhism.

Soka Gakkai: A large Buddhist layperson's organization that practices Nichiren Shoshu.

Son: The Korean term for Zen.

Soto: The largest school of Japanese Zen, which emphasizes sitting meditation.

sutra: A primary Buddhist text, usually attributed to the Buddha himself.

tantra: Oral and written practices and teachings that utilize advanced techniques.

Tara: The female Tibetan embodiment of compassion, related to Avalokiteshvara.

Tendai: A large, eclectic school of Japanese Buddhism that influenced many other groups.

thangka: A Tibetan religious painting.

Theravada: One of the two primary schools of Buddhism. It is overall more conservative, older, and more monastically oriented than Mahayana. They eschew worship of esoteric Buddhas in favor of concentration on the historical Buddha and his original teachings.

Thien: The Vietnamese school of Zen.

Three Jewels: The Buddha, dharma, and sangha, the primary objects of reverence in Buddhism.

Tibetan Buddhism: A catch-all term for the esoteric Buddhism practiced in the Himalayan region.

Tipitaka/Tripitaka: The Pali and Sanskrit terms for the central Buddhist texts.

tulku: A Tibetan lama who reincarnates in order to continue leading people to enlightenment.

upaya: The doctrine that there are many different types of Buddhism designed to assist the many different sorts of people in the world. More specifically the skillful application of those methods.

Vajrayana: A subschool of Mahayana Buddhism that practices tantra, including Tibetan Buddhism, Shingon, and Tendai.

Vinaya: The rules of the Buddhist monastic order, part of the Tripitaka.

Vipassana: A popular meditation technique that involves observing and labeling mental states.

Won: A Korean form of Buddhism that emphasizes progress, peace work, and the laity.

zazen: Zen sitting meditation.

zazenkai: An all-day Zen program, often including meditation, ritualized meals, and sermons.

Zen: A meditation-based school of East Asian Buddhism.

zendo: The hall or room where Zen meditation is practiced.

INDEX